THE
GREAT
FLOOD

Also by Edward Platt

CITY OF ABRAHAM:
History, Myth and Memory:
A Journey through Hebron

LEADVILLE:
A Biography of the A40

THE GREAT FLOOD

TRAVELS THROUGH
A SODDEN LANDSCAPE

Edward Platt

PICADOR

First published 2019 by Picador
an imprint of Pan Macmillan
The Smithson, 6 Briset Street, London ECIM 5NR
Associated companies throughout the world
www.panmacmillan.com

ISBN 978-1-4472-9819-9

1 3 5 7 9 8 6 4 2

A CIP catalogue record for this book is available from the British Library.

Map artwork by ML Design Ltd

Typeset by Palimpsest Book Production Limited, Falkirk, Stirlingshire
Printed and bound by CPI Group (UK) Ltd, Croydon, CRO 4YY

Visit **www.picador.com** to read more about all our books
and to buy them. You will also find features, author interviews and
news of any author events, and you can sign up for e-newsletters
so that you're always first to hear about our new releases.

For my parents

Contents

PART TWO: NOAH'S WOODS

SCOTLAND

Morpeth
Wansbeck
Tyne
Newburn
The Winnings
Cockermouth
Cocker Greta
St Johns in the Vale
St John's Beck
Thirlmere Reservoir
Keswick

Hull
North Ferriby
Hull

Anglesey
New Brighton
Mersey
Elwy
Neston
St Asaph
Dee

ENGLAND

Boston
The Wash
Happisburgh
Horsey

Borth
Old Bedford River
New Bedford River
Ouse Washes
Denver Sluice
Littleport
Easton
Bavents
Southwold

Source of
the Severn

Severn
Avon
Worcester
Kempsey
Tewkesbury

Ouse
South Level
of the Fens

WALES

Paviland Cave

Thames Barrier
Westminster
Thames
Cookham
Maidenhead
Windsor
Shepperton
Canvey
Island
Sunbury

Jaywick
LONDON
ARRAY

West Huntspill
Moorland
Glastonbury Tor
Burrowbridge
& Burrow Mump
Tone
Langport
Muchelney
Thorney
Parrett
Bournemouth

Medway
Teise Beult
Yalding

Ramsgate

Felpham

Dawlish

Chesil
Beach
Isle of
Portland

English Channel

North Sea

DOGGERLAND

THE SUNKEN
HUNDRED

75 miles

100 kilometres

FRANCE

PART ONE: THE DEEP

Ever the river has risen and brought us the flood,
The mayfly floating on the water.
Epic of Gilgamesh

The summer holds: upon its glittering lake
Lie Europe and the islands; many rivers
Wrinkling its surface like a ploughman's palm . . .
Calm at this moment the Dutch sea so shallow
That sunk St Paul's would ever show its golden cross
And still the deep water that divides us still from Norway.
W. H. Auden and Christopher Isherwood,
The Dog Beneath the Skin, or Where is Francis?

What in water did Bloom, waterlover, drawer of water, watercarrier returning to the range, admire?

Its universality: its democratic equality and constancy to its nature in seeking its own level: its vastness in the ocean of Mercator's projection: its unplumbed profundity in the Sundam trench of the Pacific exceeding 8,000 fathoms . . . its violence in seaquakes, waterspouts, artesian wells, eruptions, torrents, eddies, freshets, spates, groundswells, watersheds, waterpartings, geysers, cataracts, whirlpools, maelstroms, inundations, deluges, cloudbursts . . .   James Joyce, *Ulysses*

1: The Anchorage

The canoe scraped against the tarmac and floated free. The gateposts of Thorney House rose through the water like the markers on a kayaking course. We could have veered between them, paddled up the drive and moored in the porch. Instead, Glen turned the canoe into the main channel running through the village.

Apples bumped against the side and disappeared behind us, spinning as they sank. I leant over – careful not to lose my balance, as I almost had when I climbed aboard in the road in front of the Wards' flooded house – and let my fingers trail through the water. It was grey-green, flecked with grass and leaves, and glossed with an oily skin. It looked like a rich, semi-tropical stew, but it was so cold that I took my hand out straight away.

The water got deeper quickly: it was ankle-deep beneath the windows of the Wards' house, which occupied a narrowing triangle of land between the flooded road and the swollen river, but, by the time we reached the stone wall of their neighbour's house, I couldn't see the tarmac anymore; it had become a faint shadow, a dark backing to the water's greasy mirror. The water was even deeper in the garden; the glass wall of the conservatory would have cracked under its weight, if there hadn't been an equal weight pressing against it from the inside.

The reflection of a tall, narrow house with pale rendered walls shivered and fell apart as we eased across it. The water lapped at the sills of its downstairs windows. It was very quiet: all I could hear was the drip and splash of Glen's paddle, and the hum of the pumps draining the flooded houses. I knew how traumatic the flood had been for the people who lived here – and, when I had forgotten, Glen had reminded me – but I couldn't help thinking how natural it seemed: it was easy to imagine that Thorney had always been like this, a village of mouldering palazzos beside a still canal.

It wasn't such an absurd idea; the first settlements in the Somerset Levels were built in lakes, and, until recently, the land was flooded for much of the year. Yet it wasn't Thorney's past that I was seeing as I looked around me at the doubled houses and the still, deep pools of water that stretched between them, contained by the old stone walls and garden sheds of an English village; it was its future, and the future of the other places that will one day find themselves submerged by the grey tide that had engulfed Thorney.

~

Even the name seemed significant. There are many places in Britain called Thorney, which means Isle of Thorns: there is a Thorney in the Fens, where I had been in December 2013, a month earlier, on the day when the winter storms began, and it was a Thorney Island in the Thames that became Westminster, the seat of Parliament, and home to many branches of government.

The Environment Agency – the quasi-independent body responsible for managing flooding – occupies an office on the fringes of Thorney Island, Westminster, and, since the people in the Levels blamed it for the floods that had swept through their homes two years in a row, I came to think of Thorney, Somerset and Thorney, Westminster as twin towns, of a kind. The trajectories they have pursued in the last thousand years obscure their common origins as islands in marshland, and give them contrasting roles in national life, at the margin and the centre. But they also bind them together by making one subject to the other. The inhabitants of Thorney, Somerset, and the neighbouring villages resented the arrangement: they felt, at best, ignored by the bureaucrats of Thorney, Westminster – and, at worst, subject to a form of neglect that amounted to deliberate malice.

It wasn't only marginal places that flooded – on the day I arrived in Thorney, there was flooding in the Home Counties of Essex, Kent and Hertfordshire, and, in Berkshire and Surrey, the Thames had burst its banks and was spreading across the lawns of the grand mansions that stood beside it. Yet, in less exceptional times, it was reclaimed land on marsh and fen, on the shores of estuaries and on the floodplains where new estates are often built that was affected first and most severely, and I came to think of Thorney as emblematic of them all.

~

I hadn't planned to go there.

I was trying to see how close I could get to Muchelney, the neighbouring village, which had been cut off on all sides. I had tried approaching it from Langport, the unofficial capital of the Levels, which lies three miles north from Thorney, at the northern limit of the flood. The River Parrett was just within its banks at the western entrance to the town, and there were sandbags piled against the doors of shops and houses in the high street. 'It's not here yet,' the woman behind the post office counter said, 'but it's getting close.' I walked through the car park at the back of the shop and found myself on the edge of the lake that had risen out of the river. The wooden benches, ankle-deep in water where the banks used to be, were the only indication of the river's usual course. There were no corresponding banks on the other side; the wide brown lake stretched as far as I could see.

The road to Muchelney had flooded as well. I walked down it as far as I could go, past a flooded house and an abandoned car, the water gripping my ankles as it got deeper, and then wrapping my thin rubber boots tightly around my shins. Beneath its surface, grass swayed like seaweed, combed into strands by hidden currents. Noises echoed strangely in the flooded tunnel – the cry of a seagull was loud and then vanishingly faint, as if it had been flung away in a gale, and the chugging echo of a tractor in a field at the top of the lane sounded like a speedboat careering around the bend towards me.

Even people who knew the Levels seemed disorientated. As I walked back up the lane, I met a man coming the other way. He was looking for the boat that was taking people in and out of Muchelney. Since its location was no secret, I assumed he was an outsider, like me, but he lived in Muchelney, and hadn't been back since it had been cut off. 'I've been sleeping in a hotel,' he said, as if hotels were notoriously isolated, like the medieval monastery established in his village in the eleventh century. Or perhaps he meant to emphasize the sleeping: perhaps he had nodded off ten days ago and had woken up to find the Levels flooded and all the familiar landmarks changed – some doubled, like the Instagram-friendly trees rooted in their own reflections, branches spreading across the silvery surface of the water, and others erased, like the fields and roads, which were only marked by the tops of hedges, gates and fence posts.

Another road led towards Muchelney from the west. I reached a farm that stood on an outcrop of high land facing the lake that used to be its fields. An empty house with a flooded garden stood beside a bridge that had become a slipway, its walls pointing across the water towards the tower of the Church of St Peter and St Paul, next to the ruined abbey. Muchelney had been established on one of the islands in the Levels that used to remain dry all year round, and the winter rains had made it an island again. A car with a canoe on the roof drew up, and a man in a wetsuit got out. He normally went out on the Bristol Channel, but he didn't want to be at sea today. Even the water around Muchelney concealed hazards – as a child, he used to punt across the Levels in canvas boats that often tore their fragile skins on signs and gateposts. He took down the canoe and life jacket, stowed his car keys and phone in a waterproof pouch and set off, steering down the middle of the avenue of trees that marked the course of the flooded road. Ten minutes later, he reached the other side and stood up, rising unsteadily through the rubber skirt that fringed his waist.

I wondered how he would be received. When Prince Charles went to Muchelney, he was driven through the water on a throne set up on the back of a trailer, like a folkloric king seeking shelter in the marshes, but the residents of Muchelney had not welcomed the model, sent by the *Sun* newspaper, who had turned up with a photographer and a crate of beer. I understood why Muchelney had become an object of attention, for I wanted to see it myself, and yet, in some ways, Thorney had suffered more. Muchelney had been cut off, but its houses hadn't flooded, like the ones in Thorney. Muchelney was an island, but Thorney was a reef, washed over by the tide that had risen across Westmoor.

I circled the edge of the lake covering the central part of the Somerset Levels, and found myself on the road to Muchelney from the south. I drove past the first of the red 'road closed' signs that had proliferated on the verges of the Levels several miles outside the village, but, for once, I wasn't forced to stop. I followed the narrow winding lane until I reached the houses on the edge of Thorney and saw the water filling the road ahead. Its grey-green surface was mottled or pebbled, like a cobbled street. It wasn't until I parked and got out that I realized it was full of apples – red and green baubles, like misshapen Christmas tree decorations. There were more apples washed up on the road and embedded in the rotting mulch that had collected at the high-water mark. I stepped on one and felt it give way beneath me, its rotten flesh subsiding within the papery envelope of its skin.

The water reached the flower beds of a thatched cottage on the bend. According to the sign that protruded photogenically above the floodwaters, it was called the Anchorage, and it had become an anchorage again. There was an upturned rowing boat and a canoe resting on the grassy verge beneath its windows, and a man and a woman were loading bags of shopping into another canoe drawn up in the mouth of the channel.

It's easy striking up conversations on the edge of a flooded street or field. The presence of water breaks down inhibitions and allows people to talk to one another in the way they might on a stranded train. Even so, I hesitated before I said hello. I thought the residents of Thorney might have got tired of visitors to their flooded village. I needn't have worried; they couldn't have been friendlier if they had been hosting a party on the improvised pontoon. They lived in a house at the far end of the village, at the furthest point the water reached. They told me that you could still reach it on foot, by the path that led round the back of the village, beside the swollen River Parrett, and they said they would meet me there. Sue climbed aboard and Glen pushed off, standing up in the back like a gondolier, stirring up a wake that washed into the flower beds of the Anchorage. I waited until they reached the flooded porch of the house where the channel swung right and disappeared, and then I turned and walked up the road, past my car, looking for the path to Thorney Mill.

~

To an outsider like myself, it didn't seem surprising that the Levels had flooded. It was 6 January 2014, the middle of the wettest winter ever in the south of England, according to the Radcliffe Meteorological Station, which started keeping records in 1767, and the Levels were prone to flooding even when the weather was less extreme.

At the end of the last Ice Age – or the beginning of the current interglacial period, 20,000 years ago – sea levels were a hundred feet (thirty metres) lower than they are today, and Britain extended far beyond its current shores. When the Red Lady of Paviland – who was, in fact, a man, wrongly identified as a prostitute by an Oxford professor of geology – was interred in a cave on the Gower Peninsula, 34,000 years ago, the sea was seventy miles away, and the Bristol Channel was a marshy plain. As the glaciers melted and retreated, the seas rose and pushed inland, building a ridge of clay and sand on the Somerset coast and depositing silt in the saucer of low-lying land beyond. Over the centuries, dying plants and reeds laid down a layer of peat, and the land rose gradually, though from time to time it was washed over by more floods as 'the creeping growth' tried to 're-establish the solid in this would-be liquid world,' writes Adam Nicolson. The Somerset Levels are 'a *poured* landscape,' he says, more liquid than solid, a brackish bog held in place by the 'corrugations of the hills'.

Even the rivers that drain the Levels were formed by floods. For most of its length, the Parrett has no slope to carry it to the sea; in the eleven-mile stretch between Langport and Bridgwater, it drops by eleven and a half feet (three and a half metres) – a gradient of one in 5,280. Its meandering progress is too slow to carry its freight of silt, which drifts towards the beds, narrowing the channel and making it more prone to flood – and when it does, the overflowing silt collects on its banks, raising them above the moors and increasing the destructiveness of the floods.

Humans help the process by building the banks higher still, which improves the flow of 'these hopeless rivers', as Nicolson calls them, chidingly, as if they were recalcitrant children. Even when they reach the sea, the rivers have difficulties to overcome: the tidal rise in the Bristol Channel is the second largest in the world, and, twice a day, the fresh water drifting downstream meets the salt water flowing the other way, forcing it upstream, where it would, if permitted, spill out across the land in loops and brackish pools. At equinoctial tides, the rivers often come to a complete halt.

The locals knew all this, of course; it was partly their awareness of the rivers' failings that made them so insistent they had to be properly maintained. Locals believed the Environment Agency had neglected its duty to dredge the channels of the sluggish rivers and keep them flowing. The Parrett was ten feet (three metres) below its banks at Bridgwater, a local farmer called Julian Temperley said in an article in the *Daily Telegraph*, but, five miles upstream, it was overflowing. The floods were not a natural disaster, he said – they were man-made.

~

It is not a new complaint. The management of water has always been politically contentious. Civilization evolved in river valleys of Egypt and the Middle East, where water sustained life, and periodically overwhelmed it too. Herodotus called Egypt 'the gift of the river'; it was so dependent on the rise and fall of the Nile that its year was divided into three seasons: akhet, the season of inundation, when the fields were flooded; peret, the season of growth, after the waters had receded; and shemu, the harvest, when the crops were gathered in before the waters began to rise again.

'Normally the Nile would start to rise in late June until it reached a peak in mid-September, leaving behind a rich layer of nutrients,' writes John Withington in *Flood: Nature and Culture*. But if the water rose too high, then Egypt was 'converted into a sea, and nothing appears but the cities, which look like the islands in the Aegean', Herodotus wrote. Yet drought was equally destructive. In the thirteenth century, the rise in the river needed to be between twenty-eight and thirty-five feet (between 8.5 and 10.5 metres) to produce a good crop; more meant flooding, less meant drought and famine. 'In 1200, for example, it rose less than 23 feet (7 metres), precipitating a terrible hunger which took the lives of at least 110,000 people,' John Withington writes.

The dykes and levees built to contain the rivers, like the Tigris and the Euphrates and the Nile, represent some of humanity's earliest attempts at civil engineering. Withington argues that the coordinated effort required to build them 'stimulated the development of unified governments and organised societies in places like Egypt'. The German sociologist Karl Wittfogel believed that the system of centralized political control required to organize large-scale irrigation projects in fertile but flood-prone lands had led to despotism. Wittfogel, who 'went from being a devout Marxist to an equally impassioned anti-Marxist', in Simon Schama's phrase, saw parallels between a Mesopotamian tyranny closely tied in with a system for managing water and the great dams built by Stalin and Mao to assert their power. 'The colossal dam and the hydroelectric power station as emblems of omnipotence were for modern despots what the Nile irrigation canals were for the Pharoahs,' Schama writes, in *Landscape and Memory*.

Wittfogel's ideas have been dismissed as 'grandiose' and 'overdrawn', but the story of Yu the Great, who established China's first political dynasty by containing the Yellow River, which floods so destructively it is known as 'China's Sorrow', suggests the management of water was sometimes a path to political power.

Yu was the son of a man called Gun, who had tried and failed to contain the Yellow River by building dykes. The king lost patience with Gun and threw him into prison. Yu was asked to take over, and he tried a different approach: inspired by the lines on a turtle's shell, he dredged the rivers and built a system of canals that diverted water into the fields. 'Heaven commanded Yu to spread out the soil, and to cross the mountains and dredge the streams,' runs the inscription on a tureen, dated to *c.* 900 BC.

Most versions of the story praise his dedication. He had been married for four days when he started work. The first time he went past his house, he heard his wife in labour. The second time, he heard his son crying. The third time, he saw a young man in the garden he didn't recognize. Even when he realized it was his son, who had grown up in his absence, he didn't stop. 'Each time, Yu told himself that countless people were still being driven from their homes by floods and that he had no time to interrupt his work,' writes John Withington. Emperor Shun was so impressed by his dedication that he appointed Yu to succeed him in place of his own son, and Yu went on to establish China's first real dynasty, the Xia, which lasted for more than 400 years.

Yet even Yu the Great could not contain the Yellow River for long; according to some estimates, it has flooded 1,500 times in the last 3,000 years. In 1938, the nationalists deliberately breeched the levees along the Yellow River near Kaifeng to delay the invading Japanese troops; some reports claim 300,000 people drowned in a deluge that has been called the worst ever man-made natural disaster. At other times, the Yellow River's floods and disruptive shifts in course have prompted dynastic changes and rebellions, for they are seen as proof that 'the mandate of heaven', by which rulers govern, has been withdrawn.

Christian mythology acknowledges the spiritual signifi-cance of floods, as well. The Royalist antiquarian William Dugdale, whose *History of Imbanking and Drayning of Divers Fenns and Marshes* mapped the topography of seventeenth-century England with a completeness I did not aspire to match, said that 'works of Drayning are most antient and of divine institution'. He pointed out that drainage appears in Genesis before Noah, for the command to 'let the waters be gathered together, and let the dry land appear' was the third act of creation. His perception of God as a kind of universal drainage engineer might explain why He (or She) used water to reboot the design after the first model failed: 'Again, after the Deluge, it was through the Divine good-ness, that the waters were dried up from off the Earth, and the face of the ground was dry.'

People sensed the hand of God at work in the Somerset Levels, as well; they were going to church to pray for the floods to end, Julian Temperley said, though he believed they were petitioning the wrong authority; the only thing that God could be blamed for was 'not giving the Environment Agency any brains.'

It wasn't surprising that Julian Temperley was angry; his father – a ninety-eight-year-old professor of mathematics, who had given his name to a branch of algebra – lived in Thorney House, the Georgian manor that stood at the far end of the village, opposite the Wards' house. Thorney House hadn't flooded since 1924, and now it had flooded twice in little more than a year – once in December 2012, and again in January 2014. The water had started rising on New Year's Day. It began as a trickle, but it soon became a torrent, and the water in Thorney House rose so quickly that Professor Temperley was evacuated before the end of the day.

~

It was dark by the river, beyond the light cast by the unflooded houses at the southern end of the village. I had to use the cold metal handrail on the bridge above the weir as a guide as I crossed the Parrett behind Thorney Mill. The water pouring through the weir was smooth and black; I could hardly see it, until it hit the surface of the pool, where it stirred up a head of yellow-flecked foam that drained into a fast-flowing channel. The Parrett, which got so low in the summer that Glen's canoe would catch on the bottom, was nearly at the top of the raised bank dividing it from the gardens that backed on to the river. Hosepipes snaked through the flooded lawns and sank into the fast-flowing current. The Parrett hadn't flooded Thorney – the water had come across Westmoor, sweeping through an orchard and picking up its cargo of windfalls – but it had come close, and it showed how precarious Thorney had become that the owners of the houses were draining water into a river that would send it back if it rose much higher.

The narrow, trampled path veered away from the river and, ahead of me, the land dipped towards a clump of buildings, lit like the superstructure of a container ship, moored in the flooded fields. I felt a momentary panic; it didn't seem very sensible to be stumbling deeper into the Levels as it got dark, and I was relieved when I came round a curve in the river and saw Glen pulling his canoe on to the raised ground at the back of his house. His cheerful wave made my anxiety seem foolish.

I paused for a moment when I came up on the road beside the bridge, relieved to be back on solid ground again. To the north, the road was clear as far as I could see, though it must have slipped underwater before it went much further, for it was the road that ran through Muchelney and on to Langport – the one I had walked down earlier in the day. I turned and crossed the bridge into the village. The water reached the foot of the bridge and lapped at the fringes of the sodden, apple-thickened mat of compost it had laid down in the Wards' drive. The house was a low, whitewashed building with metal windows; its simple lines seemed out of place among the Georgian farmhouses and post-war red-brick semis that I had seen elsewhere, and yet it was an authentic product of the Somerset Levels, for it used to be a withy factory, where the reeds that grow in such profusion in the waterlogged fields were woven into baskets.

Most of the houses in the village were empty, but the Wards hadn't left. At first, they didn't think their house would flood; the year before, the water had reached the middle of the street, and they didn't think it would come any higher. 'But it just kept coming and coming and coming,' Glen said. The trail of apples in the drive suggested the path it had taken. Glen had boarded up the front door, but the water seeped upwards through the floor. Even then, they hadn't left: they had moved into the granny flat that stood on the raised bank between the river and the garden. 'We were luckier than some,' Glen said, with what seemed like characteristic resilience. Some people had only just got back into their houses, after being flooded the year before, when they had been forced out again. The fact that the Wards could stay and tend the pump meant they had been able to keep the water down – if they hadn't, it would have been much worse. Since he couldn't lift the water over the bank into the river, he had drained it into the lawn, where it lay, ankle-deep, in another pool filled with rotting apples.

Six days after the water had first come up, Glen thought it was finally going down; it was several inches below the mark on the back wall, which showed the highest point it had reached, though it got deeper quickly in the road, where it ran past the front wall of the house. I edged into it, until I was standing on tiptoes, and peered inside. I couldn't see the water until I tilted my head. It was a still, grey layer, glossing the floor like wet paint. I had been travelling round the country for a year, visiting places that had flooded, but I usually arrived after the water had gone down – sometimes, years after, sometimes when the clearing up was going on. I had met many people who had been affected and heard their stories of the floods. But I had never been inside a flooded house.

'Can we have a look inside?' I said.

Glen had been so welcoming that I assumed he wouldn't mind, but he said he had to check with his wife. As he crossed the sodden, apple-strewn drive to the lighted room on the bank, I waited in the shadows by the back door, conscious of the expanse of water pressing in from three sides. I expected Glen to return with a set of keys, but he shook his head as he approached: 'I'm sorry; it's private,' he said, as if there was something shameful and intimate about being flooded.

I was surprised, though I shouldn't have been, for I knew that flooding affected people in profound and unpredictable ways. Being forced to watch, helplessly, as polluted water pours through your doors or windows, or seeps upwards through your floors, destroying your possessions and turning your home into a sodden, stinking cave: it didn't take much imagination to understand how upsetting that must be. Yet flooding seemed to induce a degree of anguish that could not be explained by a rational tallying of its effects: as one civil servant said to me – off the record, as all those conversations were, for no one would speak officially, for fear of making things worse – it was 'disproportionately upsetting'.

People have always told stories of great floods that sweep the earth and drown its people, and stories of lost lands beneath the seas, and the primal fear provokes primal reactions. People are drawn to water for many different reasons

– spiritual and emotional, as well as practical. We cherish the sea view and the sound of running water.

> If I were called in
> To construct a religion
> I should make use of water

Philip Larkin wrote, in a poem called 'Water', which attempts to define a liturgy for the spiritually uncommitted. Baths and fountains are an enduring emblem of civic good. Yet flooding turns a substance that we depend upon and revere into something malign and unfamiliar. Floodwater isn't soothing or beguiling, like rivers or streams, nor is it awe-inspiring, like the sea. It is dirty, cold and destructive, and when it erupts from the channels in which we seek to contain it and invades people's homes, it leaves stains that cannot easily be erased.

~

I am lucky; I have never been flooded, though I have lived in flood-prone places. The Northumberland town of Morpeth, where I lived as a child, had flooded twice in the five years before I visited the flooded Levels – once, the water reached the bottom of the street where we used to live. The Wirral Peninsula and the Hampshire town of Winchester – two other places where I grew up – would also flood in the course of the winter of 2013–14, and the seas would encroach on the shores of Essex, where I was born.

For the last fifteen years, I have lived on a hill in North London, though even that is not as safe as it might appear, for floods are not only caused by torrential downpours or once-in-a-decade storms; it only takes a blocked pipe or an overloaded sewer to fill a street or flood a house. Sometimes, our ageing Victorian infrastructure gives way, and buried streams re-emerge with sudden force.

Such events will become more common, as climate change takes effect. As a child, growing up in the north of England in the seventies, I lived through cold wet winters and mild damp summers. Long hot summers, like the one of 1976, were memorable because they were so rare. My enduring memories are of rain-streaked windows and the smell of the morning air after a night of rain. The rubbery scrape of a windscreen wiper evokes the atmosphere of childhood holidays in Scotland or the Lakes.

The qualities that the British value most in themselves – resilience, a tendency to self-mockery, an ability to find consolation in defeat – derive from seeing the world through a haze of drizzle. The weather was moderate, like the British themselves; it rarely 'got out of hand' or acted excessively; it pre-empted extremes in us. Yet the floods and storms that marked the beginning of the twenty-first century seemed of a different order altogether, and it is not just nostalgia that makes me say so. 'For anyone under the age of 30 – more than half the world's population – the experience of a stable climate is entirely unknown,' wrote the author Brian Stone in the *London Review of Books* in 2018. 'That is to say, not a single month in their lifetime has fallen within the limited

range of temperature, precipitation or storm activity that
governed the planet for the previous 10,000 years.' According
to Met Office figures, nine of the ten warmest years on
record in the UK have occurred since 2002 – and, since a
warmer climate holds more water, they have also brought
more floods.

The same pattern holds elsewhere: globally, the last twenty-
two years have seen the twenty warmest years on record,
with the same effects that we have seen in Britain. Low-
lying countries like Bangladesh and island nations like the
Seychelles are threatened by the rising seas, and cities like
Miami and New York are increasingly exposed to devastating storms.

I couldn't go everywhere that had been affected. Work
and family kept me in London, and when I could get away,
it wasn't for long. I didn't resent the constraints; Britain is
the place that I know best, and the place that I have always
felt most compelled to explore. Besides, its intricate coastline, its winding rivers and its variable Atlantic weather
have laid down a long history of floods and flooding, preserved in art, literature and folklore. But, above all, it was
the memories of the people who had been flooded that I
wanted to record. I hoped that they would want to tell
their stories – though not, perhaps, when they were struggling to cope with water coming through the door. I didn't
want to be intrusive. But I did want to understand the
nature of an experience that more of us will be forced to
endure.

I was fascinated by the flood maps the Environment

Agency produced that showed how water spread through streets and fields, and I wanted to make a version of my own. My map would be shamelessly subjective and incomplete, deeply etched in some places and blank in others, less preoccupied with the point the water reached or the rate at which it went down than with the emotional and psychological marks it left behind.

I didn't plan where I was going in advance; I knew that people would pass me on to other people they thought I should meet, and tell me about other places I ought to go, and I wanted to let my journey develop a momentum of its own. It was only afterwards that I saw a pattern had emerged. By the time I arrived in Thorney at the height of the winter storms, which had begun when a 'great tide' travelled down the east coast on the night of 5 December 2013, driving the sea higher than it had been since the Great Tide of 31 January 1953, when 300 people in the east of Britain and 3,000 people in Holland had drowned, I had completed a clockwise circuit of the country that took me from the flood-prone towns of Gloucestershire and Worcestershire, through Wales and along the west coast to the Lake District and the North, and back to London along Doggerland's fraying shores.

~

I was pleased when Glen offered me a lift back to my car in the canoe; perhaps I hadn't offended him as much as I had thought. Or perhaps he wanted to get rid of me before I fell in the river. In any case, I was glad to see what the village looked like from the perspective of the water.

It didn't take long. We passed the flooded house on the bend and the dark channel of water that used to be the drove leading on to Westmoor, and then the lighted windows of the Anchorage came into view. The water got shallower quickly – the stained surface of the tarmac rushed towards me seconds before the canoe scraped against it and grounded in the soft bed of compost. I got out unsteadily, and Glen turned the canoe round and pushed off, standing up in the back, feeling for the surface of the road he used to walk on every day. 'See you when we get over this,' he called out, as his upright figure faded into the dusk. 'If we ever do.'

He was right to be cautious; some of the people I had met in the course of the year said the process of 'recovery' was worse than being flooded, though I doubted it would trouble Glen much. Apart from his understandable reluctance to let me look inside the house, he seemed remarkably unperturbed by living in a flooded village and going home by canoe. At the risk of overtaxing his hospitality again, I planned to take him up on the offer to go back to Thorney; though, by the time I got back there, seven months later, I would have learnt something that made me think about the flood – and the complaints of his neighbours about its cause – in a different way.

2: A Stone Ark

Tewkesbury was the first place I went to, for the small Gloucestershire town was the capital of our newly flood-prone country until the villages of the Somerset Levels displaced it.

It gained the title during the floods of the summer of 2007, when torrential rain swept through the North and the Midlands. Tewkesbury was cut off for days; thousands of houses and businesses flooded and three people drowned, including a father and his son who were overcome by fumes when they were trying to pump out the basement of a rugby club.

Yet it wasn't the individual tragedies or the statistics that earned Tewkesbury global fame of a kind it never wanted – it was an aerial photograph of the town marooned in the dark brown lake that had risen up around it. The water enclosed the close-packed streets of the town on all sides. It stretched beyond the edge of the frame, its surface broken by telegraph poles and curving lines of trees that traced the route of submerged roads. Tewkesbury Abbey was in the bottom corner of the frame: the water had risen through its lush green grounds, which was the only open space visible in the town, and was lapping at the base of its tower, which stood like an old stone lighthouse in the flood.

The photograph was transmitted around the world: it became as famous as the picture of the dome of St Paul's rising through the smoke of the Blitz, the vicar of Tewkesbury Abbey told me when I went to the town for the first time, in November 2012. Britain, which was used to watching climatic disasters unfold on the other side of the world, had found itself the object of attention. When the water went down, the first people to enter Tewkesbury were members of a film crew from Al Jazeera.

I had never been to Tewkesbury before, but I had grown up in provincial towns that looked very much like it and I understood why people were fascinated by the photograph: it signalled the end of a way of life denoted by the trinity of church, marketplace and river. It confirmed that the future no one wanted to contemplate was happening now.

~

Most of the time, I find it easy not to think about climate change. I used to think about it more. I remember lying on the lawn in the back garden of our house during the heatwave that struck Northern Europe in the summer of 2003, seized with panic at the thought of the ecological disaster we were inviting: the rising seas, the droughts and floods, the influx of refugees from the south – these did not seem like abstract possibilities anymore; they were present in the humid warmth on my skin and the sound of our neighbours' voices drifting through the doors and windows of the fetishized Victorian houses of North London, which had been temporarily relocated to a climate where life was lived outdoors.

My sense of impending disaster didn't last. The usual excuses prevailed: I didn't want to change the way I lived, and I didn't think it would make any difference if I did. Besides, I had other things to think about. As the years passed, I became the kind of person who did the school run in a T-shirt in November and passed it off with a joke about it being nice for the time of year. But even I found it hard to ignore the floods.

For years, meteorologists had warned that climate change would bring warm, wet winters, but it was the summer floods of 2007 that made me think about our new weather. There were more floods in subsequent years, often in places that I knew and loved: Morpeth flooded in 2008; the Lake District towns of Cockermouth and Keswick in 2009; Cornwall in 2010. Thousands of people drowned in China in May and June 2010, adding a new chapter to the Yellow River's history of destructive floods. In January 2011, 700 people drowned in Brazil, in its worst ever floods, and, in April, the Mississippi burst its banks.

In Britain, 2012 was another year of climatic extremes of the kind we were getting used to. It started with a drought: there were hosepipe bans in March, but April was the wettest on record and flooding inevitably followed. Summer brought more freak weather: hailstones the size of golf balls fell in the Midlands and a downpour dubbed 'the Toon Monsoon' struck Newcastle, leaving a block of flats in the east of the city poised on a set of fragile stilts on the edge of the cascading torrent that had swept away the ground beneath it. In November, New York was left without power for days when Hurricane Sandy crashed into the eastern seaboard, sending water coursing through its streets and flooding its subways.

Autumn in the UK was mild at first. A 'blood rain', thickened and tinted by dust from the Sahara, was forecast for Halloween, but it turned out warm and dry. We told our kids they had to wear something beneath their polyester witch's dress and skeleton onesie, but they could have gone out in ripped sheets and make-up, like their grown-up counterparts, who followed the glowing trail of pumpkins from door to door, with joke-shop knives through their heads and faces smeared with gore. Crowds of ghouls gathered on street corners. Apple bobbing – the only Halloween ritual I remember from my childhood – was not an ordeal. If it hadn't been for the fading light and the leaves that tumbled around our feet as we walked, it would have felt like a celebration of spring, instead of a welcoming of winter.

Two days after Halloween, it started raining again, and the temperature dropped. The leaves turned crisp with frost and then collapsed into a slippery mush that glossed the pavement and made it shine like a trout's slick, speckled skin. Outside London, rain fell on saturated ground. One man drowned after his car was washed down a flooded

brook in Somerset, and another when his car overturned in
Devon. Three hundred flats and houses flooded in England
and Wales in the course of a single day, and a cliff collapsed
in Whitby, taking several houses with it. Morpeth flooded
for the second time in four years, and the town of St Asaph,
in North Wales, was engulfed when the River Elwy burst
its banks. I would go to both of these places in the course
of the year. Yet it was the news that Tewkesbury had flooded
again that interested me the most. I had had a copy of the
photograph of Tewkesbury in the summer of 2007 pinned
to my wall since I started reading about flooding, and when
I heard that the rivers that converge upon the town had
burst their banks and were rising towards the abbey again,
I decided to go and see it for myself.

~

I left London on an early train. There was flooding on the
outskirts of Reading. The banks of the Thames had disappeared beneath a grey sheet of water. An avenue of
half-submerged trees showed where the river used to run.
There was no sign of a current beneath the placid lake.
Goalposts confirmed the function of a field and plumbed
the water's depth. Moored boats swung in line beside us, as
close as carriages on an adjoining track.

The station at Tewkesbury was two miles outside town.
A poster advertising *A Party on the Beach* hung on a fence
sealing a derelict plot of land on the edge of an industrial
estate beside the station. I crossed the bridge above the M5

and followed a long straight road lined with modern and Victorian houses. *Welcome to Tewkesbury: Historic Riverside Town*, a sign said. The turning to a village called Walton Cardiff had flooded: a Severn Trent Water sign said work was due to start in September, but the water was too deep to come from a burst main. It filled a lane that ran down the side of a new estate to a playground. It reached the top of my boots, but lay below the lip of the concrete plinth on which the houses had been built. The fields were placid ponds, sealed within the embankments that carried the roads. A stream passing beneath a bridge had become part of the lake. These were the city's floodplains, the vicar of Tewkesbury Abbey would say, and the sunlight reflecting off the silvered fields was beautiful when you drove into town – so long as the water stayed within their confines.

The worst flooding was in the street behind the hospital, where a narrow tributary of the Severn, called the Swilgate, had burst its banks. It had been even higher earlier in the week, said a man standing on the metal bridge above the branch-clogged torrent. If I had come the day before, I wouldn't have been able to get out of the hospital, for the dark brown water lapping at the verges of the road had risen as high as its back door. They were building a new hospital on an adjoining site; work had resumed for the first time in several days, and the skate park was drying out. Yet the water was only just passing beneath the bridge; it had spread out so far that the man couldn't tell where it normally ran.

My friend – who told me his name, but asked me not to

use it – had lived in a block of flats on the far bank since 1975, and he had only seen the Swilgate as high as this once before. 'They said 2007 was meant to be a one-off, but this is looking sinister as well,' he said. It was a well-chosen word: it conveyed the sense, which many people seemed to share, that flooding was not a natural phenomenon, but the consequence of a conspiracy directed against them. Yet he had no interest in the climatic changes that may have contributed to the downpours. 'Global warming, global cooling: they have no idea what's going on,' he said. It was the first time I had come across the disdain for expert advice that would become so apparent in the Somerset Levels in the winter of 2013. All he knew was that they got the rain that fell in Wales three or four days earlier – and there had been a lot of it.

It had come up without warning, said a man sweeping a tidemark of dirt off his drive, further down the road. He had woken up on Saturday morning to find the water lapping at the drive, and had taken out his boat, paddled across the cricket pitch and taken pictures looking back at his house, which had become a lakeside villa. He spoke with a rich Gloucestershire accent, but he was dressed like a biker from the American South, with a quiff and a cut-off denim jacket adorned with a Union flag. There was a motorbike with low-slung handlebars parked in the drive and a photograph of a woman riding one like it hung inside the front door. He hadn't been living in Tewkesbury in 2007, but his wife had, and she'd had eighteen inches (almost half a metre) of water in the house. He didn't think it would get high enough to get over the lip of the front door this time, though he was worried that it might rise through the drains at the side and flood the workshop where he kept another bike.

The Mill Avon, the river that the monks of Tewkesbury Abbey had built to drive water through their mills on the western edge of town had also burst its banks. I walked along the edge of the lake that had emerged from the river, trying to guess the layout of the submerged streets and footpaths by the objects that broke the surface. The top half of a postbox marked the position of a pavement, a *Resident Permit Holders Only* sign indicated parking spaces, and a set of steps leading down into the water marked a riverside path. A sign warned of boats manoeuvring for the locks, though I couldn't see the locks themselves, for the water had submerged the apparatus designed to subdue it. Boats had become clumsy objects, tethered in awkward postures by their foreshortened ropes: a barge had drifted against a metal fence, and a dinghy was dragged down at its bow – any further rise in the level of the water would sink it. The water was barely passing beneath the arches of the bridge at the end of the high street. The arches were not a conduit anymore: they were a barrier. The Mythe Bridge, half a mile out of town, carried a single lane of traffic over the Severn, where boat-club dinghies were beached on the muddy shore. Beyond it lay the solid red-brick mass of the Mythe Water Treatment Works, which had flooded in 2007, leaving thousands of people dependent on water from bowsers. Water had spilled through its gate and lay in puddles in its grounds.

I walked back towards Tewkesbury and turned into a cul-de-sac of terraced houses called King John's Court. It occupied an island between two arms of the River Avon – though, for the time being, the layout of the rivers was obscured, as well as the layout of the streets. Judging by the way the railings diminished in height as they sank into the water, the street sloped downhill, though it rose again in front of the lock-keeper's cottage in the middle of the stream, where a submerged bench looked out across the drowned fields.

The way the water mirrored the trees and clouds made me think of the descriptions of 'the Lake', the 'inland sea' that covers central England in *After London: or, Wild England* by the Victorian naturalist Richard Jefferies, which imagines the collapse of modern civilization, and the feudal society that replaces it. 'At the eastern extremity the Lake narrows, and finally is lost in the vast marshes which cover the site of the ancient London,' writes the novel's unnamed narrator. He does not know exactly how the Lake formed, but he speculates that 'changes of the sea level' threw up great sandbanks at the mouth of the Thames, while a 'broad barrier of beach' obstructed the mouth of the Severn; once the respective eastward and westward flow of the rivers was blocked, they 'turned backwards . . . and began to cover hitherto dry land.' London becomes a foul, decaying swamp, but 'the Lake' is as 'clear as crystal, exquisite to drink, abounding with fishes of every kind, and adorned with green islands.'

I was contemplating Tewkesbury's 'Lake' when I became

aware of a man watching me from the window of a nearby house. I walked over to him and he opened the window just far enough to be able to speak.

'Can I help you?' he said, in the English way that implies he did not want to help at all.

'I'm just looking at the water,' I said, which must have sounded equally indirect.

He was more concerned about burglars than flooding; his neighbour's car had been stolen the previous day and he was worried the thieves might come back. He seemed reassured that I was not a threat, but his manner didn't change, for he was sceptical of flood tourists, like me, and other people who fail to appreciate that Tewkesbury always floods. His house was perfectly safe, he said, despite being located on a promontory enclosed on three sides by water. 'These houses were built with flooding in mind,' he said, indicating the slab that raised the front door half a metre above the ground.

He conceded that the water was higher than usual and was taking longer to subside, but he said he had never been concerned, for an enormous volume of water was required to affect a rise in the level across the thousands of acres of floodplain in which Tewkesbury was located. A family had had to be rescued in Sandhurst, Gloucestershire, ten miles downstream; flood defences failed in Kempsey, Worcestershire, twelve miles upstream; and even the White Bear, which stands on the main road, had flooded – but King John's Court had remained untouched. 'Personally, I don't see a problem for us, here,' the man said. 'There is a problem in other places, but that's the subtle difference with Tewkesbury: we don't try and stop the water; we just let it flow through.'

I was impressed by his confidence, though I was not entirely convinced that he was right to be so calm, for the margins seemed very fine, despite all the efforts made to raise the houses above the water's reach. Yet it wasn't until I went back to Tewkesbury, on a spring day in May 2013, six months after my first visit, that I realized how the water had transformed the town, even in the course of a flood that some people insisted was routine. It was the Swilgate that surprised me the most. The wide brown lake that the biker had boated across was revealed as a cricket pitch, with covers and sight screens – vertical and horizontal squares of gridded white slats – arranged beneath the tower of the abbey, which stood on a hill, far from water of any kind. The Swilgate, which had been a dark brown, slow-moving current, spilling across the skate park and the road and lapping at the doors of the hospital, had subsided into the bottom of a deep, thickly grassed channel that wound through the meadow below the abbey and on into the sheep-dotted fields on the edge of town. It was so narrow that there were places where I could step across it. If I hadn't seen it for myself, I wouldn't have believed how high it had risen or how far it had spread – and yet it had been even higher in 2007.

~

The early summer of 2007 was unusually wet: between May and July, 414 millimetres of rain fell across England and Wales, making it the wettest period since records began, in 1766. When it started raining again at the end of July, there was nowhere for the water to go. Two months' worth of rain fell in Tewkesbury on the afternoon of Friday, 20 July and during the next two days, the town was hit by three floods of escalating severity.

The Swilgate was the first to burst its banks, for it was swollen by water pouring off the saturated fields. 'At first, no one was unduly concerned,' said John Badham, a local councillor and retired head teacher, who lived in Abbey Terrace, a row of Georgian houses beside the main road leading south, towards Cheltenham. Local wisdom says that as long as you can see the benches on the high ground on the far side of the Vineyards, the field that lies below Tewkesbury Abbey, then there is no need to worry. I had noticed the benches during my first visit, in November 2012, when the Vineyards were under water, and they were visible at seven o'clock on the evening of Friday, 20 July 2007. Mr Badham and his wife went out for a curry, and, by the time they got back, there was a foot (thirty centimetres) of water in their house.

The current was so strong, it was hard to stand up in it. It picked up a heavy wooden table and shifted it across the room. 'It was very frightening,' he told me, when I arrived at his house, having followed the thin blue thread of the Swilgate through the Vineyards to Abbey Terrace. 'It came up so high,' he said, indicating the top of the Aga. It was nearly a metre deep – roughly the height of one of the two black Labradors that were bustling around the kitchen, bouncing off each other and clanking their warm, heavy heads against my knees. He showed me a framed black-and-white picture of a cart standing outside Abbey Terrace during another flood, in 1924: the water came halfway up its wheels. 'It was deeper than that in 2007,' he said, before apologizing and correcting himself with a joke that he also apologized for: 'I mustn't exaggerate. I must be careful. I am a natural exaggerator. My great-grandfather was an Irishman. It was his fault.'

John Badham was in his sixties, a tall man, dressed in cords and a sweater. He was a former prep school head-master who had taught in London and Hereford before he retired and moved to Tewkesbury. It was not new territory for him. He was born in Cheltenham, eight miles south following the road that ran past his front door, and his family owned a chain of chemist shops nearby, including one in Bishop's Cleeve, the village where the Swilgate rises, seven miles to the west. John had profited from the area's post-war development through the growth of the family business, though the water that flowed through the drains ended up in his front room.

I thought he was entitled to regard himself as a local, but the locals didn't agree. When he had started a campaign to relocate the war memorial from its inaccessible spot in the middle of the high street, one 'old boy' had told him that they were running a campaign to relocate him back to Cheltenham. He told the story with relish; he liked the idea of himself as outsider and contrarian. He was a Conservative councillor, but he called himself an unconventional Tory, at odds with the mainstream of the party. UKIP had just won a swathe of council seats in the local elections, and he was pleased with its emergence: not because he agreed with its policies, but because he liked the idea of the British voter saluting the British establishment with 'two nicotine-stained fingers'.

It was a typical digression – he talked incessantly, laughing at his own jokes, and pursuing random thoughts before hauling himself back to the story of the flood. 'This is way off beam,' he kept saying, though it didn't stop him when another idea caught his attention. He talked about family, history, politics and religion, but it was his wife who showed me the floodgates that fitted to the front door, and pointed out the Ercol furniture they had chosen for its light wooden frames. Other more substantial adaptations were apparent in the kitchen: the floor had been tiled and the plug sockets were set higher up in the wall, above the point the water reached.

Tewkesbury has always flooded, for it lies at the junction of the Severn and the Avon, and at the heart of a 'confusion of small brooks' and 'snaking waterways', in the words of the author John Moore, who was born in a house near Tewkesbury Abbey in 1907. It 'was isolated even in summer,' he wrote, and in the winter it was often cut off altogether: 'milk was delivered by rowing-boat and people punted through the back streets'. Yet, even in a flood-prone town like Tewkesbury, Abbey Terrace was notoriously prone to flooding. When I had been there in November, a woman in the estate agent's office had tried to convince me that the floods were normal for the time of year. Sure, she said, there are a few car parks and country lanes under water, and a few houses in Abbey Terrace are being pumped out – but that's only to be expected.

John Badham knew all the stories. He liked to joke that he was the only man in England who had bought a house in 2000 that was now worth less than he paid for it. It didn't make any difference, because he couldn't sell it anyway. 'Any entry of water into your home, no matter how tiny, has to be disclosed – probably quite rightly,' he said. 'The first question anybody asks when they buy a house in Tewkesbury is obvious: was it flooded? Well, I would ask the same thing.'

Abbey Terrace was not only vulnerable from the front; at the back, it bordered the Mill Avon, which had burst its banks in the winter, flooding the western edge of town. The windows of Mr Badham's study, on the top floor of his house, revealed another transformation: the grey lake that I had contemplated from King John's Court was now a managed riverscape of locks and gates that contained the narrow strip of water dividing the town from the water meadow called the Ham, its lush green grass invigorated by its winter drenching. It was like going backstage in a theatre and seeing the old-fashioned machinery that was used to raise and lower the flats. It was the industrial end of town, John Badham said – though, when the water came up and the locks and gates disappeared, it was like living in Switzerland.

Their house hadn't flooded in November 2012, though it had come close: water from the Mill Avon had filled the garden and come halfway up the steps of the renovated kitchen. It had been higher in 2007, for the Mill Avon was the second river to flood Tewkesbury, after the Swilgate; it had burst its banks on Saturday morning and added to the depth of water already in the houses in Abbey Terrace. John Badham, who chewed nicotine gum throughout the time I spent with him, used to be a heavy smoker, and he had been stuck in the house without any cigarettes. 'So I rang my friend, who was very hostile to smoking, and I said, "I'm desperate, I have to have a packet of fags." He had a pair of galoshes, and he decided that, in the circumstances, he would go and buy me some.'

Yet even cigarettes couldn't persuade the Badhams to stay. One of their neighbours had a boat and, at lunchtime, he sculled up to the front door and collected them. They left with a suitcase. 'The dog swam – there was only one, in those days.' There were now unmistakably two, and they made the kitchen seem very small as they circled in a constant search for food or affection. The Badhams had had a cat as well, which they had been happy to leave behind. 'It was a horrid cat.' Mr Badham laughed. 'One of my friends called it cook-ing fat, which is a spoonerism. It was a dreadful cat – used to savage you at the slightest provocation.' They thought they would be back within a day, but it was three or four, and they had to ask the RSPCA to save the cat.

Hundreds of houses had flooded by then, though some things went ahead as planned: there was a wedding in the abbey on Saturday, and the bride arrived in a four-by-four. The Reverend Canon Paul Williams, the vicar of Tewkesbury Abbey, went across the road to the pub, which was another relic of the old monastic establishment, and asked people to help him move furniture beyond the water's reach. He returned the favour by helping people sandbag houses and businesses. John Badham, who became a Catholic when he went to college in Oxford, partly to irritate his Presbyterian businessman father, said he didn't belong to 'the vicar's flock', but had nothing but praise for him all the same. He remembered the vicar padding about with a teapot, visiting people stranded in their cars. On Saturday evening, he held a service at the gates of the abbey, and people came out of the nearby houses to listen.

I had met the Reverend Williams in the abbey on my first visit to Tewkesbury. It was only half past three when I got there, but it was getting dark already; the yellow-tinted light falling through the stained-glass windows had faded, matching the tone of the burnished pews and flagstone floor. The Reverend Williams was standing at the end of the nave. I recognized him from a photograph on the website, which included knitting patterns and cake recipes as well as accounts of Tewkesbury's history and statements of theological identity, though the dog collar marked him out, anyway. We walked round the outside of the building to his study, in the vicarage. There were comfortable armchairs and shelves of books on theology, and a tray of tea was delivered discreetly from the recesses of the old building. Yet the Anglican warmth and civility contrasted with the cold, dark expanse of water that filled the Vineyards and rose to within metres of the windows.

People came up with ingenious ways of getting through the flood of 2007, the Reverend Williams said: they rigged up a pulley system to reach the inhabitants of the Abbey Mill, which had been cut off, and sent across essential supplies, such as champagne. 'What makes human beings unique is that ability to work together for the common good,' he said. 'It was awe-inspiring, the care for one another that emerged.'

I was fascinated by the stories of life in the flooded town. I had studied the aerial photograph of Tewkesbury in 2007 so often that I felt I could have found my way through the streets revealed by its elevated perspective, but I had no idea what was going on in them. The town looked deserted – that was part of the strangeness of the photograph. I could see the tall Georgian houses of Abbey Terrace, knee-deep in water at the eastern edge of the narrow isthmus of land to which Tewkesbury had been confined, the flats of the converted Abbey Mill, which were cut off from the rest of the town, and the windows of the vicarage where I was sitting with the vicar, but I couldn't see the Badhams climbing into the boat with their dog, the pulley ferrying champagne to Abbey Mill, nor the bride arriving in a four-by-four. And I couldn't see the congregation that had formed in the streets outside the abbey to listen to the service. Now that I had heard the way sound rebounded from the surface of the water, which lay at the end of the streets, and seen how it glossed the walls of the alleys running off the high street with a faint grey glow, I could imagine prayers and chanting drifting around the flooded town on the evening of 21 July 2007, and I didn't doubt the vicar's claim that it had been 'a powerful cultic event'.

'You could see the force of ritual holding a community together,' he said. 'We had people who were trapped in their cars and slept overnight here. We had 200 in the abbey, 200 in the hall, and people dotted around about – people ran for shelter, and it became an ark.'

~

According to Mesopotamian mythology, the gods used to live on earth and provide for themselves. They even dug the channels that carried the life-giving waters of the Tigris and the Euphrates. Yet, as the years passed, they got tired of looking after themselves:

> The gods' load was too great
> The work too hard, the trouble too much

says a poem dated to 1700 BC, which also contains the earliest recorded story of a survivor of a flood. The gods made fourteen humans from clay and blood to be their slaves, but they bred too fast and the noise of their chattering and arguing rose up to heaven and irritated the gods. They tried to reduce the humans' numbers through plague, drought and famine, before a god called Enlil decided to settle the matter with a purging flood. In the *Epic of Gilgamesh*, which contains the fullest version of the story, another god, Ea, learns of Enlil's plan and passes on a warning to a man called Uta-Napishtim. Speaking to him through the wall of a reed hut where he is sleeping, Ea tells him to build a boat in which to ride out the flood:

> Abandon wealth, and seek survival!
> Spurn property, save life!
> Take on board the boat all living things' seed!

Enlil's deluge was so overwhelming that 'even the gods took fright' and retreated to heaven, where the goddess Ishtar 'cried out like a woman in childbirth' at the agonies of the humans:

> It is I who give birth, these people are mine!
> And now, like fish, they fill the ocean!

When the flood was over, 'all the people had turned to clay.' Uta-Napishtim said, 'the floodplain was flat, like the roof of a house.' The ark, filled with breeding pairs of animals, came to rest on a mountain called Nimush, and, on the seventh day, Uta-Napishtim sent out a dove to look for land. It couldn't find any and came back. So did a swallow, but a raven didn't:

> . . . it saw the water receding,
> Finding food, bowing and bobbing, it did not come
>   back to me.

The similarities with the story of Noah are not coinciden-
tal. Irving Finkel, an expert in Mesopotamian cuneiform at
the British Museum, who was recently given a Mesopotamian
tablet with specifications for an ark and built a serviceable
version of it for a TV documentary, believes the Jews heard
the story during their exile in Babylon, in the early sixth century BC, and imported it into the Bible, with few modifications.

The story has been transported into other cultures, too.
There are at least two versions in Greek mythology, including one in which the ark lands on Mount Parnassus and a
husband and wife, Deucalion and Pyrrha, repopulate the
earth by throwing rocks over their shoulders. And it has
travelled beyond the Judaeo-Christian realm of the
Mediterranean: there is an Incan Noah who survives the
flood in a sealed cave; a Hindu Noah called Manu, who is
warned of the flood by a fish, which grows so large that it
tows his boat to its resting place in the Himalayas; and a
Polynesian Noah, Nu'u, whose boat lands on a mountain
in Hawaii, and who 'sacrificed kava, pig, and coconuts to
heaven.' *The Oxford Dictionary of World Mythology* says the
legend is a mixture of Biblical and local borrowings, but
'there is no reason to suppose that independent stories did
not exist prior to the arrival of missionaries.'

In Mayan mythology, the creator-god Hurricane was so
disappointed with his early attempts to carve humans out
of wood that he drowned them in a flood, while the sun-
god, Nakuset, of the indigenous Canadian Mi'kmaq people,
was so saddened by mankind's wickedness that he wept
tears that became a global deluge. The people attempted to

escape in bark canoes, but only one man and one woman survived.

Yet it remains best known in the Christian version. Michelangelo depicted the sinners escaping the rising waters on the ceiling of the Sistine Chapel, and Raphael painted a fresco in the Vatican loggias of Noah supervising his sons building the ark. There are versions of the flood in most of the great galleries of the world, including several on the theme of *The Deluge* by J.M.W. Turner, which hang in Tate Britain – the Thameside gallery that flooded in 1928. Recently, the filmmaker Darren Aronofsky retold the story in his movie *Noah*, starring Russell Crowe, in which he mined the great storybook of Genesis for all its strangeness and violence.

Novelists have revisited the myth as well. In two recent re-imaginings, it is not the flood that wipes out most of the human race, but disease – though, in both cases, the waters rise all the same, and shrink the survivors' worlds.

The characters in Clare Morrall's *When the Floods Came* are the last remaining inhabitants of Birmingham, isolated in tower blocks that become islands in the seasonal floods, while Margaret Atwood's trilogy of post-apocalyptic novels, *Oryx and Crake*, *The Year of the Flood* and *MaddAddam*, tells the story of a benign cult, called 'God's Gardeners', who live in rooftop communes in the chaos of the 'pleeblands', the slums outside the compounds of the biotech companies that have devastated the planet through a mixture of accident and design.

God's Gardeners disguise themselves as religious fanatics

in the hope that they will be left alone in their 'sheltering Ararats', though their recycling of Biblical tropes and environmental beliefs and practices is, in part, sincere. 'God had promised after the Noah incident that he'd never use the water method again, but considering the wickedness of the world, he was bound to do something: that was their reasoning,' Atwood writes in *MaddAddam*, the concluding book of the trilogy. While they prepare for the plague they call the 'Waterless Flood', the seas are encroaching on the continental United States. Santa Monica has become the 'Floating World', and 'nearby Venice was living up to its name'. On the east coast, New York has given way to New New York 'on the Jersey shore, or what was now the shore.' New York has not been entirely abandoned – it is 'officially a no-go zone and thus a no-rent zone, so a few denizens were still willing to take their chances in the disintegrating, waterlogged, derelict buildings.'

Sometimes, the story is re-enacted outside the realms of fiction. In 2015, a flood swept through a zoo in Tbilisi, Georgia, drowning three keepers and releasing hippos and tigers into the streets, in a reversal of the pattern all children learn of the breeding animals ushered into the ark, two by two. I sometimes wondered whether the story's enduring prominence explained our attitude to global warming: to those affected, being flooded feels like the end of the world, but, to the rest of us, there is subliminal reassurance in the knowledge that there have always been floods, and, one way or another, we have come through them. True believers may relish the prospect of a cleansing, apocalyptic flood, but even those with no religious convictions find it hard to resist the irrational belief that they will be the ones to be saved. There may be room for only one family on the ark – one pair of breeding adults to accompany the animals – but we like to think that it will be us.

Even the way the vicar of Tewkesbury invoked the Christian version of the ancient Mesopotamian myth to describe the calamity that overtook a small English town in the first decade of the twenty-first century confirmed its significance. On the face of it, it made no sense to describe Tewkesbury Abbey as an ark; even Winchester Cathedral, which was saved from sinking by a solitary diver who dug out its foundations and resettled it on a kind of raft, could hardly be described as a boat. Yet the ark that Ea told Uta-Napishtim to build, as he slept on the floor of his reed hut in the marshes of Iraq, is a universal metaphor – though it has an added local resonance, Reverend Williams said. 'The idea of the abbey as a refuge is something very deep in Tewkesbury.'

It hasn't always proved effective. One of the decisive battles of the War of the Roses was fought in the fields south of Tewkesbury, when the Yorkist forces led by King Edward IV overtook the Lancastrians, who were trying to cross the Severn and retreat into Wales, and defeated them in a battle that is re-enacted every year. Many of the Lancastrian noblemen sought sanctuary in the abbey, but they were dragged out two days later and executed.

The abbey was supposed to be a refuge in another sense, too. Tewkesbury was founded by a pilgrim from Newcastle called Theoc, who lived in a hermit's cell on a spit of land where the Severn and the Avon meet, and the abbey stands on the same spot. 'The monks knew where to build,' the Reverend Williams had said, as we stood in the nave of the abbey. In its 900-year history, the abbey had only flooded once, in 1760, when one of the Reverend Williams' predecessors had paddled a boat down the aisle, but on Sunday, 22 July 2007, it flooded for a second time. The gauge on the Mythe Bridge over the Severn, half a mile outside Tewkesbury, had reached its highest level in the floods of 1947, but on Sunday morning it set a new record: 5.43 metres was more than ten times its normal level. 'When I woke up, it was eerily quiet,' the Reverend Williams said. Yet there were firemen in the streets, and, when he went outside, he saw the water rising through the grounds of the abbey and entering the building he had described as an ark.

3: Sweet Sabrina

I walked to the source of the Severn a week after I went to Tewkesbury for the second time. It was a rainy day in late May. I followed a well-trodden path through Hafren Forest until I reached a trail of stone steps dug into the damp black earth of a moor sprinkled with late-blooming snowdrops. *Tarddiad Afon Hafren*, said the vertically stacked letters on the post in an area of the bog that had been paved with stones; if the context hadn't supplied their meaning, their fluid rhythm might have. There was no sign of a stream, though the ground was soft underfoot – springy and buoyant in places, sodden in others. Wisps of dark, fast-moving cloud rose from the valley and drifted across the moor, as if the spirit of the river had been transfused into a veil of mist and rain.

According to one story, the Severn is one of three sisters who meet on the slopes of Mount Plynlimon in Wales and debate the best way to the sea. The River Rheidol takes a direct route westwards, the Wye takes the picturesque route, but the Severn stays close to the 'haunts of men' on her 220-mile journey to the Bristol Channel. She wanted 'to visit all the fairest cities of the kingdom,' says Bill Gwilliam, in *Worcestershire's Hidden Past*. Or perhaps she wanted revenge; according to another story, the river is animated by the spirit of a murdered girl called Sabrina, the illegitimate daughter of one of the sons of Brutus, the mythical founder of Britain. Sabrina was drowned in the river by her father's estranged wife, who was seeking revenge for her husband's infidelity.

Her death wasn't final. Rivers are the '*fons et origo*, the "spring and origin," the reservoir of all the possibilities of existence,' writes the historian of folklore Mircea Eliade, and 'the symbolism of the waters' implies both death and rebirth. 'Contact with water always brings a regeneration,' he writes. John Milton describes the rebirth of Sabrina in *Comus*. He says the 'guiltless damsel flying the mad pursuit / Of her enraged stepdame' did not drown when she fell into the Severn, for water nymphs picked her up and washed her 'in ambrosial oils' until she revived,

> And underwent a quick immortal change,
> Made Goddess of the river.

The Severn has flooded many times. On 29 November 1620, sixty-eight people drowned on their way to Bewdley Fair, near Kidderminster, when the Severn burst its banks, and in November 1768, it turned all of Herefordshire and Shropshire into 'a perfect sea'. In 1795, the floodwater in Shrewsbury rose 'higher than was ever remembered by the oldest inhabitants', and in 1852, 'the whole vale of Gloucester was one wide-spreading sea'. On 11 November 1875, the floods were 'out again as far as the eye can reach west of Gloucester.'

There is visible evidence of the height the river can reach engraved in the wall of the arch that leads from the riverside walk into the precincts of the cathedral in Worcester, fifteen miles upstream from Tewkesbury. Mary Dhonau, the flood campaigner, who calls herself 'Flood Mary' because 'Mary was synonymous with flooding', took me to see them when I went to Worcester in June 2013. I was in search of further evidence of the effects the Severn has on the places through which it flows, and on the lives of the people who live beside it. There were marks recording floods in 1886 and 1947, and a cluster in the previous twenty years – in 1990, 1998, 2000 and 2007. Yet the highest mark dated to 1770, when a long winter of heavy snow was followed by a rapid thaw. The plaque recording this level was a foot above my head, while the river was several feet below the banks on which I stood. It was hard to imagine the river that originated as a diffused, ghostly absence beneath a peat bog in Wales and emerged in Hafren Forest as a gushing, sparkling stream could ever summon sufficient force to rise so high. Yet there was further proof of its volatile nature in the adaptations people had made to their homes.

~

When I first walked into the sitting room of Dunmoppin', which stands beside the Severn in the middle of Worcester, half a mile upstream from the cathedral, it took me a moment to realize what was strange about it. It looked like a normal room, and yet the ceiling was lower than it should have been, and the window that overlooked the road between the house and the embankment that protected it from the Severn started at my knees, meaning my feet were level with the roofs of the cars outside. The shortened radiator filling the gap beneath the sill added to the sense that I was standing on a podium, looking down on the street below. Dunmoppin's ground floor had been raised by at least two feet (sixty centimetres).

The Severn ran beyond the embankment, or bund, on the far side of the road, at the bottom of a deep channel, flanked by banks thick with ferns and grasses. On the far side, steps that belonged to a rowing club led down into the water; they looked like the ghats on the Ganges, though they were used for launching long-oared boats that would glide across the water, instead of corpses or garlands of flowers. Beyond it, there was a racecourse, which became a lake when the river flooded, as it had done twice in the last ten years.

Mary Dhonau had introduced me to Andy, the owner of Dunmoppin', and he told me how he had raised the house himself in order to protect it from the threat of another flood. He had worked at the local paper for thirty years, which had offices just down the street, but he had been laid off a few years ago and, since then, had been doing home and garden maintenance. He was wearing a blue sweatshirt and workman's trousers. He had moved to the house after he 'ended with the girl I was with,' he said. It had flooded for the first time in 2000, and the insurance company had put it back exactly as it was. He had to live in a rented house for a year. When it flooded again in 2007, he knew what was in store; he left the house and took a bucket with him, because he was going to be sick.

'You cried when the news team from BBC Worcester came to interview you, didn't you?' said Mary, helpfully.

She knew what it was like; her house had flooded so many times that she had lost count, she said – though, when I pressed her for a number, she guessed a dozen. The first time was in 1996, when she had been living in her house in Worcester for eighteen months, but it was the flood of 2000, when she got three feet (a metre) of sewage water in her home, that impelled her to act.

Severn Trent Water refused to help, but she got the city council involved and sent a report to Downing Street. By then, 'Worcester woman' had become the archetypal voter the political parties wanted to attract, and Mary thought it might have an effect if a representative of the type went to Downing Street and made a fuss. 'And Downing Street rang Severn Trent Water and said we have had this unholy gaggle of very angry women in the street – what are you going to do about it?' Severn Trent Water built a sewage pumping station, which has reduced the risk of flooding in her street. Yet she wanted to help other people as well. She set up Worcester Action Group, which started as a research project, but so much of its work involved discussions that it inadvertently became a support group. 'People need help and advice – and who better to give it to them than people who have been flooded themselves?'

Her house flooded again in 2007, and she had other challenges to face as well. She was working at the National Flood Forum (NFF), which was overwhelmed, and she was also trying to put her autistic son into residential care, as well as going through a divorce. She has five children, three with her first husband, and two with her second husband, including Charlie, who was sixteen and as tall as I was, but with a mental age of eighteen months. She blamed the MMR vaccine for causing his autism: 'Medical science has proved me wrong on that,' she said, but she plainly didn't believe it, or didn't want to believe it. She said he had been normal at eighteen months: he could point, and he had nine or ten words. He had the jab, and, a couple of days later, he had a fit and got the flu. He was never the same again. He used to wake up every night between two a.m. and six a.m. and smear poo around his room. Mary had to get up and change the curtains.

It didn't seem surprising that the marriage collapsed. She tried to sell the house, and couldn't, so her husband bought her out. Since then, it had flooded twice, but 'in a very minor way.' Her new house, which she moved to in 2011, hadn't flooded yet, though she didn't discount the possibility: 'Never say never.' She left the NFF, which she said was one of the worst decisions she ever made, both for her and it, for it had changed since she left. The chairman and the board had never been flooded, and Mary believed they were driven by 'getting in money.' It was the kind of complaint often made by founding members of an organization, which didn't mean it wasn't true.

Yet, even if the NFF had 'lost sight of its reason for being,' as Mary put it, she was intent on continuing its work in a freelance capacity, and she had never been busier. John Badham, who I'd met in Tewkesbury, and who lived between the Swilgate and the Mill Avon, would become mayor of the flood-prone town; he was conscious of the lasting effects of the floods on people who didn't earn very much and faced enormously increased bills on their insurance, if they could get it at all. But Mary Dhonau's campaigning was not restricted to a single place.

She had been to Dunmoppin' before, and she sat on the sofa while Andy showed me the changes he had made. He had raised the ceiling in the kitchen and conservatory by propping the walls on supports and putting in another layer of four or five bricks. It had been 'a health and safety nightmare,' not helped by his accident-prone dad – he had dropped a patio door, which had fallen over his head without touching him, Buster Keaton-style. Andy had also raised the decking at the back. Steps led down to the lawn, matching the ones at the front and the ones leading down into the garage. The multiple layers added a kind of improvised grandeur to the house. There were koi in the pond at the back – three of them had survived the flood. Andy had scooped them out of a pool of shitty water, but the others had escaped into the polluted lake that subsumed the concrete-lined pond, streaks of yellow and gold that flickered briefly in the murk.

~

The word 'bund' is another legacy of Mesopotamia, the 'land between the rivers' that produced the Noah story. The embankments beside the Tigris in Baghdad were called bunds, and the term was exported by Jewish Baghdadi exiles, like the Sassoon family, who were known as the 'Rothschilds of the East'. David Sassoon was the son of the chief treasurer to the pashas of Baghdad, but his family was forced into exile by a new ruler. He was a successful businessman and established outposts across Asia, including in Shanghai, where he built Sassoon House on an embanked quay known as the Bund. Since then, the term has travelled around the world. The French engineers who raised the embankments to protect New Orleans from the waters of the Gulf of Mexico and the Mississippi called them 'levees', but they are 'bunds' in Britain, and the word carries an echo of Mesopotamia, even when it applies to flood defences in the centre of Worcester, or in the village of Kempsey, five miles down-stream, where Mary Dhonau took me after we left Dunmoppin'.

Kempsey's bund was the product of more than twenty years of campaigning by the Oram family, who owned a flood-prone cottage in the middle of the village. Rex Oram saw Tudor Cottage for the first time in 1976, when he was planning to move his family back to England from Ghana, where he had been teaching. It was used as a hospital for Cromwell's men in the Civil War and it has a thatched roof and timbered walls. Its front windows are set below the level of the street, so you can see people's feet as they go past – an element of its antique charm, which came to seem less charming. Rex thought it was the perfect place to live, within easy reach of Birmingham, where he would be working, yet he did not realize that Hatfield Brook, a tributary of the Severn, which runs through a wood on the other side of the road, had a habit of backing up and flooding the village – and that, when it did, it would, inevitably, cascade into the subterranean sitting room of Tudor Cottage.

The house flooded for the first time in 1979. Cathy Oram, Rex's daughter, came downstairs to see the carpet billowing and everything floating. 'It seemed very exciting at the time,' she said. They considered moving – they even looked at other houses – but, in the end, they decided to stay and adapt as best they could. They built an extension that was two feet (sixty centimetres) higher than the original house, and they fitted a pump in the corner of the sitting room, which was not only the lowest point in the house, but the lowest in the village. When Tudor Cottage flooded, as it did every two or three years, they would go and stay with friends. 'Mum just got on with it,' Cathy told me, when I met her at her house on the edge of Kempsey, a short walk from Tudor Cottage, which she was trying to rent out. 'She put the furniture on trestle tables, mopped and cleaned and just

got on. It wasn't a big deal. The water could come in and it
would just be little swirls across the floor – and it would be
pumped out through the gate.'

Yet, since the turn of the century, the floods had got
worse: in 2000, the water was a metre deep and the extension flooded for the first time. The electricity was cut off
and they were forced to move out. In July 2007, more than
150 homes and businesses were flooded in Kempsey and the
A38 was blocked for two days. Tudor Cottage would flood
six times in the course of the year – once, a week before
Cathy's sister's wedding. They had planned her hen do at a
pub down the road, which had also flooded. 'And we just
carried on really, preparing for the wedding, walking into
the cottage in our waders,' Cathy said.

Yet by then, her parents had had enough: 'Anyone can
cope with a flood, but you can't cope with six in twelve
months,' Cathy said. They couldn't get insurance anymore,
and they knew it would be hard to sell it; even Mary
Dhonau, who had pointed it out to me as we drove through
the village, did not want to take it on. She had considered
it when it was for sale at a knock-down price, but her partner, who is older than her, refused. He said he might curl
up and die if he got flooded, which was hardly surprising,
given the way she talked about it. Cathy's parents considered demolishing it, but instead, her dad gave it to her, and
in 2007, they took on the task of fitting it with pumps and
flood gates. 'It was great to be back in the village. And it
gave me an opportunity to really get to know Dad better.'
They spent three years fixing up the cottage, and in the

meantime, they were also campaigning for flood defences to protect the village.

When Mr Oram proposed the idea in 1991, it seemed crazy, Cathy said. 'He thought you could put a gate across the field. Everyone thought he was bonkers – the parish council laughed at him. But he kept writing letters. My dad had this idea that people act with integrity – he believed that, if we were one of the worst-flooded villages in the country, then the Environment Agency would do something about it.'

In 2009, Cathy took on the task of running the campaign 'against her better judgement', and with Mary's help, she set up Kempsey's Flood Action Group. Some people told her she was wasting her time. 'They said, "Good luck, my dear – it has always flooded here, and it always will."' Mr Oram died unexpectedly in 2009, but his persistence was vindicated posthumously: three years later, the bund he had campaigned for was completed.

A long, flat embankment now runs through the middle of the field between Kempsey and the Severn. It passes round the back of the church, where the bones that were unearthed in its construction had been re-interred, and crosses the narrow channel of Hatfield Brook. Its profile feels as timeless and unobtrusive as the grassed-over outline of an Iron Age hill fort, though the massive sluice gates that bracket Hatfield Brook are modern: when we went to see it the stream was a trickle, and the flood gates were open, for the Severn was low, but when it rises, they close, and pumps lift the water from Hatfield Brook into the field beyond the bund to stop it backing up and flooding the village.

Cathy's mother and the local MP cut the ribbon at the opening ceremony. Five months later, Kempsey flooded again. 'It was as bad as it had ever been,' Cathy said. 'Everyone went to bed thinking they were working – and, in the night, they were flooded.' Yet it wasn't a structural failure or a fault in the concept that had caused a flood; it was a computer glitch, which switched off one pump and failed to switch on another. Cathy was confident that it would pass the next test, which might come very soon: a month's worth of rain was forecast for the next day, and it had already started to fall as Cathy's two-year-old son, Rex, peeled away from our group and started running across the field, past the bench dedicated to his grandfather in memory of twenty years of letter writing, towards the sunken thread of the Severn.

~

Heather Shepherd, who now ran the National Flood Forum, was another victim of Sweet Sabrina. She lived in the upper catchment of the Severn, in Herefordshire, but she spent most of her time travelling around the country, and she had agreed to meet me in a village on the coast of Sussex, which was exposed to flooding from both fresh water and salt.

I took the train to the coast. As it wound through the fields inland, on a raised track, I could see how vulnerable the coastal plain would be. At Pulborough, we crossed a bridge above a terrace of houses with lush green gardens that ran down to a dark, slow-moving river. It was a bright June day: the marshes felt mutable and fluid, as if their spongy beds and peaty paths were stapled together by the railway tracks, though the process of reclamation began long before the Industrial Revolution. In his famous book *The Making of the English Landscape,* W. G. Hoskins says that 'Offa's Charter', which was written in the eighth century, 'speaks already of ditches in the Pevensey Levels' in West Sussex, though '300 years later the tide water still flowed freely over most of the Sussex marshes.' In the twenty-first century, some of the reclaimed land is being relinquished. In Medmerry, new defences have been built a mile inland, and the sea will be allowed to advance towards them, creating a new wetland habitat and reducing the risk of flooding for hundreds of homes elsewhere on the coast.

Yet, other parts of 'poor old West Sussex' will remain prone to flooding, Heather Shepherd said. She had been in Lancing in the morning; when she arrived, there had been a bit of flooding, but, by the time she left, water was spouting through the tarmac 'like geysers'.

'It was coming out all over the place,' she said, with such enthusiasm that I wondered if she had been misreading the chain of cause and effect: she thought she was following the floods, but perhaps the floods were following her as she travelled around the country, a modern-day Enlil, god of mops and sodden carpets, conjurer of storms and spouts of gushing water.

~

Heather's house had flooded for the first time in 1998, two years after she had moved to a village called Pentre, in Herefordshire. It is several miles from the river, but the water builds up behind an *argae*, or embankment, like an earthen bund, which was built in the nineteenth century to facilitate farming. It was several miles long, though it was tied into the landscape in a way that made it hard to see, even at the point where it crossed the road. When the house flooded for the first time, she could hear a distant roar, like the sound of a storm at sea, though she didn't know the water was on its way towards her – nor that she had two hours before it got there.

Even if she'd known, she wouldn't have realized how it was going to feel to have water in her home. 'You have all these visions in your head, but it's difficult to understand the concept until it happens to you. It came in at different levels. We couldn't stop it. It came in through the walls, in little spurting fountains; it came in through the floors; it came through any opening it could find.' It kept rising all day, covering the hedges and gates. At the end of the drive, it was chest deep. She spent the day trying to save what she could, carrying on by torchlight after the electricity failed. The adrenaline kept her going, but when she opened the fridge door and saw that everything was ruined, she burst into tears. She and her husband carried the kids to the neighbours' house, which had been raised on stilts to escape the floods, and they drank a couple of bottles of red wine. 'God, if you ever need alcohol in your life, it's then. But, of course, you have to face it all in the morning, and that's really just the beginning.'

Builders were brought in to do the repairs, but proved inadequate. One team left live wires in the wall; another team cooked breakfast on camp stoves and then went to the pub; another admitted that they usually worked on the railways, laying sleepers. One day, she found two builders preparing to demolish a sixteenth-century staircase. 'They said, "It's all right, you'll get a brand-new one – it's contaminated." And we said, "It's been contaminated for the last several hundred years: it will survive."' The damp and the dehumidifiers drove the family out, so they lived in a caravan in the drive. It was like bereavement. Broken relationships were common. Heather had been married for thirty-five years – if it had been much less, she and her husband would have got divorced.

'It consumes you completely,' she said. 'There is no other life. There's always something to be done. It's incredibly stressful.' She rarely talks about her own experiences, she said, because she doesn't have the strength to. The last time she had done an interview, three years before she spoke to me, she had burst into tears. Besides, she said, people who had been flooded didn't want to hear what had happened to her – though, sometimes, it was helpful to prove she had been through it too. Yet she had no doubt that the experience inspired her devotion to the cause. 'It's very much why I'm in the National Flood Forum,' she said. 'I don't think it ever really leaves you. I often ask why I do what I do – nobody in their right mind would do it – and I think that's what drives me.' She used to be a special-needs teacher before she became involved in the Flood Forum, and she now worked all the time. 'It's twenty-four seven. I usually start at seven a.m. and don't stop till ten at night, and I work weekends regularly. But it has been cathartic for me, helping other people deal with it, and I feel very passionate about it.'

Once she started talking, the stories poured out of her with such fluency and force that the woman whose story I was supposed to be hearing was reduced to the role of listener, like me. Jane Smeaton came from London, but she had moved to the south coast in her early twenties to work in the Portsmouth naval base, where she met her husband. 'It was a classic case of a temporary job that results in thirty years in the civil service,' she said. She and her husband moved to Felpham in 1996, though Jane knew the area already, for she used to go to West Sussex on holiday as a child and she had family nearby. They bought their house from her cousin, who had owned it since 1982; they knew it hadn't flooded since then – though, in the past, the sea had often flooded the streets and fields behind the beach. When she moved to the area, there had been piles of shingle on the beach, which were being used to construct new defences. Yet keeping out the sea was only half the challenge, for the water that collects inland has to drain as well.

There is an outfall pipe at the end of their road, which collects surface water and takes it out to sea, but, in 2009, it broke: the flap at the end that seals it at high tide fell off, and the pipe cracked. Seawater surged into the pipe, spilled out in the street and flooded Jane's neighbour's house. Three years later, the equation was reversed: on 12 June 2012, six weeks' worth of rain fell on Felpham in a day, and the 'tide-flex' valve that had been fitted to keep out the sea didn't open enough to let it out. Jane watched the downpour from her bedroom window: 'I went to bed at eleven o'clock and the rain was torrential: it was hitting the gutter and bouncing out like a waterfall – I was concerned, but it only lasted about twenty minutes, so I went to bed and thought, Fine, that's all over.'

At two in the morning, the neighbours woke her up to say they had flooded, and the water was coming Jane's way. She spent the rest of the night trying to bale the water out of her garage with a dustpan and brush. When the builders' merchant opened at seven a.m., Jane's husband fetched sandbags. They were keeping it at bay, but only just. The water had backed up in the pipe and overflowed into the drainage ditch that ran down the side of the house. Jane was measuring its rise against the bricks in the wall that enclosed the far side of the ditch.

We went to look at it when we left the pub. It was a shallow, unevenly grassed ditch, lined with rubble: it looked like a path running down the side of the houses, but Heather Shepherd greeted it with a cry of recognition: 'It's so typical,' she said. 'It looks like it never had water and never will, but when water hits it, it comes up so fast – nothing to overflowing in a matter of minutes.'

At one point, the water stopped rising and went down half a brick. They thought they were okay. 'Then it just went *whoosh*, as if someone had pulled a plug upstream,' Jane said. It was an inch, then two inches, and it still kept rising. Within an hour, there was a foot and a half (almost half a metre) of sewage-tainted water swilling about the ground floor of their house.

~

I had seen for myself the destructive power of seemingly inconspicuous sewers, drains and culverts in the Newcastle suburb of Newburn, which had flooded several times in the course of 2012, once on the night of the Toon Monsoon that struck the north-east on 28 June, two weeks after Jane's house in Felpham had flooded. Newburn's floods had begun quietly. In May 2012, a hole six metres deep and four metres wide appeared in a road that ran through a transport depot owned by the Duke of Northumberland's estate. The culvert that carried a stream called the Winnings beneath the depot had collapsed. The estate rerouted the stream into a steel pipe that ran above ground through the estate, and, for a while, no one was particularly concerned. Yet it was only the beginning of a catastrophic sequence of events whose effects had still not been resolved when I arrived in Newburn on a cold winter's day in March 2013. A block of flats had been undermined and nearly swept away, its residents had been dispersed across the city and the valley was still sealed within a series of building sites that restored it to a simulacrum of how it must have looked in its industrial heyday. In the meantime, the council and its contractors continued the laborious process of threading the Winnings back into the culvert in order to ensure it wouldn't flood again.

Culverts are a legacy of rapid urbanization in the Victorian era. When the expanding cities found themselves restricted by natural dips and hollows created by streams and rivers, engineers sank the water into a tunnel and filled in the land. Many are forgotten, though they are never entirely lost. London's buried rivers 'still exert an influence upon the world above them,' Peter Ackroyd writes, in *Thames: Sacred River*. 'They can make their presence known in odours and in creeping dampness; the buried Fleet, for example, can still flood basements along its course.'

I once walked the course of the Fleet, from its source on Hampstead Heath to the point where it pours into the Thames beneath Blackfriars Bridge, with a man who had a quixotic plan to restore it to the surface. He checked its course by going into shops and asking if their basement flooded. 'The lost rivers were once deemed to be responsible for ague and fever, and their valleys (now carved between the streets and buildings of the city) were peculiarly susceptible to mist and fog,' Ackroyd writes. 'In more recent times the presence of the underground waters has been blamed for the prevalence of allergies in their vicinity.'

Other sources say the number of psychic incidents and ghost sightings in areas bordering the city's buried rivers increase after heavy rain, as their secret swollen flows evoke mysterious apparitions. There are physical traces in the names of streets, in the contours of the roads, and in unexpected flowerings, such as the reeds that appear near the railway tracks in Barons Court, close to Counter's Creek, one of fourteen tributaries of the Thames.

Even when they emerge, they are hard to spot – many of the people who stand beneath the pipe that carries the River Westbourne above the platform of Sloane Square Station will not know what it is. The culvert that carries the Winnings through Newburn is not a secret, for the stream's upper and lower stretches are above the ground, but its middle section flows beneath the deep weight of rubble and spoil that fill the valley.

Newburn has always been a significant place, for it lies on the most easterly fordable point of the Tyne, but it began to grow rapidly after the Industrial Revolution, when Newcastle became one of the great shipbuilding and engineering centres of the world. In 1822, John Spencer established a steelworks on the upper reaches of the Winnings, and, as it grew to meet local demand, he reshaped the valley in the pragmatic place-making style of the time, sinking the stream into a culvert and filling in the land to build on. 'Basically, they threw a load of waste material into the valley and put a pipe through it,' said Mick Murphy, technical director of Newcastle council, when I met him outside the linked sites that cascaded down the hillside, enclosing the many locations where the repairs were underway.

The valley was never particularly beautiful, Mick Murphy said, but at least it was dry. Yet the fact that the Victorians had made no effort to align the man-made section of the valley with the land upstream created the conditions for the floods that erupted nearly 200 years later.

It started raining heavily in June 2012, and the raised edge of the depot became a wall that held back the water that couldn't drain through the blocked culvert. The water collected in a pool in the woods, and grew wider and deeper, until it was a brimming lake, poised ominously above the buildings lower down in the valley.

At first, the water spread backwards into the trees, filling the valley and flooding a stable, but then it overtopped the escarpment and poured downhill, flooding houses and forcing the evacuation of two blocks of flats in an estate called Spencer Court. Worse was to follow, two weeks later. Fifty millimetres of rain fell in two hours on the night of 28 June, in the storm that became known as the Toon Monsoon. It was Newcastle's heaviest storm since the 1940s: 500 properties in the city flooded and thousands of homes lost power. Shopping malls and Metro stations were forced to close. Drivers abandoned their cars, and landslides blocked both main east- and west-coast rail lines. Lightning struck the Tyne Bridge, supplying a vivid televisual demonstration of the power of the storm, and, in Newburn, the pool formed in the woods by the Winnings overflowed again.

Water poured through the depot, sweeping away the ground beneath the block of flats closest to the place the stream emerged from its culvert, leaving the building poised on a few fragile-looking pillars. The water separated into a series of waterfalls and, as the 'Niagara effect' worked its way backwards, it ran close to two other blocks of flats and undermined the ground at the sides of the valley, threatening flats and houses that had been built years before Spencer Court. Further down the hill, the rubble-choked water flowed into the mouth of another culvert, which carried the stream beneath the main road. It backed up, flung aside the concrete lids that covered the stream and spread out in a rubble-thickened torrent that reached hundreds of metres along Newburn high street. The downhill flow burst through the doors of a business centre on the other side of the road and knocked down the back wall, taking desks and computers with it as it rejoined the lower reaches of the stream, which wound through the sparsely wooded slopes, towards the Tyne.

When the water went down, the rubble was waist-deep against the shuttered door of the bike shop beside the stream. It took a team of workmen, with three machines and two wagons, two weeks to clear it all away. There was more rain on 26 September, and the pool formed by the Winnings overflowed again. 'I woke up at quarter to five this morning, and I heard a trembling,' said a woman who lived in a house in the valley. She couldn't see anything at first, but when she looked out again, she saw the water pouring towards her. Soon, it was running like a tide through the front door.

I had watched video footage of the water cascading through the grounds of Spencer Court, but it wasn't until I stood above the pool in the Winnings that I realized how frightening it must have been. A wooden platform had

been built across the lip of the man-made dam that contained the lake at the top of the valley, and there was a hut,
like a bird hide, above the brick arch that formed the mouth
of the culvert. Looking down on it, far below, made me feel
dizzy. Yet, looking upstream, at the lake in the woods, did
not make me feel much safer. Admittedly, the water was
within manageable limits: according to the depth gauge
anchored like a giant buoy in the middle, it was three metres
deep – though, two days before, it had reached eight. When
it reached fifteen metres – five times its current level – it
would overtop the lip of the dam, which was the beginning
of the man-made section of the valley, and pour downhill
through the estate.

Larger pipes had been installed to carry the overflow.
They jinked downstream in a giant rusting chain, a steam-
punk river, taller than I was, out of all proportion to the
narrow woodland stream that the Winnings had been.
Further down the hill, a shaft that resembled the founda-
tion for a skyscraper had been dug to reach the collapsed
section of the culvert.

In November 2012, the pool in the Winnings overflowed
again. It was the fifth flood since May, but, by then, the
council had built an overflow channel made of concrete
blocks, which took the water between buildings, past the
spot where Spencer Court used to stand, and let it pour
down the side of the valley, which they had clad in 'rock
armour' – row upon row of dark grey boulders, clamped in
place by steel nets. It was a brutally functional piece of
landscaping, in keeping with the spirit of the place, and it

had worked as expected. It was like a giant water feature, Mick Murphy said, an industrial rockery – and he plainly liked the idea of having created the emblem of the suburban garden on such a scale.

The bill came to more than £12 million, and the Duke of Northumberland had to auction heirlooms from his family homes in Northumberland and Kew to meet the cost. Lots included a painting by Jan Breughel the Elder, called *The Garden of Eden*, which went for £6 million, and a first-century sculpture of Aphrodite, which went for £10 million. The auction raised £32 million. The estate set aside £10 million to compensate the people in Spencer Court and others that had flooded. Any surplus would be invested in its long-term heritage projects, it said. Yet it saw no return on the £22 million it had spent: three months after the auction, it sold the depot in Newburn for one pound.

The cost was nothing compared to the bill that would follow if one of the bigger culverts in Newcastle were to collapse, Mick Murphy said. The culvert that carries the River Ouseburn through east Newcastle, from Jesmond Dene to the Tyne, was used as a bomb shelter in the war; it was so big that it accommodated a platform above the water, on which thousands of people had slept. If that one went, it would make Newburn look like a vicar's tea party.

Such disasters are inevitable, Heather Shepherd said, for we live in a crowded country, and our ageing infrastructure can no longer take the strain of the changing climate.

~

Jane Smeaton and her husband had stayed in their flooded house in Felpham for a night. 'It was horrible; it was cold and smelly, and we could hear the water moving about downstairs. So we decided one night only.' The water took thirty-six hours to go down: 'It wasn't sudden – it didn't whoosh away. The area was tidal locked; the flap put in to stop the sea coming up was stopping the water going out, so surface water that would normally feed out to the sea was locked in situ – nothing could go out.' Once she had the cats – there were nine of them – and she knew she and her husband were safe, she felt calm: 'I thought, well, it could have been worse.' It wasn't until the water went down that she recognized the extent of the damage. There was black-grey slime over everything, and anything that could absorb the water was ruined. The kitchen lino was buckled and wavy. The hardwood floors were ruined. The kitchen cupboards were swollen. The carpets were gone and the water had been soaked up into the walls from underneath, so the whole of the house, up to a metre's height, was drenched.

The cost came to £100,000, and at first they weren't sure that the insurance company would pay. 'It turned out there was a clause in our contract which said we weren't covered if we were within 200 metres of a whole list of watery things – streams, watercourses, tidal, anything you can think of that has water in it – and we'd said no, because we thought we weren't.' The insurance company sent a man to look at the property and assess their claim. 'And, I'm not kidding, he got a tape measure out to measure the distance from the back wall of the house to the high-tide mark.' It was 120 metres. For six weeks, they didn't know if the insurance company would accept liability or not – though, they did, for the house hadn't been flooded by the sea.

A neighbour let them stay in his holiday home initially, and then they moved into a caravan, which they parked in the drive, so they could be closer to the house, partly to protect it from the people driving round in white vans. When I visited, they were still living in the caravan, although they had moved back into the pebble-dashed house to sleep. The washing machine had been plumbed into the hall, guarding the entrance to a series of stripped and empty rooms, given over to the cats. There was one cat sleeping by the fireplace in the sitting room that overlooked the garden, and another scampered through the kitchen as we went in. There were paw prints in a strip of freshly laid concrete, and piles of cat food and cat litter in the old kitchen. It smelt of cats, though Heather dismissed Jane's embarrassment by saying it added to the 'flavour' of the flooded house. The tang made the sea air outside seem even cleaner.

We walked down to the beach to see the pipe that had blocked. It was larger than I expected – a solid steel tube, like the ones that had been threaded through the building sites at Newburn, which ran a hundred metres down the beach to a point below the high tide. Water trickled from its mouth. There were two pumps in the side of the concrete bunker behind the promenade, so, if the pipe became tide-locked again, they could pump the water over the promenade and straight into the sea.

~

The tide was out, but the sand between the groynes was glossed with streaks of water that gleamed in the evening sun. The poet William Blake had lived in Felpham in his only extended spell outside London, in a house between the Fox Inn, where I had met Jane and Heather, and the beach. He had never been to the sea before, and he relished living so close to it, according to his biographer, Peter Ackroyd.

Blake 'who was heavily influenced by beliefs in the lost city of Atlantis, of which the British Isles were the only remnant' watched the sea 'at all times and in all seasons'. He was on the beach one day when he had a vision that expanded 'Like a Sea without shore': he became entranced by what he called 'the shifting lights of the sea', and, all along the shore, he saw the spirits of poets and prophets, '"majestic shadows, grey but luminous, and superior to the common height of men" . . . as if the light of the sea itself had acquired human form.'

~

We said goodbye on the promenade. Jane was going back to the caravan in the drive, but Heather had other places to visit. She was staying with family in Oxford and then

going on to a village in Essex, where another blocked culvert had flooded an estate, but, before that, she had
another meeting in West Sussex and she was planning to
walk along the coast to get to it. 'I love walking,' she said,
in her usual enthusiastic way, and she set off along the
promenade, heading east, pacing out another dimension
of her floodable domain.

4: Forgotten City

Sandy Henderson and Jacqui Dixon, two women from Hull – a city poised, like the village of Felpham, between fresh water and salt – had responded to the floods of 2007 by forming a different kind of group from the ones set up in Sussex and on the banks of the Severn. Theirs was not political. It was not concerned with securing new defences. It had a purpose that I approved of and understood: prompted by a researcher from Lancaster University, whom I met one day in London, Sandy and Jacqui attempted to deal with the emotional and psychological effects of the flood that overwhelmed Hull by writing about it, as if setting down their memories on paper was the only way to contain them.

The subject of memory was particularly significant for Sandy Henderson, for she had grown up on the Hessle Road, in west Hull, the centre of the old fishing community, which used to flood all the time. Recovery was simpler in those days, she said; people used to get out the carbolic soap, get down on their hands and knees and scrub the floors. 'Not everyone could live like that,' she said. 'They were hard people. They would go to sea for three weeks, come back for two days, get drunk and then go off again.' But there was something to be said for it, because there was no fuss, and 'you could recover.' Yet the old sense of the inevitable rise and fall of the waters had gone. Naturally, she welcomed the construction of the barrier on the River Hull that put a stop to flooding in the middle of the city, but she also felt that it had made people forgetful and complacent: flooding didn't mean anything to anyone anymore – a significant absence in a city that was partly created by flooding.

By the tenth century, deposits of silt and mud left behind by the inflowing tides had created dry land on the coast, though the freshwater marshes – or carrs – inland were permanently sodden. Meaux Abbey was established on islands between the River Hull and the River Fleet in 1150, and the monks began the process of reclaiming land, despite opposition from the locals, who feared the loss of fishing grounds and pasturage, in the same way they would in the Fens and the Levels. The southern area was most easily drained and defended, though there were periodic setbacks: in the thirteenth century, reclaimed land at Myton collapsed into the Humber and was never recovered.

Keeping the seawater out was not the only challenge, for the rivers that meandered through the carrs had to be allowed to drain. That was especially difficult at high tide, when the gates in the sea walls were closed, or at times of exceptional rain, when water built up behind the defences, as it did on 27 June 2007, forming a shallow lake that spread across the city. Yet, even in less testing times, there was little margin for error, for the dykes and channels that supplied

Hull with drinking water had to be kept full to ensure a steady flow. In 1409, people in the villages of Anlaby, Ferriby and Swanland, west of Hull, complained that their meadows had flooded, because the 'Julian dyke' in Anlaby hadn't been kept clear. But it wasn't neglect that caused flooding; it was the 'flatness of the land', write Edward Gillet and Kenneth MacMahon, in their book, *A History of Hull.* Since the hamlet of Wyk, which became Kingston-Upon-Hull in 1293, stood in an area of 'rough common land' which often flooded from both sides, 'there were seasons in which the town was virtually an island in a sea of flood water.'

The pattern continued into the twentieth century. My father, who took accountancy articles in Hull in the 1950s, said the river overtopped its banks so often that you had to watch where you put your feet in the city centre. The barrier on the River Hull, which was completed in 1980, helped Hull live with its river, a council official said to me, as if the river was an antisocial teenager, causing disturbances on a street corner. But the floods of 2007 didn't come from the river, the official said. They came from the sky.

May 2007 had been the wettest month in Yorkshire since 1882, and the downpours continued in June. The Lord Mayor's Parade was cancelled in the middle of the month because of flooding, and sewers overflowed in Hessle, in west Hull. It was a taste of what was to come, people said. 'We asked ourselves: could it happen again?' the council official said to me. 'Would it happen again? By God, it did happen again.' What's more, it happened within a month.

~

Sandy Henderson and her husband were on holiday when it started raining. They put their caravan into storage in Cottingham and came home. There was a lot of surface water on the road when her husband went to work the next day at half past seven. 'I took the dogs out and came back,' Sandy said. 'I was going to do the ironing, but I went out again, and the water was lapping on the pavement and coming up the road. Next door came out and said there was water in the garage. We were trying to pick things up and put them away. I telephoned Paul and he said, "That bad? I'll come home." And the wash of the car as he came into the drive sent the water over the threshold.'

It was July 2013, and we were sitting in the conservatory at the back of their house in Bransholme, a suburb in the drained marshes in north Hull. There was no sign of the damage that the flood had done six years before. The garden was a neatly gravelled square, with plants in pots and a swing seat, and the inside was just as tidy: it had white walls, grey radiators, wooden kitchen cabinets.

Sandy was proud of the house, for it was the first place she had settled. She was born on the Hessle Road on the Queen's twentieth birthday, which meant she was sixty-one in 2007. Her mother was half-Welsh, half-Scottish and her father was a Canadian from Alberta, who had come over during the war. 'I was the result, but they never married,' she said. She never had any contact with her father. Her mother was grateful when Sandy's stepfather proposed, but he turned out to be a womanizer and there were always problems. 'I was eighteen when I was told he wasn't my father – I was only told because he had lung cancer and he was ill, but it all fell into place.' She moved to east Hull aged five, where she went to school, and then to Beverley, where she met her husband. They lived in various places, depending on where he was working. 'You weren't allowed to buy a house in the early days in the police force, because they moved you around so much,' she said. 'I think we have been a bit like gypsies.' They moved to Hull twenty-one years ago, and twelve years ago, they bought the house in Bransholme.

It was the lowest in the street, and, since it stands on piles in the marsh, the water came up through the floorboards as well as through the door. They managed to save the sofa in the conservatory and other pieces of furniture, but by the evening the hall was completely flooded. 'It went up about three stairs – two feet – sixty-five centimetres of water,' Sandy Henderson said, with practised fluency. She showed me photographs of the dark brown water filling the house. They were not yet aware of the scale of the calamity that had overtaken the city: one of the pumping stations that lifts water into the River Hull packed up, meaning it couldn't drain, and the city's 1950s watercourses were overwhelmed. Even the River Hull contributed: it rained so hard that groundwater began to emerge – and, by the time it stopped raining in the afternoon, more than 10,000 houses and flats in Hull were flooded.

~

Sandy Henderson was standing at the sink of her house in Bransholme, on 26 June 2007, when she felt something nudge her leg. It scared the life out of her, she said. Even shallow water evokes terrors. It might have been a shark or a sea snake that had swum into her flooded home through the channel that had been opened to the deep, but in fact it was a koi carp that had escaped from her neighbour's pond. The Hendersons stayed in the house for the first night. It was like being on a ship, Sandy said; there was creaking and groaning as the furniture shifted and swelled, and, in the middle of the night, they were woken by a crash. Downstairs, the floorboards had popped up and tipped over the table on which they had piled many of their possessions.

They stayed in the flooded house for three or four nights in total, but the staircase was unsafe, and they had no power or furniture, so they moved to a Premier Inn, where many of their neighbours were staying. 'It was like a reunion – we'd all eat together in the evening and come down for breakfast together,' Sandy said.

Three nights later, they had to move again, for the kennels where they had left their dogs had also flooded, and they couldn't have them in the hotel. Sandy rang the Bridlington Caravan Centre, which is on the coast, near Flamborough, thirty miles north of Hull, close to the source of the River Hull, and asked if she would be able to have a static caravan on her drive. The salesman said yes – and they were lucky, because it fitted across the front of the house. 'He came to see us, measured all the houses, and, within a couple of days, we had seven static caravans in the close.'

In many places, the water trapped behind the river defences had still not gone down: large parts of one of England's largest cities were still flooded, and yet the rest of the country had barely noticed. 'It was flooded in pockets right across Bransholme,' Sandy told me, 'but no one knew – no one knew.'

Years later, she still found it hard to comprehend – though, in one sense, it was not particularly surprising. Hull has always seemed a marginal place – to the rest of the country, at least – overlooked in its unglamorous estuarial location at the end of road and rail routes. Sometimes, that works to its advantage: Philip Larkin, Hull's most famous twentieth-century resident, said it was 'in the world yet sufficiently on the edge of it to have a different resonance'. But its isolation worked against it after the Cod Wars of 1975–6, when the fishing industry that had sustained several generations of Hull families, including Sandy Henderson's collapsed. The loss of fishing was an industrial catastrophe comparable to the demise of coal or shipbuilding, people in Hull said, but the city didn't get the kind of help that was given to Sheffield or Glasgow, and, in June 2007, as the floods moved south and west across the country, it found itself overlooked again.

'The council didn't bother with us – no one had bothered with us for quite a while,' Sandy said. Then a Sky News helicopter passed over Hull, on its way to 'something or other', and they looked down and saw all the caravans lined up in the Hendersons' close. 'And, the next thing we knew, there was a Sky van outside.' Sandy laughed. 'It all snowballed from there and we became quite famous.'

~

Gordon and Jacqui Dixon were also on holiday when it started raining. Their son-in-law texted them in Menorca to say that East Ella Drive had flooded, but their house hadn't. *It's going down*, said the next text. *Don't come back*, said the third. *East Ella Drive has been evacuated, and you can't get in.* But they went, anyway – they couldn't resist, Gordon said. They flew back and tried to drive home, though the M62 was closed and they had to go around the south side of the Humber and across the bridge.

They got to East Ella Drive at one o'clock in the morning. It was as dark as it had been in the war, Gordon said, though the blackout hadn't been imposed to disorientate enemy planes, like the one that dropped a bomb through the roof of the house, in east Hull, where he had grown up. The water was ankle-deep at the top of the street, but, by the time they reached their house, it was level with the top of the bay.

The Dixons stayed with their sister-in-law and went back in the morning. 'It wasn't very nice water to wade around in,' Gordon said. It was waist-deep inside as well – even the dishwasher was full of water. 'We lost everything – literally everything – on the ground floor. We have been married for fifty-two years now, and we lost things we were given as wedding presents,' Gordon said. 'Our daughter's wedding videos. The insurance guy said it was all a write-off – all had to be replaced.'

Their fish had escaped as well – but they found their way back. Gordon and Jacqui were surveying the damage the water had done when a couple of lads knocked on their door and said they had found their goldfish. Gordon gave them two quid and they came back with a bucket of fish. When the water went down, he put them back in the pond; after all, he didn't know that the fish weren't theirs.

They moved back in after two nights, and lived in a room upstairs, because Gordon didn't want to leave the workshop in the garden unattended; anything you put down disappeared. Some of the plundering was officially authorized. In the morning, East Ella Drive was full of white vans clearing possessions. The Dixons were upstairs one day and watched from the window as 'this army of big guys with big muscles walked down the middle of the street, picking things up. It was quite frightening. They were volunteers from the prison – they spent all their time in the gym. It was a weird sensation, seeing everybody's belongings crushed. The people on the other side of the street had antique furniture that used to belong to their parents: it all went in the skip.'

Gordon had rewired the house so the upper floor was on a separate circuit to the downstairs, and their middle bedroom became a sitting room. People dropped in at all hours. The street was dark at night, since most of their neighbours had left, but it was never quiet, for the industrial dehumidifiers ran twenty-four hours a day, draining moisture not only from walls and furniture, but also from the air. 'We could hardly speak for three months, because of our throats,' Gordon said. The owner-occupiers of west Hull got no help from the council, the Dixons said, though the Red Cross gave them a microwave. It was a welcome gift, though it added to the sense they were living through a disaster.

Yet it was the builders appointed by the insurance company that upset Gordon the most. 'I don't mean to insult you, but they were from the south,' he said, as if I might have known them personally.

'I'm not insulted,' I said, but he didn't seem to believe me. It wasn't personal. It was a matter of regional pride. He was a joiner and a cabinetmaker in a city known as a centre of joinery. The insurance-company builders were cowboys from Maidstone.

'I don't know where these guys served their time,' he said. 'I could get my fingers behind the skirting board.'

'And they're not small fingers,' his wife said.

Gordon Dixon was in his late seventies or early eighties, but he was still a solid-looking man, barrel-chested and with a big white beard. Like Sandy Henderson, he had grown up in a flood-prone part of town, in the docks in east Hull; he remembered rolling up the coconut matting on the floor of his childhood home in the docks and watching the water trickle through the front door. There were disadvantages to the approach, he said, such as high rates of diphtheria and scarlet fever, but he shared Sandy Henderson's view that at least it meant you recovered quickly. Even after fifty years of marriage, he couldn't stop himself reminding his wife that she'd 'had it easy', for she had grown up in the wealthy streets of west Hull, which never flooded. 'A bit of flooding round here didn't bother me as much as it did you,' he said, though it wasn't clear he meant it, for he was not as robust as he looked.

He had had a major operation in 2000 and, ten years later, he had succumbed to a condition called cauda equina or 'horse tail' syndrome, in which the spine closes up, leaving him with no feeling in his legs. 'I only told you that after I drove you, didn't I!' he said, with a shout of laughter. I wasn't surprised that he had offered to pick me up, for Hull is a place where you rarely have to walk. Sandy Henderson had picked me up at The Deep, the museum that commemorates the city's relationship with the sea, and, one afternoon, I was driven around by the council official tasked with improving the city's flood defences. I had tried to walk to the Dixons', but I misjudged how far it was down the Anlaby Road, which runs parallel to the Humber, inland from the once flood-prone fishing community where Sandy Henderson had grown up, and, since I was late, I rang Gordon, and he said he would come and pick me up.

He drove in the same way he spoke: rapidly and impulsively. When he turned into East Ella Drive across a two-lane road, he accelerated so wildly that I was thrown back into my seat. I wasn't surprised to discover that he couldn't feel the pedals. He drove by memory and hearing. 'Completely numb!' he said, delighting in my surprise. Yet, despite his habit of 'nearly popping it', he had been on the 'up and up' when the flood struck, and he felt it had knocked him back: 'It took a big chunk out of our lives,' he said. 'I don't know how many years I have got left, but I couldn't afford to give any away.'

~

The Hendersons were luckier than most; they knew a builder who used to live next door, and they rang him up the day after the flood and asked him to do their house. Even so, Sandy wasn't sure how she managed not to slit her wrists. 'People bickered, they got divorced, several split up. Another moved to Australia. One had a heart attack and died. Until you have had it happen to you, you really can't understand.'

There were loss adjusters to deal with as well – official ones, and unofficial teams of freelancers who offered to negotiate with the insurance companies on behalf of those who had been flooded. It was hard for people to take control, one person said. Even after the water had gone, they felt like flotsam, cast adrift on the currents. One of the Dixons' neighbours was 'tipped over the edge' by the flood and had been in a home ever since. Another man burst an artery in his leg and nearly bled to death: 'The kitchen was like a butcher's shop,' Gordon said, with a certain relish. Many got ulcers from padding around in the polluted water, and Gordon had to endure the spectacle of the hapless southern builders trampling through a house that he had always taken care of himself.

They were lucky as well: the insurance company covered the cost of repairs to the house, but the money didn't solve all the problems. The house had evolved over many years and couldn't be remade in one go: they couldn't get the curtains without the sofa, and they couldn't get the sofa until they knew the colour of the walls. Eventually, they had to decide it all at once. 'It was all thrown at you, and your mind was spinning with it all,' Gordon said.

Other people felt a deeper unease about the influx of new possessions. I had met a retired nurse from Bransholme who said she had relished buying her furniture piece by piece because she knew she had earned it. If she didn't have the money, she didn't buy it. Being given the money to buy her kitchen all at once was an affront. The builders started work in East Ella Drive in October, and most of the work was done by December. The first meal Jacqui cooked in their new kitchen was Christmas dinner, which they ate on an improvised table, made from trestles and a sheet of MDF. Yet it didn't feel like home. 'I turned on the TV and sat here like I was in a hotel room,' she said. 'You're a long time before you get everything back to where it was.'

~

Jacqui had been feeling like 'a caged animal' in their upstairs rooms, and when she was invited to join the writing group, she relished the chance to get out and talk about the flood. To begin with, it had forty members, and even when the Lancaster University project ended after eighteen months,

Jacqui rented a room where they could meet. Sandy Henderson also went to the first meeting and kept going. The writing group saved her life, she told me. She and Jacqui became friends and six years later, they were still in touch. But, gradually, the cathartic effects of writing things down began to fade. It had helped Sandy through the ordeal, but it wasn't helping anymore; in fact, it was keeping the trauma alive. If it started raining heavily, she would grow anxious, fearful that the house would flood again, and she told Jacqui that she didn't want to keep going. 'It's past, it's gone, and I've finally got to love my house again.'

Jacqui was not so determined to move on. When the diarists' thoughts were published in a report, she was invited to speak at conferences across the country, and she also went to London to address the Cabinet Office. 'If I can do a bit of good going and talking to people, I would rather die knowing I had tried,' she said, modestly. Years later, she was still concerned with testifying to the effects of the flood. While her husband was talking to me, she went out of the room and came back with a box of papers and photographs, which we looked through together.

I was fascinated by the writing group, and the complementary impulses of remembering and forgetting that it served – remembering, in Sandy's case, aiding forgetting, which seemed to me the ultimate aim of 'recovery'. But I also wanted to understand how the experiences that Jacqui and Sandy had recorded sat within the wider context of the city, and its estuary and river. I walked into Hull when I left Sandy Henderson's house, following the banks of the River

Hull as it wound through the marshes, past the pumping station that had failed on the day of the flood. Factories, warehouses and wrecking yards closed in around the river, accumulating like barnacle-encrusted mussels on a rope. The next day, I caught the train to North Ferriby, a town beside the Humber, eight miles west, and approached Hull from another direction, along the shores of the Humber.

~

My grandmother lived in Ferriby, as it is usually known, for forty years, but that wasn't the only reason I had chosen it as my starting point. Ferriby is the site of one of the oldest boatyards in the world, where boats capable of navigating the estuary and the North Sea were built. The first one was discovered in 1937 by a nineteen-year-old amateur archae-ologist and palaeontologist called Edward Wright. He was searching for dinosaur bones on the foreshore at Ferriby, where I had played as a child, when he saw 'three massive wooden planks projecting at a shallow angle' from the intertidal mud flats. He took the timbers back to the family house, which stood behind my grandmother's in Turner's Lane. Her house was still there, but the Wrights' wasn't; the old brick wall that had marked its boundary now contained the houses of a new estate.

Ferriby was smaller than I remembered: places that you knew as a child always are when you go back as an adult. It was quieter, as well. A girl on a horse rode past me when I got off the train and walked up Station Road. Yet there was concern about overcrowding, even here: *Save Our Ferriby*, said the yellow stickers plastered to lamp posts and windows. The locals were campaigning against a plan to build 600 homes on waterlogged land north of the village; they said it would force water downhill and overload the drainage systems of the village, which already could barely cope. I heard the same story in many places I had been, and I wasn't surprised to hear it in Ferriby as well, for it had always seemed a characteristically English place, as robust and unselfpitying as my grandmother, its apparent insularity belied by the great waterway that flowed past its feet.

It was early. I waited until the florists opposite the church had opened, so I could buy some flowers for my grandparents' grave, and then walked down to the shore. The outline of the boat engraved on the bank of the estuary was larger than I expected: it was a flat-ended oval, braced by eleven cross pieces, long enough for eighteen oars and a mast. The original had been built from trees split into planks with wooden wedges, stitched together with yew branches and waterproofed with moss. It was sixteen metres long and weighed four tonnes empty. It would have been propelled by eighteen paddlers, capable of making six knots in short bursts.

At first, Edward Wright thought it was a Viking boat, left by the people who had founded 'the village by the ferry' on the north shore of the Humber in *c.* 900 AD, but it proved to be much older: it has been dated to 2030–1780 BC, which means it was almost as old as the Humber Estuary itself. Until the end of the last Ice Age, the area had been covered by a lake; yet, as the glaciers retreated, the water that had been dammed inland cut a channel to the sea, and the estuary formed. Until 2500 BC, its banks were covered by forests of oak and alder, but, as the sea levels rose, the salt water poisoned them.

The boats were an adaptation to the changing landscape of the Humber. Some people believed they had been left by immigrants from Egypt, where the only boats older than the ones in Ferriby had been built, but the theory has been dismissed, and I prefer to think of them as prototypes of the cargo ships, trawlers and ferries that generated Hull's prosperity – and that of families like Edward Wright's. His grandfather had been chairman of the Hull Dock Company, though Wright himself had worked for Reckitts, another great Hull institution. My grandfather and great-grandfather had worked for Reckitts as well, and it had paid for the information board beside the boats.

The tide was out. A row of exposed posts that looked like the remnants of a bridge or jetty trailed away into the water, tracing a dotted line towards the wind turbines on the far shore and the towers of a factory or refinery beyond. Upstream, the estuary narrowed and disappeared out of sight. Downstream, the vertical pillars of the Humber Bridge, and the lines of the cables that supported its decks, framed the view towards the open sea.

~

I followed the dead-straight cinder footpath that ran beside the Humber for the next six miles, only leaving the dark brown water when I reached a stretch that was being repaired. I had to duck through a hedge on to the railway line; the train that I had caught to Ferriby at half past seven rattled past at terrifying speed, whistle screaming. A digger backed, beeping, into view through a gap in the hedge, and I fell flat on my face to make sure I wasn't seen. Beyond the workmen, I scrambled down the bank into a deep, over-grown ravine, and climbed up the other side, on a fallen metal fence as springy as a trampoline.

The sun was coming out as I reached the Humber Bridge. Lorries rumbled over the decks and descended into Hessle, where a man had drowned, in July 2007, when he got trapped in a storm drain. Hessle was the site of the first sea defences on the Humber, but it might not be protected for much longer. Hull and Grimsby will be saved, but Hessle may be relinquished, as part of the policy of 'managed retreat' in the face of the ever-rising seas.

As I reached the outskirts of Hull, the path ran into the rush of oncoming traffic beside the A63. Car dealerships, business parks and supermarkets gave way to derelict plots and breakers' yards, where the cars were stacked in shiny piles that looked like they might slide into the river. High reeds shaded the path and obscured the river, and two men in black shirts sat on the steps outside a warehouse, smoking. There were horses tethered on the towpath. A graffiti artist was tagging the walls of an old warehouse and, further on, the metal frame of a new warehouse rose from an empty site.

At St Andrew's Quay, I passed the memorial to the trawlermen who had lost their lives at sea and entered a long tract of derelict docks. My father began his career auditing businesses in St Andrew's Quay, but there were none left anymore; the empty warehouses reminded me of photographs of the bombed-out cities of Europe at the end of the Second World War. A teenager in a hoodie emerged from a doorway carrying a piece of corrugated metal. He threw it into a trolley pushed by another boy, and they trundled off ahead of me, leading the way into Hull.

As I approached The Deep, the museum which stands at the confluence of the River Hull and Humber Estuary, I thought about a man I had met earlier in the week, at a community centre in Bransholme. Jeff Dixon – who was no relation of Gordon and Jacqui – had been a sapper in the Royal Engineers, and had then worked on the railways and the buses. Until he retired at the age of sixty-five, he had never had a day off. Six years later, he watched as everything he had worked for was destroyed by the water pouring through the front door of his house. Yet he didn't complain: 'Everyone lost something they valued, that day,' he said.

The insurance company had covered all his costs, and he didn't ask for a penny more than he was owed. He got his house back. His son, who has cerebral palsy, used to live in a room on the ground floor, but after the flood, he had moved into sheltered accommodation in Victoria Dock near The Deep.

Mr Dixon was pleased with his son's new home – it had beautiful views, and it was well maintained. They were getting the grounds done, he said, and making a nice job of it. The council official who had introduced us was happy that

Mr Dixon seemed so pleased. I had never met his son, but the warmth of the exchange that I witnessed in a community centre far from the Humber made him seem very real to me. I imagined him sitting in his flat in Victoria Dock, looking out across the estuary towards the North Sea, in the direction from which the next storm to hit the city would come.

5: The Colinda Spear

As early as the tenth century, astute observers noted that Britain's coastlines were fringed with trees that were only visible at low tide. They tended to regard the 'drowned forests' as evidence of Noah's flood, relics of the antediluvian world destroyed in the Biblical story, and it was not until the twentieth century that their true significance was acknowledged. In 1913, a self-trained geologist called Clement Reid published a book called *Submerged Forests*, in which he argued that one of Noah's woods 'stretched far below the level of the mean tide. In fact, we followed it down to the level of the lowest spring tides. Nothing but a change of sea level will account for its present position.' Observations on the east coast of England led him to conclude that the Thames and Humber estuaries were once 'flanked by a wide alluvial flat which now lies from 40 to 60 feet [twelve to eighteen metres] below the modern marsh level'.

In an attempt to verify his claim, Reid analysed a clump of 'moorlog' – the peaty substance that fishermen used to dredge up from the shallow bed of the North Sea, in an area known as Dogger Bank. As well as the compacted remains of shells, wood and lumps of peat, it contained the bones of a bestiary: bear, wolf, hyena, bison, mammoth, beaver, walrus, elk and deer. There was only one way to explain their presence at the bottom of the North Sea: 'Noah's Woods' must have once stretched far beyond the current shore, with Dogger Bank forming 'the northern edge of a great alluvial plain, occupying what is now the southern half of the North Sea, and stretching across to Holland and Denmark.'

Confirmation of Reid's theory came in 1931, when a trawler called the *Colinda*, which was fishing off the Norfolk coast, found a remarkable artefact embedded in another lump of moorlog. The crew of the *Colinda* would have thrown the block overboard, as they always did, but the master of the ship noticed that it made a metallic sound when it was struck with a shovel. 'I thought it was steel,' Skipper Pilgrim E. Lockwood said later. 'I bent down and took it below.'

He split the peaty lump open and 'an object quite black' fell out. It was a handworked antler, twenty-one centimetres long, with a set of barbs running along one side. It was a prehistoric harpoon, and it was subsequently dated to the Mesolithic age, between 4000 and 10000 BC. It had been lying in a freshwater deposit, meaning it hadn't fallen overboard during a sea voyage, but had been dropped by a hunter crossing a landscape dotted with lakes and pools. It was 'the first real evidence that the North Sea had been part of a great plain inhabited by the last hunter-gatherers in

Europe', write Vincent Gaffney, Simon Finch and David Smith, the trio of archaeologists who have made the most sustained attempts to map the area that has become known as Doggerland, in a book called *Europe's Lost World: The Rediscovery of Doggerland*. It was a remarkable discovery – though, in a way, it was not a surprise. Long before the existence of Doggerland was established, people had speculated about lost worlds beneath the seas, which they conceived in terms of another great flood myth that has been retold countless times.

~

In the original version of the story, which appears in Plato's dialogue *Critias*, the continent of Atlantis was a 'great power', ruled by descendants of Poseidon, 'a remarkable dynasty of kings', which 'arrogantly advanced from its base in the Atlantic Ocean to attack the cities of Europe and Asia'. Ancient Athens, which represented Plato's idea of the perfect state, defeated it in battle, but had no time to enjoy its triumph, for both victor and vanquished were overtaken by disaster: in 'a single dreadful day and night, all [Athens's] fighting men were swallowed up by the earth, and the island of Atlantis was similarly swallowed up by the sea and vanished'. Scholars often insist that we are not meant to take the accounts of Atlantis literally, but rather 'we should use the story to examine our ideas of government and power,' writes the philosopher, Julia Annas, in *Plato: A Very Short Introduction*. 'We have missed the point if instead of thinking about these issues we go off exploring the sea bed.'

The warning has often been ignored. Plato's first readers were not interested in the exact location of Atlantis, and early modern writers such as Thomas More and Francis Bacon explored Platonic ideals of the good society, in *Utopia* and *New Atlantis* respectively, without becoming preoccupied by questions of geography. Yet, recently, we have renounced the challenging task of interpreting Plato's layered enquiry into the nature of the good society in favour of millennial fantasies about drowned worlds. The number of stories about lost continents is 'beyond count', said the American science-fiction writer L. Sprague de Camp in 1954, in a survey of the genre, and it featured in several books I read as a child, such as Arthur Conan Doyle's *The Maracot Deep*, which is set in a miraculously preserved and inhabited undersea world. It tells the story of a group of underwater explorers who are attacked by a giant crustacean that snips the cable of their 'bathysphere', plunging it to the bottom of the sea. They are rescued by the surviving Atlanteans, who take them as curiosities to their submarine city.

Atlantis also appears in Jules Verne's *Twenty Thousand Leagues Under the Sea* – though as a ruin, not a thriving city. In one memorable scene, the occupants of the submarine *Nautilus* climb through a sunken forest on the slopes of an erupting volcano on the bottom of the Atlantic, until they find themselves looking down on a ruined town, 'its roofs open to the sky, its temples fallen, its arches dislocated, its columns lying on the ground'. Captain Nemo chalks a single word on to a rock of black basalt: 'ATLANTIS'. Aronnax, the marine biologist who narrates *Twenty Thousand Leagues Under the Sea*, marvels at the thought that he is standing 'on the very spot where the contemporaries of the first man had walked'.

The treatment of the subject was not confined to books that advertise themselves as fiction. The champion of the idea of Atlantis 'as veritable history' was an American politician called Ignatius Donnelly. He was a congressman and senator for Minnesota, but he was also a land speculator, farmer and fantasist. He proposed three implausible theories: that Francis Bacon had written Shakespeare's plays and embedded a cipher within them; that great events in the Earth's history, such as the Ice Age, were brought on by 'extraterrestrial catastrophism'; and that Atlantis was a fragment of a vast oceanic continent that used to lie beneath the Atlantic Ocean between Britain and America.

Yet it was not only a real place – it also represented all the lost paradises from which humanity had been expelled, and all the longed-for realms of the afterlife: 'the Garden of Eden; the Gardens of the Hesperides; the Elysian Fields . . . the Asgard of the traditions of the ancient nations . . . a universal memory of a great land, where early mankind dwelt for ages in peace and happiness,' Donnelly wrote in a book called *Atlantis: The Antediluvian World*. He believed that a few lucky survivors of the submergence of Atlantis had escaped 'in ships and on rafts' to populate surrounding continents. As proof, he cited seemingly uncanny resemblances between European and American plants and animals, culture and language – common artefacts and habits of mind, which he believed the Atlanteans had carried with them as they fled, east and west, from the sinking land.

He was wrong in every way it is possible to be wrong. Most of his statements were 'wrong when he made them, or have been disproved by subsequent discoveries', L. Sprague de Camp said, and, even if they hadn't been wrong, he would still have drawn the wrong conclusions from them. People on both sides of the Atlantic may have used spears and sails, got married and divorced, and believed in ghosts and flood legends, but that 'proves nothing about sunken continents'.

Yet being wrong is rarely a bar to success, especially in the realms of mysticism. Donnelly's book was reprinted twenty-two times in the eight years after its publication in 1882; it become known as 'the New Testament of Atlantism', and attracted a following among occultists such as Helena Petrovna Blavatsky, founder of the Theosophical Society. Blavatsky believed that Atlantis was one of several lost continents on which humanity had evolved. She claimed that her esoteric magnum opus, *The Secret Doctrine*, was dictated on Atlantis, and that part of humanity was descended from a 'root-race' who lived on another vanished continent, called Lemuria. Its existence had originally been proposed by an English zoologist called Philip Sclater as a way of explaining why lemur fossils were found in Madagascar and India, but not in Africa or the Middle East. Sclater believed that India and Madagascar had been conjoined on a continent that broke apart into islands or sank beneath the waves. Blavatsky made grander claims for it. She believed that Lemuria was 'the cradle of mankind, of the physical sexual creature who materialized through long aeons out of the ethereal hermaphrodites'. Her fellow theosophist William Scott-Elliot offered a vivid description of this 'creature' in *The Lost Lemuria*, published in 1904: 'His stature was gigantic, somewhere between 12 and 15 feet [between 3.5 and 4.5 metres] . . . His skin was very dark, being of a yellowish brown colour. He had a long lower jaw, a strangely flattened face, eyes small but piercing and set curiously far apart, so that he could see sideways as well as in front, while the eye at the back of the head . . . enabled him to see in that direction also.'

Once the theory of continental drift had been accepted in the early twentieth century, there was no need to propose the existence of lost continents or sunken land bridges to explain how species crossed from one land mass to another. Yet the idea of Lemuria continued to fascinate occult writers.

In 1904, the American writer Frederick S. Oliver published an influential book called *A Dweller on Two Planets*, which was supposedly written under 'spirit guidance'. It tells the story of a community of sages who escaped from Lemuria and settled on Mount Shasta, near Oliver's home in northern California. Sightings of the Lemurian community of Mount Shasta were reported during the twenties and thirties; it was said to consist of 1,000 magi living in a 'mystic village' built around a Mayan-style temple. Occasionally, they appeared in neighbouring towns, clad in long white robes, 'polite but taciturn', and they paid for supplies with gold nuggets. Every midnight they rejoiced in their escape from Lemuria in ceremonies that bathed the mountains in red and green light.

Californian luminaries such as the actress Shirley MacLaine, who recalled a past life as an androgynous Lemurian in her memoir *I'm Over All That*, and Guy Warren Ballard, founder of the religious movement I AM, were both inspired by Oliver's novel, and it still informs the philosophy of the Lemurian Fellowship, which claims 'the continents of Atlantis and Mu [often synonymous with Lemuria] did exist, and still do, sunken beneath the waters of the Atlantic and Pacific Oceans.'

Another occultist, the British writer James Churchward, claimed to have learnt the secrets of Mu from ancient tablets discovered in temples in India. His book *The Lost Continent of Mu: The Motherland of Men* was one of the last great manifestations of the mystical preoccupation with lost worlds. By the time it was published in 1926, the wild fantasies of the nineteenth-century cult of Atlantis were being displaced by a story that was no less astonishing and had the advantage of being true.

~

Doggerland was lost slowly at first, and then with terrifying speed. To begin with, meltwater from the retreating glaciers erased the edges of the land and crept through its low-lying hollows and channels. It created new habitats as well, such as salt marshes, which the Mesolithic peoples must have regarded as 'a gift of the sea', say Gaffney, Fitch and Smith in *Europe's Lost World: The Rediscovery of Doggerland*. Yet they also knew their territory was shrinking, as the sea 'reclaimed ancestral hunting grounds, campsites and land-marks'. Some would have continued to live on newly created islands. Others may have retreated to the high ground to the west, which they had previously ignored.

No one knows how many remained on Doggerland when a tsunami crashed across it, *c.* 6200 BC. It was triggered by an underwater landslide caused by an earthquake or the release of methane gas beneath the seabed near the Norwegian coast, and it replicated the pattern made tragically familiar in the tsunami that killed 230,000 people in fourteen countries bordering the Indian Ocean on Boxing Day 2003. At first, the water drew back to reveal 'an amazing bonanza' of stranded fish and shellfish, write Gaffney, Fitch and Smith, and some of those who saw it might have thought their ancestral homes had been restored. Yet what seemed like a retreat was the gathering of an irresistible force.

During the next two or three hours, four or five waves struck the coast as the seawater that had 'piled up in the depression' flowed back towards land in a series of massive waves. Anyone caught in the open would have been killed. Coastal settlements flooded. In some places, the water travelled twenty-five miles inland. Further south, the water broke through the marshes that stretched to France, and the remaining barriers between the North Sea and the Atlantic disappeared.

The way that Britain became an island, or a collection of islands, so suddenly and unexpectedly, seems all the more remarkable, given the way its sense of itself as distinct from the rest of the continent has shaped its cultural and political life. Yet the

> silver sea,
> Which serves it in the office of a wall,
> Or as a moat defensive to a house,

as John of Gaunt says in Shakespeare's famous lines in *Richard II*, is a source of danger, as well as a means of protection, for it hasn't stopped rising since Doggerland disappeared.

~

John Buxton was ten years old when the sea broke through at Horsey, on the night of 12 February 1938, and spread out in a deadening lake that engulfed all but twenty-five of 7,469 acres of his parents' estate. He was away at school, and he was desperately disappointed to miss the excitement of the flood. 'I was a small boy and I was so eager to see what it looked like,' he said.

It was July 2013 – the height of a warm, dry summer that gave no indication of the winter that would follow

– and I had driven out to Norfolk to visit some of the places that had flooded in 1938 and 1953. Horsey Hall was my first stop, though I was three hours late because my car had packed up on the Norwich ring road. Mr Buxton and his wife, Bridget, were far too good mannered and hospitable to complain; they seemed more concerned by the inconvenience I had suffered than any I might have caused. They showed me into the cool, dark kitchen at the back of the house. A large black-and-white picture of a young John Buxton deer-stalking in the Highlands hung on the wall, and the windows overlooked a moss-stained lawn. It felt peaceful and secluded – yet, at the front, it was only a short walk to Horsey Gap, which led to the beach and the restless sea.

The Buxtons had been reminded of the fragility and impermanence of the coast two years before the flood of 1938. On the night of 1 December 1936, a gale scoured the beach on the seaward side of the dune, exposing the hoof-prints of unshod horses and cattle, and the foundations of a wall. There was only one possible explanation for their position: the dunes used to lie much further east.

It was a reminder that the coastline is always changing. Two thousand years ago, Norfolk's Yare Estuary was deep enough for ships. One and a half thousand years ago, the sea level fell and the estuary silted up to form the tidal inlet of Breydon Water. A spit of land emerged where Great Yarmouth now stands. The locals harvested wood for fuel and dug peat: between the twelfth and fourteenth centuries, they dug more than 900 million cubic feet (275 million cubic metres) of peat, and the rising sea flooded the holes left behind, creating the lakes and rivers that became the Norfolk Broads.

The effect of the rising seas was particularly apparent in the south, for it was compounded by the phenomenon known as post-glacial rebound: as the temperature warmed and the glaciers retreated, the land that had borne the lightest load tilted downwards, while the land in the north that had been most heavily compressed sprang upwards. As J. E. Sainty said in a book called *The Norfolk Sea Floods*, the *Colinda* spear – which he called 'the lovely bone harpoon or fish-spear' – dredged up from the bed of the North Sea, off the Norfolk coast, 'was lost by its Mesolithic owner in swamp or shallow water; whilst the cave at Oban, inhabited by hunters at a time when the breakers could occasionally sweep into it, is now high above the surf.' As the North rises, the South sinks; and the sea encroaches on the low-lying coasts.

~

John Buxton's father, who had owned the estate for seven years by 1938, was less thrilled by the flood than his son. Instead of the drama and romance that appealed to a ten-year-old boy, he recognized its destructive effects. 'He was devastated,' Mrs Buxton said. 'He had been through a war, and now he had seen Horsey flooded. He was terribly worried about the future.'

Anthony Buxton had gone to Horsey for the first time in

1930, drawn by reports of shooting on the mere. He had always been fascinated by the natural world, though he intended to preserve Horsey as a shooting estate as well as a nature reserve – and saw no contradiction between the two. The fascination for nature was a family failing, John Buxton said. His grandfather – Anthony's father – had founded the Society for the Preservation of the Fauna of the Empire, which became Flora and Fauna International, and Anthony Buxton had inherited his approach to wildlife, which was 'typically Victorian': shoot anything that moves and then preserve it.

Anthony began his career as a brewer in the family business in Spitalfields, East London, but it was interrupted by the First World War. He served in the Essex Yeomanry, and he was so horrified by what he saw that he wanted to try to stop it happening again. In 1919, he joined the Secretariat of the League of Nations in Geneva, as a member of the British delegation, which was led by Lord Perth. There, he established a pack of beagles and found a wife: 'Mother was a cousin of the Perths,' John Buxton said, with long familiarity with the interconnectedness of aristocratic life. 'She went out to see them, met father, and they got married.'

By 1930, Anthony knew that his time in Geneva had not secured world peace. 'I suspect he felt increasingly disappointed at how ineffective the League was proving, and he was certainly looking for a change of direction in life,' John Buxton wrote, in a book that described the discovery that cranes were nesting in Horsey after a 400-year absence from the UK.

Lady Buxton, who came from Beauly, near Inverness, did not like the flat and seemingly empty landscape, but Anthony saw a pair of marsh harriers flying over the reed beds and knew he wanted to live there. 'The fun of the thing to me, and I believe to many naturalists, has been to see the struggle for life,' he wrote in his memoir, *Fisherman Naturalist*. Yet naturalists did not often own estates, and Anthony Buxton's tenure of Horsey was regarded as an oddity. 'Idiosyncratic narrative underwrites estate curiosity,' notes a book called *The Cultural Geography of the Norfolk Broads*, in an epigrammatic style that might be imitating its subject's clipped phrasing: 'Buxton projecting a singular ownership.'

~

The alarm was delivered in a countryman's muted style: 'The sea is in, sir,' Anthony Buxton was told, as he came out of the house at seven thirty p.m. It had risen to within 150 yards (137 metres) of Horsey Hall, and 'a mass of dead worms, many drowned hares, rabbits, pheasants and partridge' had washed up in the lane. One man was caught in his car on the coastal road: 'He tried to get away, but the sea beat him to it,' John Buxton told me. 'His headlights went out, and he couldn't swim – poor man.' The car was a soft top, Mr Buxton said, so he was able to cut himself out, but he spent a terrifying night on the top of his car in the middle of the moonlit expanse of water.

John Buxton finally got to see it in April, when the family

came back to Horsey from Happisburgh, nine miles up the coast, where they had been staying. By then, a second tide had poured through Horsey Gap, sweeping away the temporary defences built after the first one. The water had gone down, the evaporation making it saltier, but the coast road was still flooded. The water was above their boots, 'which meant it was so high,' Mr Buxton said, tapping his knee. He set out to explore with the son of a gamekeeper, who was a friend. He was fascinated by the stench of rotting vegetation and the endless dead fish; they had all been killed immediately, apart from the eels. Herrings, flat fish, crabs and barnacles gradually took their place. Yet his father was horrified by the 'strange and deathly silence' that settled over Horsey as his beloved marshes became a 'red-brown salt desert' that reminded him of the steppes of Asia Minor. 'The devastation and the general air of a great flat rubbish heap on which nothing can thrive, produce a feeling of intense depression,' he wrote. 'There may have been . . . some beauty about the floods, particularly at sunrise, sunset and by moonlight,' but there was none as the water receded, leaving 'a dead and smelly waste', littered with rubbish of every kind. At the borders of the flooded area, the transition was 'blatantly abrupt' – 'from bright green life to red brown death . . .'

The marsh-loving birds, like the bitterns and the harriers that had drawn Anthony Buxton to Horsey, disappeared. 'The one exception are the pigeons,' Buxton wrote: 'wood pigeons, stock doves, and in particular turtle doves, seem to thrive on salt.' He noted that the trees 'behaved in a peculiar way': many made 'repeated, in some cases violent, efforts to produce leaves and flowers,' but they nearly always failed. Only a line of oaks on a dyke and a group of young birches in the middle of a sedge marsh managed to produce normal foliage, for they were sustained by freshwater springs, and there was one island of 120 acres that the water hadn't covered. It was 'the one bright spot' where trees and plants flourished, and birds still sang.

~

The land took three months to drain, for there is no natural fall: the water had to be lifted into the high-level system of broads and dykes, through 'day-and-night pumping'. Horsey Mere was like a bath, and the marshes were the bathroom floor, John Buxton said – an analogy that became clearer when we climbed to the platform of the Horsey wind-pump, the old windmill that used to drain the marshes, and looked down on the landscape from above.

Mr Buxton has been going up and down the stairs inside the pepper-pot cone since he was a boy, and he waved away my offers of help. He had taken most of the photographs on the illustrated panels hanging on the walls of each floor, for he had inherited not only his father's love of nature, but his love of film and photography as well; having spent his childhood 'mucking about in boats on Horsey Mere' and carrying his father's cameras through the marshes, he had become a wildlife cameraman.

The last flight was the steepest of them all, but when we reached the wooden balcony at the top, Mr Buxton was far more comfortable than I was: looking down at the greenish water in the dyke below made me feel sick, but he moved around the flimsy platform with a familiarity he would never lose. It was a beautiful summer day, and the mere was busy: there were people fishing from its banks and strolling along the paths that run beside it, though they were not allowed to enter the western part of the estate, where the cranes had their nests.

Even when the salt water had been lifted out, it took a long time for the mere to purify itself; it was still salt in September 1938, seven months after the flood, and was 'likely to remain so, until many inches of rain have fallen and been in turn pumped into the broads,' Buxton wrote. The water moves slowly on its twenty-one-mile journey to the sea at Great Yarmouth, for it is propelled by nothing except the slightest of gradients and the wind. Yet the longest lasting damage was to the soil, which turned to 'a sodium clay with the consistency of putty'. Anthony Buxton went to Holland for advice, and they told him that, if he let air get into it, it would turn to cement; he was to put away his implements, pray for rain, and not try to grow anything for the next five years. One of the three tenant farmers on the estate ignored the advice: he ploughed his fields, and Anthony Buxton sacked him.

~

Horsey flooded again in the Great Tide of 1953, though not as badly as in 1938. Seawater reached Horsey Mere via Sea

Palling, but only 1,200 acres of marshes were flooded. Horsey had one advantage over other places, the Buxtons said: once the defences were breached at Sea Palling, the sea poured into the high street, but, at Horsey, it spread out across the marshes. One woman, whose family climbed on to the roof of their bungalow in Sea Palling in 1953, described the sea as 'a great sheet of water, hissing and roaring'. Seven people drowned in the village, including a baby, who was swept off her father's back, and the landlord of the Lifeboat Inn, who was trying to reach a rescue boat.

New sea defences at Horsey were completed in 1958, a year before John Buxton took over the estate. From the platform of the wind-pump, they looked like a breaking wave, rising from the livid green and brown patchwork of the marshes. In 1959, Horsey was connected to the water mains. Until then, they had used their own wells, which supplied water that was muddy at best, and undrinkable below ten feet (three metres). That sort of thing made it feel out on a limb, Mr Buxton said: 'Everyone used to say that no one in Horsey ever passed their eleven-plus. No one sensible would buy a house like this and live with the permanent threat of flooding. But we have got used to it.'

Their tenancy of the estate is set to continue; John Buxton's son recently renewed the lease until 2099, though Mr Buxton said it would only survive that long if the defences are maintained and renewed. That is not guaranteed. In 2008, English Nature, the agency responsible for managing wildlife and wild places, inadvertently released a discussion paper that considered letting the sea break through a fifteen-mile stretch of coast between Eccles-on-Sea and Winterton: five fresh-water lakes and six villages, including Eccles, Sea Palling, Horsey and Hickling, which lies beyond Horsey Mere, would be lost, and a vast bay or inlet would be created, covering one per cent of Norfolk and restoring much of the North Broads to salt marsh, which they had been 2,500 years ago, when the sea lay a mile further east.

Mr Buxton had played no part in the campaign to resist the idea. He didn't need to; the local opposition was very fierce. It was led by a man who lived in Hickling, which had flooded on St Lucia's Day, 1287, when the water rose a foot (thirty centimetres) above the altar in Hickling parish church, and 180 people had drowned. Eric Lindo and a friend had coordinated meetings, mobilized local politicians and petitioned central government; he said no one in Whitehall had come across a double act like theirs. The plan was dropped. Some people said it would have been, anyway – it was a thought experiment, which wasn't meant to be published, let alone put into practice. There was delight that the bureaucrats had been forced to retreat – and yet no one doubted that the rising seas would be harder to defeat.

~

At the end of the summer of 2013, as the hot sunny days began to turn cloudy and rain-spotted, I spent a week in Southwold, the Suffolk town that became an island in 1953, when the sea swept through the marshes behind it and cut it off from the mainland. One morning, I walked past the pier and the rows of coloured beach huts beyond the car park to reach the beach at Easton Bavents, where I could see the ramp at the beginning of the defences built by Peter Boggis, the King Canute of East Anglia, who had grown so impatient with English Nature and its failure to protect his family's rapidly eroding land that he had decided to do it himself.

Boggis had lived in Easton Bavents, the clifftop hamlet on the edge of Southwold, since he was four years old, and even when his family had rented out their house for the summer, they had only relocated to a caravan on the beach, which then lay a mile to the east. He'd only had one prolonged spell away from Easton Bavents, when he was doing national service in the Royal Navy, and it had coincided with the Great Tide of 31 January 1953. He was in Malta when he got a 'worrying telegram' saying that 300 people in Southwold had drowned. In fact, the real total was four. He moved back to Southwold in 1954 and worked for an engineering company. When his father died in 1971, he moved into his house on the edge of the cliff. Five years later, he moved out. 'My marriage had broken down, for which I consider myself totally responsible,' he said. Boggis walked out of his father's house in a boiler suit, emblem of his professional calling, but, even then, he didn't leave Easton Bavents. His grandfather had died within three months of his father, and he moved into his house, The Warren, where we met. It was set further back from the cliff, which means it will be safer for longer than the other houses in Easton Bavents.

By 2002, when he started work on his defences, the cliff had moved 160 metres inland, and the 340 acres that his grandfather had bought in 1924 had been reduced to 160. Such loss of land is not unusual. Dunwich, which lies five miles down the coast, has been reduced from a great port to a tiny hamlet, with a few houses, a church and a museum – a vestigial village dedicated to memorializing its own past. Twelve churches have shuffled off the retreating cliff edge, and now lie beneath the waters of the bay. Many other buildings will go the same way. In 2014, the Environment Agency estimated that more than 7,000 homes will fall into the sea this century, and a recent report by the Committee on Climate Change put the potential loss even higher: by the 2080s, it said 100,000 properties, 1,600 kilometres of road, 650 kilometres of railway and 92 stations will be at risk. So will ports, power stations and gas terminals. Toxic waste from 1,000 landfill dumps may fall into the sea.

Yet Boggis did not accept the erosion as inevitable. He was seventy-one years old when he started work, and he wasn't exactly running around like a three-year-old, but, being an engineer, he knew what he was doing. He said that his attempt to hold back the waves required nothing more than 'common sense', but it was plain that he regarded the term as the highest possible praise.

He used lorry-loads of rubble to build an improvised road from Southwold Pier to the clifftop village of Easton Bavents, and, once it was in place, he sent more lorries along it, loaded with material that he packed against the cliff to form a sacrificial wall that would erode instead of the land. Some people got tired of the thirty-eight-tonne lorries rumbling past their homes, and the rubble that washed down the coast. Others saw him as a hero of an inimitably English kind: self-reliant, inventive, dismissive of bureaucratic procedure, and, above all, eager for his day in court.

His real enemy was not nature, but English Nature, or 'English Nazis', as he liked to call the agency. There was an *Encyclopaedia of Planning Law and Practice* on his desk, and he was constantly referring scornfully to 'the powers-that-be, in all their wisdom'. He did not wait for their approval; by the time English Nature 'became aware that something they said could not be done was being done, and at no cost to the nation,' he had built a wall a kilometre long that had slowed the rate of erosion. Before, the land had been disappearing at the rate of ten metres a year, and, since the wall had been there, they had lost two metres in ten years. Yet the cost of fighting English Nature defeated him: in 2005, he was declared bankrupt and forced to abandon his defences. Since then, ninety per cent of his structure had been lost and the land was beginning to slip away again.

The process is not entirely one-way. Sometimes, land is gained as well as lost. The South England flood of 1287, which destroyed houses in Dunwich and swept away the town of Winchelsea, in East Sussex, left New Romney landlocked a mile from the coast. As the River Rother silted up, Rye became a port instead. Yet its status was provisional, as well. When Celia Fiennes went to Rye, some 400 years later, she noted that it had begun to lose its access to the sea: 'it does still come up to Rhye town as yet but its shallow,' she wrote. Romney Marsh, which was known as the 'Fifth Continent' or the 'Gift of the Sea', was expanding southwards and eastwards, as it was reclaimed by innings and one-way drains, so that villages like Lydd, which had been established on an island in a sandy lagoon, found themselves several miles inland.

Sea-level rise is far less even-handed. The Deep, the museum I visited in Hull, has an interactive exhibit that allows you to spin a wheel and watch the water creep across the fields of North Lincolnshire and the East Riding of Yorkshire. In most projections, the Somerset Levels and the Fens are the first to go, followed by other places that I know and love, like coastal Essex and the Wirral. Cornwall becomes an archipelago, and Scotland is cut off from the rest of Britain. In the Midlands, the enlarged Severn stretches so far inland that it almost meets the Wash, in a version of 'the Lake' that covers central England in Richard Jefferies' *After London*. Yet it is the east coast that will be affected most; in some projections, cities like Hull and Chelmsford disappear, and Norwich lies so far offshore it would take all day to reach its sunken ruins.

~

Boggis knew he wouldn't win. His first wife, who lived in one of the houses that stands metres from the cliff edge, remembered going to a party in a bungalow that lay several hundred metres further east. Boggis knows that more of us will end up with memories of dancing in gardens beneath the waves, but he remained determined not to give in.

Boggis must have been a powerful man in his prime, but he was eighty-two years old, and he had recently been diagnosed with prostate cancer. He drove me the short distance to the northern end of the disintegrating remnants of his sea wall, and when he got out of the car, I had to take his hand and help him down the slope on the edge of the corn field. He had only been allowed to keep the car because it was bought for him after he was declared bankrupt, but when his bankruptcy expired, he intended to revive the other machines through which he projected his failing strength, like the disassembled digger that hung from a frame in his back garden, and resume his fight against nature and bureaucracy.

In the meantime, he had one more defiant gesture prepared. Before I left him, he drove me to the southern end of his defences and parked beside a pile of boulders that he had drawn up on the cliff at the top of the improvised road that ran downhill, past sheep-dotted fields, to the car park beside Southwold Pier. It was a characteristically theatrical gesture: when all was lost, and there was no other hope of saving the houses on the cliff, including the one where his ex-wife lived, he would tip the stones on to the beach below, as a final barrier against the waves.

I left him sitting in his car and walked down to the beach. I couldn't see the giant rockery from below, but I could see the twisted pipes, bricks and rubber tyres that protruded through the last remnants of his defences, like the hand-holds on an urban climbing wall.

Further along the beach, I came to Easton Bavents Broad, which the sea had breached in the previous winter. The trail of driftwood strewn across the fifty metres of pebbled sand showed how the sea had reached the wide reed-fringed pool and turned its water brackish. There were purple flowers in the field behind it and lorries on the road. I passed the Eastern Broad River Outfall, a fenced-in pond of dark, still water, and followed a foot-path along the edge of a field until I reached Easton Bavents. The seaward half of the last cottage on the lane that led to the end of Boggis's defences was dark and empty, but the landward half was rented out; there was a salt cellar on the table and a dishcloth hanging from the door of the oven in the kitchen. *Danger – Keep Out – Cliff Eroding*, said the sign at the end of the lane, where the road ended abruptly.

Juliet Blaxland lived in the most landward of the three cottages. It was spare and weathered: there were faded fittings in the kitchen, and books about the sea on a shelf in the draughty downstairs bathroom. The upstairs window looked across Boggis's diminishing clifftop fields to the part of Southwold where the sea had broken through in 1953. The town would be even more vulnerable when the protect-ive shoulder of Easton Bavents was removed.

Juliet, who was an architect, admired Boggis's efforts, though she was conscious of the absurdity of shoring up the cliffs with clay dug up inland, sacrificing one part of Suffolk to the sea in order to save another. She had recently visited a church on one of the islands in the Venetian Lagoon, and she had realized that Suffolk will look the same in fifty years: a Northern European version, with farms scattered across outcrops of high land, linked by boats instead of roads, like the island villages created in the Somerset Levels two winters in a row.

Yet the ingenuity and stubbornness that Peter Boggis had displayed might slow the process. As I travelled along the east coast in the summer of 2013, visiting places that had flooded in the past and meeting people threatened by the rising waves, I was conscious of the wind turbines that had appeared on the horizon, modern versions of the Horsey wind-pump, displaced offshore and anchored in the shifting soil of Doggerland in an attempt to slow the rise of the water that had covered it.

I wanted to see them close up, so, one day, I caught a boat to the London Array, the world's largest wind farm, which was emerging in the mouth of the Thames Estuary, between the Kent and Essex coasts.

~

We left Ramsgate in bright sunshine, but, beyond the harbour wall, the mist closed in. A white bar of chalk hanging above the docks was the last glimpse of the mainland to disappear. The diverging trails of our wake were the only markers of progress as we drove across the sunken plain of Doggerland, towards Long Sand and Deep Knock, the sandbanks on the edge of Black Deep, where the London Array was being built.

I had crossed the North Sea before, by ferry, before the Channel Tunnel was built, but not since I knew what it concealed. The water was so flat and calm that I had no sense of how fast we were going; we might have been moored in a still, grey pool, no longer than the boat. I imagined walking to the side and slipping overboard. Opening my eyes beneath the surface, I wouldn't find myself suspended in the blue vault of a summer sea, lit by angled shafts of sunlight, but in a cold grey fog that matched the one above the surface, hung with twisting wreaths of silt. While the boat circled to pick me up, I would sink again, feeling the vertiginous pull of the deep water covering the drowned world below.

~

The scale of the land that was lost has only been acknowledged in the last twenty years. At first, archaeologists believed Doggerland was a land bridge, a promontory or isthmus connecting Britain to the rest of continental Europe. In the 1990s, an archaeologist called Bryony Coles proposed its true extent. She called it Doggerland, after the North Sea shoal invoked in the nightly prose poem of the shipping forecast:

> Darkness outside. Inside, the radio's prayer.
> Rockall. Malin. Dogger. Finisterre

writes Carol Ann Duffy in her poem, 'Prayer'. Coles argued that Doggerland was not a remote, uninhabited place, but the heart of the continent.

Yet there was still more work to do. Over the years, the oil companies that had hunted for deposits beneath the North Sea and built installations in its silty bed had collected seismic data mapping its terrain, but it wasn't until the turn of the century that we had the computing power required to convert it into 3-D renderings of the lost land. As Vincent Gaffney, Simon Fitch and David Smith fed the data through the computers at the University of Birmingham and revealed the course of a river, as large as the Rhine, that once ran across Dogger Bank, they realized that they were discovering 'an entire, preserved, European hunter-gatherer country' – a lost land that, at its most extensive, was as large as the UK.

Even before its submersion, it had been dominated by water: 1,600 kilometres of river channels and twenty-four lakes or marshes wound through the plain, which was dominated by the Outer Silver Pit, a lake almost the same size as the largest in Europe. The marshy plain would have seemed bleak and featureless to the modern eye, but to Mesolithic people it would have offered 'a rich living', Vincent Gaffney says. He compared it to the Somerset Levels in one of the intervals between the incursions of the sea, when the land was covered by 'extensive areas of dense reed bed, wet carr, willow, birch and alder woodland'. The reeds, or withies, that fuelled the staple industry of the Levels for centuries would have grown in Doggerland as well, and deciduous woodland provided 'edible fungi' and fuel for cooking and warmth. The inhabitants would have picked fruits, nuts and herbs – raspberries, blackberries, hazelnuts, acorns, chestnuts, sorrel, water lily and meadow-sweet – and hunted cormorants, mallards, grebes and cranes.

As the climate warmed, there would have been more animals to hunt: reindeer and horse, at first, and, later, deer, pig, wolf, hare, beaver and dog. They caught fish and gathered shellfish on coasts and beaches.

~

We reached the substation first. It appeared beside us suddenly, like an image projected on the white canvas of the fog. It was half of the wind farm's double-chambered heart, which collects the power and sends it ashore via cables buried in the Mesolithic hunting grounds on the seabed, and it was brand new, its bright yellow triangular base and multilayered deck unweathered by wind or waves. The *MPI Adventure*, the ship that installs the turbines, lay hidden beyond it in the fog, sturdy and immobile as an island on the steel legs that raise its hull above the waves. We circled it, foghorn blowing, in tribute to its improbable presence.

It faded into the mist, and, within minutes, a turbine took its place. I knew it was as tall as the London Eye, but, since I couldn't see the top, I couldn't get any sense of how large it might look on a clear day, when its position in the sea would be revealed. It might have been a post planted in an endless ocean, or an infinitely tall beanstalk rooted in a pond measured by the length of the boat. I found it hard to believe that there were dozens more like it hidden in the mist, tended by boats that buzzed between them like bees in a field of giant metal sunflowers.

By the time the remaining ninety turbines had been installed, the London Array would cover an area of a hundred square miles – though, by then, it would no longer qualify as the largest wind farm in the world, for there were already larger ones being planned and built. They were part of a new industry emerging off Britain's coasts. Like many Victorian resorts, Ramsgate had been in decline since air travel brought foreign holidays within reach for the average British person, but now the harbour was overflowing with visitors, and the town's hotels and restaurants were fully booked. The offshore site manager, who was on the boat, was a Londoner who had worked in oil and gas in Qatar before he got a job on the Thanet wind farm, further south. He lived in Brighton, but he had a flat in Ramsgate, like many of his colleagues. They had their own running group, a football team and a band.

Other cities on the east coast were benefitting from the renewables industry. As we made our way back to the shore, we stopped at a turbine to pick up a man who had asked for a lift, as if flagging down a passing cab. He was called Steven Nicholson, and was a health and safety officer for Siemens, the German electronics and engineering conglomerate that manufactures vanes for the London Array. Nicholson was from North Ferriby, the village west of Hull where my grandmother lived for more than forty years. I was so disorientated that the coincidence didn't seem surprising; I wouldn't have been surprised to discover that everyone on the boat was from Ferriby. They certainly could have been from Hull, for Siemens had opened a wind-turbine manufacturing plant in the city's docks. It was the kind of investment Hull needed, Nicholson said. In 2002, he had set up his own engineering business in Hull, having worked in the oil and gas industry since 1984, in West Africa, China and the Gulf of Mexico, but it didn't do well, and, in 2008, he had decided to go back offshore. He had been working on the London Array for a year.

He had spent the morning working on the turbine with a team of technicians. The idea of climbing up the inside of one of the tall, narrow towers, which seemed no more securely rooted than a metal buoy spinning in the current, made me feel dizzy, in more than one way. It was potentially dangerous, Nicholson said, but only because you were so isolated. But offshore work was always potentially dangerous. He had been working on an oil rig stationed halfway between the Orkneys and the Norwegian coast when the nearby Piper Alpha rig blew up in 1988. One hundred and sixty-seven people were killed. Standards had improved so much since then that you were safer in offshore oil and gas installations than on a building site onshore, and he predicted that the wind industry would soon catch up, as it continued the process of colonization that had produced successive waves of marine installation

– from forts and oil platforms to the giant yellow turbines of the London Array – and generated the data that made the reconstruction of Doggerland possible.

~

Much still remains obscure. Doggerland is 'one of the most enigmatic archaeological landscapes in the world,' write Gaffney, Fitch and Smith. They recognize that their work will galvanize fantasists as well as scientists, for it shows that the nineteenth-century occultists who were preoccupied by the idea of lost lands beneath the seas were not as deluded as they might have seemed. We did not evolve on the continent of Atlantis, but we live on the edge of a drowned world and we are descended from its inhabitants.

Yet the rediscovery of Doggerland was not only an act of forensic skill; it was also a feat of imaginative empathy. Despite their warnings against reaching for conclusions that the evidence did not support, the archaeologists did not overlook the human dimensions of their discovery: they made me appreciate the sense of loss and fear the inhabitants of Doggerland must have felt as the waters rose, though, as the boat drove on through the mist, I reminded myself that there was at least one sense in which they were better off than we were. The water from the retreating glaciers that poured into the sea, and drowned their ancestral homes, also created new territories on the low-lying land to the west and the north, which they had previously ignored.

They had somewhere else to go. At the beginning of the twenty-first century, there are no comparable havens to explore.

6: The Great Tide

I was in the Fens on 5 December – the day the weather turned. Overnight, there had been reports of a storm approaching: two people were killed by falling power cables in Scotland and there was flooding on the east coast.

Yet, even if I hadn't been warned of the storm's approach, I couldn't have failed to notice it; it was a cold, wet day, and the wind gusting through the Fens was so strong that it was hard to stand up in it. When it was blowing in my face, I had to lean forward to walk into it, in a tilted posture that seemed all the more pronounced in a landscape where the embankments of the rivers are the only vertical structures. When it was behind me, it hurried me along, lifting me off my feet from time to time, like a bouncer ushering me towards the exit. It gathered up the clouds and stacked them on the horizon in the south; I kept thinking that the dark mass beyond the spire of Ely Cathedral was a range of hills, though I should have noticed that it was getting bigger and darker as the day passed.

My guide for the day made me feel it was his pleasure to show me round the country that he loved. John Martin's

family had farmed land in the South Levels since the eight-
eenth century, and played a part in draining it as well.
William Martin was the first chairman of the Littleport and
Downham Internal Drainage Board in 1845, and other
Martins filled the role before John took it on, in 1971. Yet
the chain of memory in his family goes back even further.

He lived ten miles outside Cambridge, on a long, straight
road lined with industrial estates that carried the spirit of
the modern city into the countryside. Yet Denny Abbey
Farm stood among a cluster of buildings more preoccupied
with the past: there was a partially restored abbey, built on
one of the 'islands' of high ground that supported the first
settlements in the Fens, as they had in the Levels, and a
museum of rural life. The house lay beyond an open-sided
stable in which there was a row of farm vehicles used for
shooting. It was a modern building, white walled and regular, like the Wards' withy factory, though it stood in a
courtyard enclosed by old stone walls.

'Well done!' John Martin called out from an upstairs
window when I drew up at the front door, as if negotiat-
ing the layers of history in which the house was embedded
required an act of time travel, rather than the simple
matter of plugging a postcode into a satnav or looking at
a map. He was a former High Sheriff of Cambridge, and
a friend of a friend of my parents. I had been told that he
was interested in water management and drainage, and
that it would be worth my while to meet him. I wasn't
disappointed.

He drove me through the Fens to the house where he

grew up, near the Denver Complex, the system of locks and gates that sorts the water from the rivers of the Fens and holds back the water from the sea. It was a good day to be introduced to the landscape of the Fens, for the approaching storm was a reminder of its fragility: 'You do not need to remind a Fenman of the effects of heavy inland rainfall or the combination of a spring tide and a strong nor'easter,' wrote Graham Swift, in *Waterland*, his great novel of Fenland life – and no one fitted the description of a Fenman better than John Martin.

Before we left the house, he showed me his collection of maps and pamphlets devoted to the topography of the Fens and its drainage system. There were scrapbooks documenting the floods of 1938 and 1947, which he had witnessed, and a personal memoir of an even earlier flood, which one of his ancestors had lived through. 'Ah – how well I remember that day – 80 – no, 81 years ago,' Joseph Martin's memoir of the 'Great Drowned' began, conversationally, as he recalled the day when 'the Bank broke and all Littleport Fen was flooded.'

~

Late in the afternoon of Saturday, 11 September 1796, 'a man on horseback came round to our Farm, calling out, "the Banks broke, the Banks broke",' Joseph Martin said. Everyone knew what that meant. His father moved the stock to high ground and his mother and sister worked through the night and the next day to save the corn and the oats. They got the corn 'all sent away and only just in time, for the water was rising so fast that the roads were soon under water . . . It was a terrible time, for the wind blew and the rain came down in torrents, and in a few days, there were 30,000 acres in that district under water.'

By Wednesday morning, their house had flooded. They were preparing to leave, but, overnight, the water froze. It wasn't strong enough to walk on, and yet you couldn't push through it by boat. They stayed in the house, 'quite away from any other, with the water 7 ft. deep all around us.' The front door was frozen open; Joseph Martin used to put his skates on in the downstairs room and skate 'about the house – in doors and out – all day long.'

They were frozen in for ten days, and the weather got worse before it got better. 'It hailed and rained in great torrents, and the ice began to break up and float in great pieces' that banged against the house. One night, 'when the wind roared and the ice and lumber kept knocking against the walls', the house 'shook and groaned', and his mother 'who had kept up so bravely till then, quite broke down and said we must certainly be washed away.'

Yet, the next morning, the thaw had begun. They looked out across 'one great sheet of water, as far as the eye could reach; only broken here and there by a tree top, a hay stack, or the roof of a cattle shed, with the great blocks of ice floating about . . .'

At midday, they spotted two black specks on the horizon. As they came closer, they saw they were lighters, punted through the mud banks and the tops of trees and all the other half-submerged obstacles in the water by men from Littleport.

The family climbed into the boats with the few possessions they could take, but they were so low in the water that they thought the wind would tip them over if they turned broadside. They had to break the ice as they went, and they made slow progress, 'constantly meeting and passing great heaps of things that the flood had washed away.' They couldn't reach Littleport before night, and they stayed in a farmhouse that had become a hostel for people and a stable for their sheep and cattle. They went back to the house six months later to rescue their belongings, but they never lived there again. By the time Joseph sat down to dictate his memories, it was occupied by a labourer's family. 'I have seen other floods since then and after I was grown up and in business for myself – had my own farm under water once,' he said, 'but somehow, I seem to remember this – the Great Drowned as we always called it – best of all.'

~

The floods of 1947 left an equally strong impression on John Martin. His father had taken him to the edge of the lake that had spread out through the breaches in the banks of the rivers, and told him to make sure it never happened again. He took the injunction seriously: he became the chairman of the Regional Flood Committee that protected the east coast, from the shores of the Humber to the Thames. He coordinated local committees, went 'cap-in-hand' to

Whitehall to raise money, and trained the local people who had to decide whether or not to evacuate when they received warnings of the kind that were being transmitted along the east coast as we sat at the table in his dining room, surrounded by the archive of material he had produced. 'If you do it unnecessarily, then, after the third time, they won't go,' he said.

As we drove through the Fens, he kept pointing out the places where the water had reached in 1947, but I got a better sense of how it might have spread, and how hard it would be to contain it once it overflowed, when we reached Ten Mile Bank, the raised channel that carries the southern part of the River Ouse from Littleport to Denver Sluice.

In most places, rivers are sunken channels, but in the 'upside down world of the Fens', as in the Somerset Levels, they ride high above the fields. Ten Mile Bank refers to its length, but when I stood at the bottom of the dyke and looked up the slope, the name seemed to invoke its height. I couldn't see the river from below, and it was a surprise to scramble up the bank and find myself standing beside a wide channel of grey water. The wind was worrying at the boats tethered to the bank and stirring the surface into choppy waves. Yet it was only when I turned round that I saw how vulnerable the low-lying land would be to the mass of water contained within the banks of the river.

The fields were daubed in shades of dark brown and soft black that matched the colour of the sky. Distances were hard to judge, for there was no high ground to provide perspective, and the only dabs of contrast were the pale green patches of newly planted crops. There weren't even hedgerows to break up the view; the field boundaries were ditches that linked the pipes buried beneath the soil to the pumping stations that lifted the water into the rivers. Since there were no animals, there were no stables, barns or troughs. Here and there, a wavering twist of black climbed into the sky, rising and turning in constant swirls, like the twisters that blow through the Fens when they dry out: they were flocks of starlings, feasting on fields that had been left fallow to attract them, and they were the only vertical markers to be seen, before the land rose again to form the banks of the Hundred Foot Drain, or the New Bedford River, the second of two channels that the Dutch engineer Cornelius Vermuyden had dug in the seventeenth century, to take the River Ouse in a straight line across the Fens to the sea.

Vermuyden's attempt to drain the Fens was largely successful, though it had one consequence that no one had expected, which made his gains harder to maintain: peat contracts as it dries out, by as much as twelve inches in the first year and a slower rate thereafter, and, as the fields 'shrank away from the channels that drained them', they had to find new ways of lifting the water into the raised rivers. Steam, diesel and electric engines supplanted windmills, in a sequence you could track through the stewardship of the Martin family. Yet lifting the water into the rivers was not the greatest challenge: 'Our problem is not Fen drainage,' one of John's pamphlets said. The problem was the strength of the river embankments, which were required to hold an ever-greater weight of water.

~

The floods of 1947 were considered particularly cruel. 'The war's over. But the hardship's not over. The ration book still stands on the mantelpiece. And show us, please, the fruits of our victory,' wrote Graham Swift, in *Waterland*. Two million sheep and lambs died in the hills and 30,000 cattle on the plains during the winter snows, and, when they thawed, heavy rain and meltwater overwhelmed the rivers. 'Never in any history of which we have record, have nearly all the main rivers of the south, the Midlands and the north-east of England swollen into such deep flood simultaneously,' said *Harvest Home: The Official Story of the Great Floods of 1947*, which describes the battle to contain the rivers of the Fens as if it was a continuation of the struggle to win the war.

At Worcester, the Severn rose ten feet (three metres) in twenty-four hours. The Thames overflowed at Windsor, and gales struck London, killing two people. Water flowed through the streets of Bow, though there was none to drink, for the treatment plant flooded. In Yorkshire, the pit village of Selby was 'attacked by the Ouse from the north and by the Aire from the south', and became 'a little Venice almost overnight,' says *Harvest Home*. There were 2,800 houses in the 'town that drowned'; 2,000 of them flooded.

In the Fens, 'a long and weary struggle' to contain the

rivers began, for the modern consensus that it is better to let farmland flood if it means saving houses downstream did not prevail when the country was struggling to feed itself.

The thaw in the catchment of the Great Ouse, the main river that runs through the Fens, began on 10 March. On the eastern side of the Fens, the water rose eight feet (two and a half metres) in four days, and on 14 March, the call went out to 'stand by the banks'. The first breach was in the Great Ouse, at Over, which had never been known to over-flow. Two gangs of workmen and prisoners worked on the banks for two days, dragging bags of clay to the wave-washed summit. The wind was so strong they couldn't hear each other speak, and 'they could advance only by stagger-ing, bent nearly double.'

Nobody saw the bank burst, for the men had retreated, but people in houses that had flooded knew that something had given way. As the water in the Great Ouse poured through a breach in the bank, the level went down. The water rushed out into Willingham Fen, as far as the banks of the New Bedford River, Vermuyden's second channel, which was also threatening to overflow. One farmer rowed out to his house and rowed through the holes the waves had torn through it.

Soldiers and prisoners were drafted in to help the local labourers, as gale-force winds whipped the water into waves that broke against the collapsing banks and threw up sheets of ice-cold spray that threatened to sweep away the work-men. They were reduced to 'clinging to a fence or whatever else would yield a handhold.' In some places, the wind was so strong that it blew away the bags of clay brought in to reinforce the banks. Yet the Fenmen struggled on, facing 'darkness and a wind of hurricane strength, with their forces scattered over nearly 250 miles of threatened flood-banks, any of which might yield at any point and at any moment.'

~

The Martins thought the top floor of their house would be above water if the Ely Ouse burst its banks in 1947, but they did not want to see their theory tested. By the time the Ely Ouse flows past White House Farm, which stands beside the road, no more than a few metres from its banks, it has been swollen by several other rivers. The banks of one of its tributaries, the River Lark, were under threat, but the workers managed to save them. 'Defeats at other points provide more dramatic stories, but this success on the Lark is a greater story,' said *Harvest Home*, in its morale-boosting tone: 'Here we won.' A breach in the banks of the River Wissey, which flows into the Ouse opposite White House Farm, might have helped them, too, for it gave way a mile upstream. Instead of flowing into the Ouse beside White House Farm, the water spilled into Hilgay Fen, 'transforming it into a rising lake.'

The culverts that carried surface water from the Fens, under the road, from Ely to Kings Lynn, had already been blocked, but there was a mile-long section that the water could wash over at any point. Workmen started to build a wall of sandbags five feet (one and a half metres) high along its length. By Thursday morning, the water was lapping at the base of the bags in the wall. The water was rising six and a quarter inches (sixteen centimetres) an hour, and the wall had to be built at a rate to keep pace with it. It held all night, even as the weather worsened and a south-westerly gale whipped the floodwaters into waves that battered at the wall of bags with the force of the sea.

The wall was never breached, but the Wissey could not be contained. The water burst through one of the culverts beneath the road 'with a thundering roar, sweeping an amphibious truck half a mile across the fen, tearing down the brickwork of the culvert and . . . clawing out a great hole in the road beneath the wall,' writes *Harvest Home*. There were two houses nearby: the wave tore away the side of the nearest one, scattering its furniture across the Fen, while the owner of the other felt the 'place lift beneath him'.

~

In total, 37,000 acres of land would be left under water. The flood was 'by far the greatest and most sudden in living memory,' said the chief engineer of the River Great Ouse Catchment Board. 'It may well have been the greatest flood since the Fens were first drained.' And it wasn't only John Martin that it galvanized into action; it inspired the authorities to complete the drainage scheme that Cornelius Vermuyden had conceived, and largely carried out. In 1638, he had sketched a relief channel that would complete his plan, and, nearly three hundred years later, it was finally built. John Martin attended the opening ceremony in 1961, and, since then, the South Level had felt relatively secure.

Yet not everyone wanted the Fens to be drained in the first place, and, recently, nostalgia for the pre-drained richness that outsiders regarded as a trackless waste has been growing. In Cambridgeshire, the Great Fen is being stitched together from surviving wetlands, and patches are being restored within Vermuyden's grid of rivers in the Fens as well. It wasn't until I walked into the birch-clad visitor centre at the Welney Bird Sanctuary, which lies at the base of Vermuyden's New Bedford River, that I realized how accustomed I had become to monotonous tones of clay and peat. It wasn't just the warmth inside the building that came as a relief; the tall windows at the back overlooked a green field with grazing horses and pools of water ringed by clumps of reed, which seemed rich and luxurious compared to the flat brown fields elsewhere.

Yet Vermuyden had not entirely excluded wildernesses from his scheme. On the map, the New Bedford River – or the Hundred Foot, as it is known in reference to its original width – is a thin blue line, like all the managed rivers of the Fens, but, when I clambered up its steep bank and stood beside it, it did not seem neat and disciplined. The wind was veering along its length with bullying strength, and the ruler-straight banks seemed to be wavering and dissolving as the water within them faded to the colour of the dark grey sky. Beyond it lay the Ouse Washes, the empty space between the Old and New Bedford rivers that Vermuyden had left as a floodplain. He called it 'a room in which the water could rise' and it had become a stopping-off point for the birds who travelled on unseen paths from the Arctic, borne on the winds that rattled the open windows of the hide at Welney.

~

There was a light in the main chamber of the Hundred Foot Pumping Station. Two men were working inside, and they both remembered John. His accent changed as he spoke to them, picking up a Fenland intonation that must have been as natural as the way he spoke to me. His grandfather, Horace J. Martin, chairman of commissioners, had inaugurated a new oil engine in the Hundred Foot Pumping Station on 2 April 1926, according to a report in the *Cambridgeshire Times*. It said that Mr Martin 'has more service on the commission – 42 years – than any other Commissioner present that day.' A poem engraved above the entrance of the old engine house caught everyone's attention, the report said:

> These fens have oft times been by water drowned,
> Science a remedy in water found;
> The power of steam, she said, shall be employed,
> And the destroyer itself destroyed.

Yet, even steam, 'with all its undoubted reliability', had to 'give way to oil', and soon, oil gave way to diesel. The engine in the end room was the size and shape of a train, and it drove a massive waterwheel housed in a dark green casing with a pipe that stretched to the ditch below. The wind was rippling the water in sudden, isolated flurries; even in the lighted interior of the old pumping station the wind was visible.

~

We drove back across the Deep Fen, which was reserved for small farmers. It was divided and subdivided into plots that were a fraction of the prairie-style fields common in East Anglia. A group of cottages sheltered beside a grove of trees and the road was strewn with clumps of mud. Strips of young crops and grass on the verges unrolled unevenly on either side of the car: they were the only spots of colour between the dark sky and the rich, black earth, and they seemed to be glossed with a faint luminous sheen, as if they were already under water.

~

At seven p.m., the storm reached the mouth of the Humber, driven by the usual combination of a low-pressure system that drew the water higher and strong winds that pushed it into the narrow channel of the North Sea, which forced it higher still. The gales had died down by the time the surge reached Spurn Head, the fragile comma of land that curls across the mouth of the Humber, but, even so, the sea was almost two metres higher than expected. At Kilnsea, where the land has retreated 374 yards (342 metres) in 157 years, it picked up caravans and tumbled them together, breaking them beyond repair, and leaving a club house standing on the cliff edge. It punched through the protective bank and flooded the few buildings that stand on Spurn Head, including 'Barry's old bungalow', as one report called it, and the bird-ringing lab on the peninsula's southern tip.

The tide flowed across the spot where the port of Ravenser Odd used to stand, before it was destroyed in the 'Grote Mandrenke' – or Great Man-Drowning – of 1362, and moved inland, flooding 7,000 hectares on both shores of the estuary. The Albert Dock – the only one in the city with an eastern-facing entrance on the Humber, which I had walked through in the summer – took the full force of the surge. The pub where I had stayed flooded, and the water spread inland, flooding the Hull Arena, where people had gone ice skating. They had to wade out through waist-deep water, passing stranded cars and flooded shops. The barrage on the River Hull recorded its highest ever level. If the water had been forty centimetres higher, it would have overtopped the barrier and spread out through the centre of the city – the flood would have been as bad, if not worse, then the one six years before.

On the south bank, the surge travelled up the River Trent, and breached its banks in the Lincolnshire village of Burringham, twelve miles from the Humber. According to one eye-witness account, its high street became 'a river'. On the north bank, the water broke over the wall of a car park in Ferriby, the village where my grandmother used to live, and flooded fifteen houses.

The Fens didn't flood, though the water in the Tidal River, which I had stood beside at lunchtime, nearly reached the top of the bank. It was a reminder that you could never be complacent, John Martin said, in an email. There had been flooding throughout his old territory on the east coast, from the Humber to the Thames, and police had evacuated the Essex town of Jaywick, where sixty people had drowned on the night of 30 January 1953.

~

I drove out to Jaywick two days later.

The flood warnings were still in place on the A12, as far inland as Chelmsford, where I was born. My father had worked at the oil refinery at Coryton, on the Thames beside Canvey Island, where fifty-seven people drowned in 1953, though we lived in a village outside Chelmsford. He used to say that the A12 divided Essex in two, with the industri-alized foreshore to one side and the villages inland on the other – though, as I drove into the low sun, which cast a blurring halo across the road, I felt like I was following a line drawn between two zones of a different kind: one that was floodable and one that wasn't.

I parked on the Broadway at Jaywick and walked back to the beach. It was very quiet; there was one shop open, but the amusement arcade was closed for the winter. The sea wall rose above the level of the unmade streets. Signs warned of the dangers of soft sand. A rainbow hung above the marshes, framing the houses that faced the beach – they were of different heights and sizes, with wide windows to take in the view. Most stood on flimsy-looking stilts planted in the unpaved streets below the sea wall.

The two lads on the path by the sea wall said they had never felt at risk. They had gone to the shelter because they were told to, but they didn't stay for long. They had left at two a.m. and walked back along the shore to Jaywick. It was only two miles, but it must have felt further in the dark, with the gale shoving them inland and the sea threatening to break over the defences. Yet they were temperamentally inclined to dismiss it: 'Nothing happened,' the first one said. The cowl of his hoodie hid his face, but he made no attempt to conceal the spliff cupped in his palm. The sea had reached the wall, but it had only splashed over it. 'You don't normally get puddles on the beach,' he said. Dope smoke merged with the marine tang of seaweed and salt-soaked sand as they walked away.

A woman walking her dog on the beach said her son had ignored the warnings and stayed in Jaywick, but she had been scared enough to obey, and so had many others: there was no room in the shelter in Clacton, and she had slept outside with her dog, a Jack Russell. It was freezing – nothing like the summer evenings, when she was often on the beach until ten p.m. 'It's very untidy,' she said, as if that was the greatest concern, gesturing at the pools of standing water and ribbons of mud-streaked sand between the break-waters, which had the sleek black sheen of a mussel shell.

A man brushing sand off his porch, further down the beach, was equally relaxed. The last time the streets of Jaywick had flooded, human error was to blame – they'd forgotten to close the gate in the sea wall.

He had grown up on a Caribbean island where the lights were powered by a windmill, and it amused him that he could see the turbines of Gunfleet Sands from his front door: 'They're going back to the past.' I doubted that he would have been so dismissive if he had seen the massive turbines close up. He was more preoccupied by local distinctions than what was happening offshore. According to some measures, Jaywick is the poorest place in England. In 2011, sixty-two per cent of its working-age population were receiving benefits – more than four times the national average. For several years, it was the setting for a Channel Five series called *Benefits by the Sea*.

Yet, even within Jaywick, the Brooklands and Grasslands estates are set apart. They are the 'badlands', the man said, gesturing along the beach, towards the south, and offering a succinct explanation for their decline: 'The council keep putting crap in.' I thought it was crude to refer to people as 'crap' – though, when he said they were thieves and addicts who nicked anything they could get their hands on, I suppressed an urge to go and check my car.

~

Jaywick was established in the 1930s by a property developer called Frank Stedman, who bought twenty-four acres of

unused land on the Essex coast. He was hoping to emulate
Clacton's success by attracting Londoners who wanted to
escape the East End. He laid out the streets of Brooklands
in the shape of a Bentley's radiator grille, and named them
after makes of cars, such as Bentley, Hillman, Austin,
Sunbeam, Wolsey and Talbot. The names conveyed the
optimism of an era in which 'motoring' put the sea within
reach of millions of people.

Within the plots, owners could build how they liked.
Beach huts, cabins, chalets and bungalows, which had
entered the British architectural vocabulary in the Raj,
emerged in the unpaved streets behind Jaywick Sands,
and, despite the effects of the storm of 1953 and the antip-
athy of the local council, they had survived. Jaywick wasn't
connected to the main sewers until 1977, and, in the
1990s, the council tried to remake it completely: it built
forty new prefabricated houses on the site of a former
holiday camp beside Brooklands, with the aim of rehous-
ing the occupants of the older properties and replacing
their buildings. Yet people didn't want to be rehoused, and
only five original properties were demolished. As the
architectural historian Clive Aslet wrote, 'Jaywick has succeeded where many more architecturally prestigious
schemes have failed: it has personality, and woe betide
anyone wanting to threaten it.'

Yet it has hardly prospered. One measure of deprivation
suggested Jaywick had six of the ten cheapest streets in the
east of England, and it wasn't hard to see which they might
be. Most were unadopted, and hence unsurfaced, and they

were pitted with potholes filled with water that seeped up from below. The houses were strikingly frail: single-storey cabins or bungalows with roof spaces, which must have provided precarious shelter in 1953, fronted by wooden steps and enclosed by crumbling walls of breeze block or mortar. Some were clad in wood, others pebble-dashed or whitewashed, though most had faded to the grey of the sea. Some looked abandoned. A caravan stood in the knee-high grass in a garden plot, and telephone lines hung above the rooftops. Even the sea seemed remote, hidden by the sea wall that protected the estate, though the tang in the air was a reminder of its proximity.

There was no one in sight, and I got no answer at any of the houses. Cyclists glided past on the concrete platform high above the crumbling streets. I reached the end of the estate and climbed up on to the sea wall beside the Martello Tower, which had stood like a dark lighthouse in the flood, a useless fortification in the sea that had risen up around it. Beyond it lay the marshes that had become a channel for the surging tide on 31 January 1953.

~

An effective warning system would have saved many lives, for the severity of the storm was apparent for at least two days before it reached the east coast. Early on the morning of Friday, 29 January 1953, a trawler called *Michael Griffiths* sank off the Hebrides. None of the fifteen crew members survived. At one forty-five in the afternoon, the passengers and crew of the British Rail ferry *Princess Victoria* abandoned ship east of Belfast: 132 of the 176 people on board drowned. It was the worst ferry disaster in British history, and yet news of the accident did not precede the storm as it rounded Scotland and travelled south.

'By the afternoon of Saturday 31st January, the sea was hammering mercilessly at the eastern coastline,' writes Michael Pollard, in *North Sea Surge*. 'It smashed huge gaps in Scarborough's massive North Bay sea wall. Sweeping down past Spurn Head and curling inwards, the storm cut off the community of lifeboat men and coastguards on the headland and carried away the transmission masts of the Humber radio station. Racing on to Cleethorpes, it smashed the railway embankment and swept away buildings on the foreshore. Large areas of neighbouring Grimsby were flooded.' But, so far, this was 'merely severe storm damage,' Pollard says, 'bad enough, but within the scope of the emergency services. The worst was yet to come.'

The police in Clacton were told of the risk of flooding at 9.52 p.m. on Saturday, but they were preoccupied with events in Harwich, and three local bobbies were left to deal with Jaywick on their own. At midnight, there were reports of water breaching the sea wall behind the Broadway, and, half an hour later, 'mountainous waves' were seen rolling towards Adrian's Wall, the wall named after the chairman of the Jaywick Sands Freeholders Association.

Yet Jaywick was not only vulnerable from the front. At one a.m., a police inspector turned inland to see a river 'raging' through the marshes behind the town. The water swamped his car, and nearly swept away an elderly couple rescued by the police. Witnesses called it a 'wall of death', and a 'shining silver mass, gleaming brilliant in the moonlight'. It had poured through twenty-two breaches in the sea wall to the west, and poured across the marshes, carrying with it 'a tangled mass of debris from smashed caravans,' writes Patricia Rennoldson Smith, in *The 1953 Essex Flood Disaster*, an oral history of the events of the night. The water swamped Meadow Way and other streets behind the Broadway. Twenty-two people drowned.

Once the water had breached the walls and flowed through the low-lying streets, it couldn't drain away. Grasslands, which lies between the Essex River Board Wall and the Counter Wall, was also enclosed: 'it resembled a saucer, brimful of water, adrift in a turbulent sea.' One young boy said that his mother had got up to go to the toilet and found the carpet lifting off the floor. 'She tried to run to wake everyone, but it was like trying to run on a hammock.' Caravans were carried past on the waves, and the bungalows were shifted off their foundations, some with people clinging to them. Even huts raised on piles two feet (sixty centimetres) high were waist-deep in water. Some of the bungalows were submerged.

At midday on Sunday, the water in Brooklands and Grasslands was ten feet (three metres) deep in places, and it was still coming over the wall. 'Rescuers found people near collapse with shock and exposure, standing on windowsills and clinging to house eaves with their fingertips. Some, numbed by the cold, dropped into the water and drowned.'

An observer on higher ground watched a whole family, 'one by one, slip into the water and disappear.'

People who had taken shelter in roof spaces were hauled out by firemen, though even experienced boatmen found it hard to reach the houses; the water was full of 'hidden obstacles and live with electricity'. People were lighting matches to show their positions, unaware they might ignite the water, which was suffused with petrol.

More boats arrived, and the 'tired, dirty, soaked policemen, firemen and civilians' went back and forth to the flooded houses. At first, they used loudspeakers to call for survivors, but, by Monday, the nature of the rescue effort changed: instead of saving the living, they were retrieving people who had drowned, their bodies 'frozen in grotesque shapes'. Some had been tethered to the lamp posts so they wouldn't float away.

~

The deaths were not random: the average age of those who died was sixty-five, and most lived in prefab houses or summer homes, like the ones in Jaywick, which could not withstand the tide. Such homes were found all along the coast. The inhabitants of a Victorian terrace in Felixstowe had watched, disbelievingly, from the safety of their upper floors, as the wooden huts that occupied a site on the end of the road were borne past them. Yet the highest death toll was in Canvey Island, in the Thames Estuary. The sea broke through at Smallgains Creek, in the south-east corner of the island, in the early hours of the morning, and surged inland, through an area of 'shack-like' chalet bungalows ominously named Sunken Marsh.

Frank Harris was on leave from national service and he was staying with his grandmother and his aunt, who had a small baby, in Rainbow Road, near Sunken Marsh. He had been out on Saturday night, and he was in bed when his aunt woke him up and told him there was a leak. 'The house was ankle deep in water,' he told me. 'I thought, God, that's a big leak. And I looked out of the window and I said, "That ain't a leak – it's a flood." And I went into the bedroom just in time to whip the baby out of the cot before the water reached the mattress.'

I had met Frank earlier in the year, at the house where he lived with an old friend called Jane, who had also survived the flood. He had been at school with Jane's late husband, to whom she had been married for fifty-seven years. He had died two years before: 'He fell, or I assumed he fell, and by the time I got out of bed, he was gone,' she said. 'The doctor said there was nothing they could have done – they turned the machinery off at three minutes to ten, and he was dead by ten.' They sat in matching leather armchairs facing a widescreen TV. There were doggie snacks, a comedy beer mug (*It's my bum, I'll fart if I want to*) and a box set of John Wayne DVDs. They were both in their late seventies and talking made them short of breath.

They had lived in Canvey all their lives. The street where Frank now lived had been open fields when he was a boy

– he used to help the farmers collect the hay to make hay-
stacks, before destroying them by tunnelling into them,
and, when he wasn't doing that, he was playing in a bombed-
out house on the seafront. The memories of childhood
games made him laugh so much he cried, though they also
prompted the mournful refrain that nothing was quite the
same. Canvey had grown so much that they didn't know
anyone anymore. At one time, they could walk into the
Haystack pub and say hello to everybody – now, they would
be lucky to recognize anyone at all. Canvey was now so
densely occupied that you can't see greenery when you drive
on to the island, Jane said. That was partly true: I had passed
open fields flanking the Avenue of Remembrance, the wide
straight that led into Canvey from the mainland, but I had
soon found myself amongst a maze of streets. From the
vantage-point of Hadleigh Castle, which stands on a low
rise on the Essex shore, Canvey Island looks like a housing
estate moored midstream, but once I was on it, I had no
sense of its precarious location: most of the time, I couldn't
see the estuary or the far shore, for they were hidden by the
sea walls that rise above the houses. It felt like I was wandering through the streets of a low-rise prairie town, exposed
to the overarching sky, rather than a seaside resort, threatened by the rising tide.

Frank's grandfather, who had driven the first bus across
Canvey, used to tell Frank there was no need to fear flooding,
for only the very highest tides could breach the walls, and, by
the time they did, the water would be going down. He was
wrong. Yet Frank had been lucky – his grandmother's house

in Rainbow Road had a first floor. Many houses didn't; some people broke into the roof space, but others were trapped in ground-floor rooms, which filled to the ceiling. Some people climbed on to the roof; some stayed there all night, others slipped into the water and drowned. Even the first-floor rooms of Frank's grandmother's house flooded, but they climbed on to a wardrobe, and watched the water rise towards them. Frank's 'normal clothes', which he had come home in, were wet, because he had left them on a chair: the only dry thing was his army uniform, so he put that on.

Jane had been woken by the noise of barking dogs. She called her father, who told her she had left the tap running. 'I said, "Dad, there's a fish in the living room," and he said, "Don't be so bloody stupid, woman."' She was forced to shelter on the roof. 'I cried all night,' she said, adding that it was freezing, and she was on her own, as if her anxiety needed any explanation. Some of her neighbours slipped off and drowned.

Her husband-to-be, Frank's schoolfriend, was also on military service. He got back before his mother knew there had been a flood. The water was six feet (1.8 metres) deep in Hainault Road, where they lived, so he went in by boat, and found the occupants of the house asleep upstairs. In Rainbow Road, Frank sat on the wardrobe with his grandmother and his aunt and her baby for four or five hours until the police arrived. They put the women and the baby in the boat, but Frank walked up to the main road in his army uniform and was requisitioned by the police, who told him to tell his unit that they were keeping him. There were still people trapped in houses in Sunken Marsh. No one knew which ones were occupied, and eyewitnesses remembered the shouts of the rescuers as they rowed down the flooded streets, where gas lamps glowed beneath the water.

~

Sunken Marsh has changed its name: it is now called Newlands, and, like most of Canvey, it has been covered by a brick mesh of post-war houses. I wandered through it, trying to identify the location of a photograph of a rescue boat drifting down a flooded street, but it had changed so much, it was hard to be sure. There was a floodgate at the entrance to Smallgains Marina, where the water had broken through. The tide had encrusted the sides of the creek with deposits, natural and man-made: tractors, jetties, wooden boats on stands, and broken-hulled barges. Canvas dinghies full of old tyres settled their backsides in pillowy beds of green-brown mud. The harbour-master's office was a shipping container – an emblem of one of the great trade routes in the world. Further up, the water faded to a trickle that exposed the fat ridges of sea-sculpted mud, but it was easy to imagine a surging tide filling the channel and sweeping away the scaffolding that braced its sides.

I didn't have to go far to reach Canvey's undefended shores. The waves were breaking noisily on a sloping peb-bled wall, and the railings around Concord Beach paddling pool were almost submerged. Families in swimming gear were camping on the benches on the path and on the small scrap of beach. The Thames was a rich, dark green, laced with white horses. A tanker moved slowly through the mouth of the estuary. Beyond the Island Yacht Club, I found a path lined with shells that crackled underfoot, which led out on to a marshy promontory, sprinkled with samphire and sea lavender, where two men were collecting winkles. A line of rotting posts marked the remnants of a sea wall built in 1623.

Essex is England's driest county, but no point of it is further than thirty-four miles from tidal water, and it is defended by 300 miles of man-made defences that have been built up over the last 800 years, says *The Great Tide*, Hilda Grieve's account of the events of the night of 31 January 1953 in Essex. 'The walls run in almost unbroken sequence, from the muddy saltings of Judas Gap, at the head of the Stour estuary, right round to the wharves, warehouses and docks of the Port of London,' she writes. 'They front the open sea boldly, and wind interminably round the creeks, only interrupted, here and there, by a short stretch of clay cliff, a quay, "hard", wharf or seaside promenade, or, on Thames-side, a plateau of refuse "tipped" on the marshland.'

Yet large stretches of the defences were destroyed on the night of 31 January 1953. On Mersea Island, the local 'wall walkers', who monitored their stretch of the hundreds of miles of sand dunes, groynes, sea walls, and clay and shingle banks that fortify the coast of Essex, went out at dawn on 1 February 1953, and found a scene of devastation: 'At approach points, what looked like a vast calm lake hid roads and deep marshland drainage ditches,' yet gates and fences were 'submerged obstacles and traps,' and, in places, the sea wall had collapsed or been washed away, 'leaving nothing but salting levels.' The same was true elsewhere, for defences had been damaged along three quarters of the coastline: 'the bank between Kings Lynn and Hunstanton, with its formerly neat line of beach huts and bungalows, had been reduced to a shambles of driftwood,' writes Michael Pollard in *North Sea Surge*. 'The north Norfolk villages of Salthouse and Cley . . . had become waterside settlements . . . Foulness and Canvey had become half-submerged offshore islands.'

It would take many months, and in some places years, to repair the damage, though the sea subsided as soon as the storm passed through. The MP and author Tom Driberg, who used to own a house in Bradwell-on-Sea, on the Dengie Peninsula, which he called 'the most beautiful house in Essex, and *therefore* the most beautiful house in England, and *therefore* the most beautiful house in the world,' had gone wall walking on Sunday, 15 February 1953, two weeks after the Great Tide, and found everything peaceful: 'All quiet, water gently lapping the base of the wall,' he wrote in his diary. 'Home to bed 3.30 am.'

~

I had been planning to go back to Norfolk after the great tide of 5 December 2013 passed through, but, as usual, Norfolk found a way to frustrate my plans. My car had broken down when I had driven up to the coast in the summer to visit the Buxtons at Horsey, and, this time, it was me that packed up. I got a bug and went to bed. It didn't matter; I followed the coverage on the radio and online, and I was lying in bed when I heard that Bryony Nierop-Reading's house, in Happisburgh, Norfolk, had been swept into the sea.

Bryony was another great survivalist of the east coast, like Peter Boggis – though, unlike him, she had no plans to save her home, beyond the impractical-seeming idea of seeding the cliff-face with weeds and grasses, in an attempt to bind it together.

When I had gone to see her in the summer of 2013, she had measured out how far the cliff in front of her house had receded since she bought it in 2008, by laying out the posts of the fence she had been taking down as the ground beneath it gave way. Laid end-to-end in the grass, they were twenty-eight feet (eight and a half metres) long – more than the remaining distance from house to cliff. She had lost more than half her garden in the last five years, though the rate of erosion wasn't steady, and she hoped that the house would last several more years. She had got so used to living near the sea that she couldn't imagine moving, though she found the wind intimidating, especially at night, when it infiltrated the frail, weather-beaten walls of her bungalow and made it wheeze like an accordion. The furniture and the books and tools that filled every shelf and surface in the bungalow and in the workshops and greenhouses and spilled out into the garden above the beach did not seem enough to anchor it against the weather.

She said it was absurd that we had resisted invasion over

the years, and then let the sea eat away the land, bit by bit. Yet the forces at work are inexorable, as Happisburgh makes plain; the Thames used to run through it when it was a tributary of the Rhine, some 800,000 years ago, and, when the English Channel was formed, 450,000 years ago, Happisburgh lay fifteen miles inland, on the grassy banks of an estuary where the River Thames and the Bytham River met. The pine forests in the valley were home to rhinos, hippos, bison and their predators – sabre-toothed cats, lions and hyenas – and the eroding cliffs that threatened Bryony's home periodically reveal moments of great significance in human history.

In May 2013, six months before the storm, the oldest set of hominid footprints ever found outside Africa were discovered in a layer of sediment beneath the cliffs. There were fifty in all – twelve of them more or less complete. They had been made by a group of five individuals, both children and adults, of the species *homo antecessor*, who were between two feet eleven inches (seventy-eight centimetres) and five feet seven inches (170 centimetres) tall. They were walking south along the mudflats of the estuary, hunting for shellfish, or going to or from an island that provided refuge from the animals in the woods and plains onshore. Archaeologists mapped and photographed the footprints before they were washed away, and their existence was not announced until the winter storms had passed through, scouring away another scallop-shaped segment of cliff and leaving Bryony Nierop-Reading's house hanging precariously above the beach where they were found.

~

I got better, so I went to Boston, the Lincolnshire town that had flooded on the night of 5 December 2013, thanks to the effects of the surge. The storm had reached the Lincolnshire coast soon after it passed Hull. In the centre of town, the water reached the top of the wall of the tidal inlet, called the Haven, paused long enough to reassure everyone it wasn't going any further, and then heaved forwards, pouring through the graveyard of St Botolph's and spilling through the streets beyond.

I caught sight of the 'Stump' – as St Botolph's is affectionately known, thanks to the lantern tower that rises high above the flat landscape of the Fens – as the train approached Boston, and I didn't lose sight of it for the rest of the day. Daniel Defoe said that sailors used to steer by it; he called it 'the largest and highest' church tower in England, and said it was 'strange' that it stood in a country that 'has no bottom'.

It was low tide, and the water was seven or eight metres below the top of the bank that enclosed the Haven, which connects the once great port of Boston to the sea. The river was no more than a narrow grey stream at the bottom of a slick, muddy channel, but it wasn't hard to imagine the graveyard waist-deep in churning, ice-cold water, for the saturated stones still exuded a steely dampness. Everywhere was damp: pavements, window ledges, even the trees. There were heaps of wet leaves and piles of sooty earth among the gravestones commemorating the pilgrim fathers who had founded another city called Boston on the other side of the Atlantic. When I put my notebook on the wall, it got wet. The dark tidemark on the wall of the Stump was higher than the engraved marks that recorded the levels of previous floods that had hit the town. They had been getting higher over time: the floods of 1978, 1953, 1810 and 1781 were all neatly ranked in ascending order, the most recent at the top.

The cobbles of the surrounding streets and the market square were wet as well, slick and black, encrusted with a residue like flakes of salt, and the air smelt briny, as if I was standing on the muddy foreshore of a secluded creek.

Police officers had begun to arrive in anticipation of a royal visit. I stood beneath a dripping tree on the edge of the graveyard and watched Princess Anne and her entourage pick their way through it. They did what I had done: looked over the wall at the Haven, inspected the flood marks on the tower, ascending so neatly over the years, and looked inside the sealed doors of St Botolph's. Not surprisingly, the church was closed, though a man who called himself a 'gopher' let me look inside. Cardboard walkways had been laid down across the floor, and pumps and dehumidifiers were at work, heating the air so that it rose upwards and dissipated through the inverted funnel of the tower.

~

I had lunch in a Mexican restaurant run by a Portuguese woman, in a narrow street outside the gates of the churchyard.

The woman had lived in Wales and Norwich before she had moved to Boston in 2001 – for, instead of exporting people, the town now imported them. As I walked through its streets, I overheard conversations in so many languages that I didn't recognize, let alone understand, that I wouldn't have been surprised to have been told that I had fallen asleep on the train and woken up on the other side of the North Sea. Yet Boston's immigrants do not only come from the countries of Eastern Europe to which it used to be connected through the trading alliance of the Hanseatic League, for the Haven is a saltwater road that runs into all the oceans of the world.

The owner of the restaurant was a trained chef, but she had worked for a company that made car cables before she decided to go into business on her own. She had been hoping to open the restaurant on Saturday, 7 December 2013, and she was doing the final preparations on the Thursday before, when the police told her to go home. That night, the Haven burst its banks and began to pour across the narrow, cobbled alleyway towards the front door of her restaurant. She was lucky: she was at the higher end of the street. The water had reached the doorstep, but didn't come in.

The neighbouring buildings had not escaped. The newspaper office on the corner had flooded, and so had most of the shops on the other side of the street, which backed on to the Haven. The chalk mark on the wall of Nevermind was just below the CD racks. It was just as well, the owner said, as he leant on the counter at the back of the dark, narrow shop, which stood in the middle of a jumble of

Victorian and Georgian buildings. 'I wouldn't be here if that lot had got wet.'

The record shop had been knee-deep in water on Saturday morning, but the owner was determined to remain open. The water had come in at seven thirty in the morning and had gone down by eleven. He had lost a lot of stock in the basement, but he had worked hard to stay open. Nevermind sold more than records: there were racks of jewellery hanging from the walls, and the shelves were filled with T-shirts, hoodies, boots and dolls from horror films and video games. The pervasive dampness suited the clutter of gothic props and toys. 'When it happens to you, it feels personal,' the owner said. 'But I hate feeling sorry for myself.' He'd grown up with a severely disabled brother, and he had always been told to get on with things: 'If I got ill, I was told to run it off – play football, have a hot toddy, go to bed and sweat it out.' Besides, he had other things to worry about: his daughter was in hospital with a recurring condition. 'If this is the worst thing that happens to me this year, I'll be okay.'

~

It wasn't only businesses that had flooded. The surge had travelled along the Haven, hit the barrier upstream and rebounded, in a widening current that spread out through the streets of Boston. Once the water was high enough to overtop the tree-lined path on the westward bank of the Haven, there was nothing to stop it. It poured down the slope and crashed through the doors and windows of the houses below. One woman had been in her kitchen when she saw the cooker rise from the floor and sway in the air, before swinging towards her with a kind of leisurely violence that seemed all the more threatening for being unexplained: she thought it had moved of its own accord, until she saw the current that was carrying it, and felt the icy water around her feet. Most of the houses were still empty, their gardens strewn with rubbish. Discarded sandbags littered the slope of the Haven. Three old-school red phone boxes, without their doors, were arranged in a back garden further down the lane. Two lads were rolling a spliff in an alley, and a pink-legged girl in a short skirt sat on her doorstep, smoking a cigarette.

'It happens,' said a man helping one of his tenants move out of a flooded house on the other side of the Haven.

'Not very often,' I replied.

He shrugged. 'About once every thirty years.'

The devastation wasn't confined to the first row of houses. The water had poured through their windows and through the gaps between the terraces, spreading out into the streets beyond. Damp furniture and rotting carpets were piled on the pavements in Irby Street. Many of the cars had Czech number plates. One woman had been in Prague when the water flowed through her terraced house, leaving an ankle-deep tidemark on the walls. She didn't seem particularly surprised. The houses in Irby Street are officially under water for several hours a day, for they lie below the level of the high tide in the Haven, and perhaps the flood seemed less like a

disruption of life in Boston than a confirmation of the min-
gled elements that sustain it.

Not everyone was affected. One of the rectors of St
Botolph's lived in a modern house at the end of the road. He
had missed Princess Anne's visit because he was home with a
cold, but his wife showed me the view from the kitchen windows, where she was baking. At high tide, the Haven was the
level of the ceiling, and the lawn that stretched to the tree-
lined bank at the end of the garden looked like it was under
water, even now, for the light falling through the kitchen
windows made it glow like the sea beneath a dock at night.
Yet the water had followed its usual capricious path: it had
flooded their neighbours' houses and bypassed theirs entirely.
There was a bitter joke doing the rounds the day after the
flood, she said: Boston had finally drowned under its weight
of immigrants. And yet the people who had turned up to
help clean up the Stump weren't local.

7: Little Venice

It was not an easy Christmas for the residents of Yalding, which lies six miles south-west of Maidstone, in Kent. As the storm subsided on the east coast, it began to rain inland, and the three rivers that converge upon the village burst their banks, in a series of unkindly timed floods. The first was on Christmas Day; the second, a week later, at New Year's; and, when I arrived in the town on 4 January 2014, the Environment Agency was considering evacuating the Little Venice Caravan Park for the third time in two weeks.

The water was ankle-deep inside the park, but deeper in the garden of the cafe, which adjoined a flooded field. Upturned plant pots, gas canisters and plastic chairs had washed up inside the gates, and there was a pair of waders hanging out to dry. *Humidity Restoration Disaster Recovery Specialists*, said the sign on the van parked in the entrance, a short walk down the hill from the station. The residents of Little Venice were used to knee-deep water, for the park often floods, but they had never seen it as high as it was on Christmas Day. 'It was the scariest thing I have ever seen,' said the man who lived in caravan number sixty, inside the entrance.

Usually, the water comes across the fields at the back, from the River Medway, which was so far out of its banks that it came halfway up the handrails of the riverside paths, but, on Christmas Day, it had come from another source: the canalized section of the Medway, which runs down the far side of Hampstead Lane, past the caravan park. The water rose six feet (1.8 metres) in four hours, until it was higher than the garden shed that stood beside the caravan with its back to the main channel of the Medway. The caravan had risen with the water, as it was supposed to; the park floods so often that the caravans are classified as houseboats. Yet it didn't stop rising until it was two feet (sixty centimetres) above the railings that contain it within its mooring, and it was knocked over by the downdraught of the helicopter that came to evacuate the residents in the middle of the night.

The owner of number sixty hadn't been there for long. He and his partner had got engaged in May and sold their properties to buy the caravan. 'It was our dream home,' he said. 'Now it's like bloody Beirut.'

They had moved out for four days, and they had only just got back in when they were told to go again. Now, they were expecting to go again. He didn't blame the Environment Agency, for he knew it was dealing with 'exceptional weather', but he didn't want to leave. He was worried about looting, because people knew the park was empty. The police had been slow to arrive, but, when they did, they made their presence felt – there were two stationed on motorbikes beside the bridge above the Medway, further down Hampstead Lane.

The meadow beyond the bridge was flooded, and there was rubble strewn across the pavements in the high street: remnants of the first flood on Christmas Day, when the River Beult had burst its banks and poured down the high street in a waist-high torrent. People were carrying possessions in and out of their homes, and I could see furniture stacked on the tables in ground-floor rooms. Some of the houses were empty. Some were fitted with floodgates. The George Inn, which stood beyond the bridge, on the banks of the Beault, was closed. A group of four or five men had gathered in the doorway of a flooded house on the other side of the road, and, when I tried the door of the pub, one of them came over and asked what I wanted. He wasn't very friendly.

'I was hoping to get some lunch,' I said. It was one o'clock, and there was nowhere else open.

He was a balding, thickset man in his fifties or early sixties, dressed in a leather jacket. He laughed. 'You'll be lucky to find that open,' he said. I knew he was worried about looters, but I didn't think it was very likely a looter would try to break in the front door of the pub in daylight, and in full view of a group of possessive-looking blokes. He had reason to be possessive; he had been the landlord for more than thirty years. Flooding wasn't uncommon. Yalding had flooded in 1968, a year after he arrived, and again in 2000, when the George had been shut for several months. We chatted for a few minutes, but I still didn't feel he trusted me, and he watched me as I walked away, until I reached the turning that led to the bridge across the Beult, the river that had backed up and swept through his pub on Christmas Day.

~

George Parker and his wife, who lived in a fifteenth-century cottage on the far side of the narrow bridge that spanned the Beult and the grassy meadow that served as its floodplain, had started moving belongings upstairs on Christmas Eve, after the Environment Agency issued a warning for Yalding. It was only a precaution: they didn't think the town would flood, for the forecasts had been wrong before. 'Since three rivers meet at Yalding, it means you have three different catchments and three different sets of rainfall, so there are lots of different scenarios,' Mr Parker said.

Besides, the water had a long way to rise. Even on a day like today, when it was far above its usual level, it was contained within the wide expanse of low-lying land that lay beneath the full span of the bridge. Yet, on Christmas Day, it had reached the windows of the house that stood on the far bank, below the church. Workmen from one of the many branded vans that I had seen in the town had been carrying furniture out of the front door when I went past.

'I bet its value has just gone down,' said an elderly man standing on the bridge, leaning on a stick. He had a Kent twang to his voice that made him sound like Mick Jagger. He seemed rather pleased by the thought of falling property prices.

'How's your house?' I said.

He laughed. 'My house didn't flood. We'd all be in trouble if my house flooded.' He pointed out George Parker's house and told me to go and speak to him. 'He's a friend of mine, and he's had a terrible time,' he said, with the same curious relish. 'He'll be pleased to see you.'

It was a strange introduction; he was like a storm crow, conjured into life by the flood, that had come to rest on the bridge. Mr Parker said he didn't know who he was – and he wasn't particularly pleased to see me, either, for reasons I understood. He didn't talk to journalists or the BBC, he said, but, since I was writing a book, he agreed to speak.

His house was set back from the river, but it was lower than the neighbouring buildings, and the area in front of it often flooded. Sometimes, the water reached the top of the bowed step that led up to their wooden porch, but it had come inside the house only once, in the summer of 2000. Since then, it hadn't even reached the steps. There were no records of floods in Yalding, but there was evidence that people put down wooden boards to stop the water coming in.

'In those days, they would have expected it – and they wouldn't have had so many possessions. They wouldn't have had the electrics, either.' The carpet had been lifted up to expose a red stone floor. There was a dehumidifier in the fireplace, which was big enough to stand up in, and he was surrounded by boxes of possessions, including a crate of toys.

He was in his sixties, I guessed, with grey hair and an earring. He was a retired teacher, who had set up a school in the Zambia, and he was a keen sailor – which had not reconciled him to the prospect of water in his house. He looked tired, which was hardly surprising, given the Christmas he had endured. In 2000, there had been eighteen inches (forty-six centimetres) of water inside the house, and when it started coming up through the floorboards on Christmas Eve, they didn't expect it to be any worse this time. Some of their neighbours came round to help them move their belongings upstairs, and, in hindsight, they wished they had taken more.

The Environment Agency said that the river would peak on Christmas Eve, but it didn't stop raining, and, by Christmas morning, the water inside the fifteenth-century sitting room was three feet (one metre) deep. They couldn't get out of the front door, for the water had filled the area in front of the house and was climbing towards the steps of the church and the windows of the library on the other side of the road. They rescued what they could from the study, and, at nine thirty on Christmas Day, they escaped through their neighbour's back garden.

'We came back on Boxing Day, but there was still water in the house, so we decided to go and stay with our daughter. We came back early, the day after Boxing Day, and started clearing up.' It would be a long process; the walls were made of lime plaster, which will dry out, unlike modern gypsum, which has to be stripped out and replaced, but it takes months, and having been through it before made the prospect harder to bear. Mr Parker had begun to think that he would never feel entirely safe in the house again, and he wondered how he and his wife would cope as they got older. 'We thought 2000 was a once-in-a-lifetime thing, and it would never happen again, but we will never have that feeling again.'

~

Edward Raikes, who lived in a converted oast house on the banks of the Medway, would not have tried to convince George Parker that his house would not flood again. But he might have tried to persuade him that the risk was worth taking. Mr Raikes had a profound attachment to his house, which he had inherited from his grandmother, but it coexisted with a rigorous assessment of the chances of a flood – and an unsentimental disdain for its effects.

'Is your book going to be anecdotes or statistics?' he asked when I arrived at the house, and there was no question which he preferred. The way people talked about flooding made him impatient. 'People always ask whether the water is still coming up, or has it stopped and is it starting to go down again?' he said. 'And they say, "Yes, it's still coming up, because it was up to the third brick and now it's up to the fourth brick in the wall of my yard." But there was no good means of making the measurement.'

After the floods of 2000, he had come up with a two-part plan to address the lack of accuracy. He wanted to persuade the Environment Agency to put a gauge on the upstream side of the main town bridge, and then set up a surveying service, so people could see how high they were above the water. 'We had no takers.' Mr Raikes seemed baffled by the lack of logic. 'No one wanted to know. And I think that's why we have such appalling consequences from floods. People are in denial. They don't want there to be any relationship between their house and a flood.'

He was right, though I thought the denial was less conscious than he implied. Collective amnesia ensures that every flood is entirely unexpected: 'Floods are forgotten, until the next one occurs,' writes Peter Ackroyd, in *Thames: Sacred River*.

Mr Raikes also wanted to put markers showing the height the water had reached on the side of the library, opposite George Parker's house, but people didn't like that idea either. He had been doing what he could to address the lack of information, for he had been keeping records of rainfall in Yalding since 1991. He published the results in the parish magazine and posted them in the window of the library. I had seen the December update when I left George Parker's house, and I was so intrigued by the neatly tabulated figures and the dispassionate summary of the weather that I had gone inside and asked where I could find Mr Raikes of Parsonage Oasts.

~

The house had flooded over Christmas, which wasn't surprising, given its position on the banks of the Medway. The
Environment Agency had an office at the end of the lane,
which was a sign in itself, and the Sea Scouts kept canoes
in a pillbox on a strip of lawn between Mr Raikes's gravelled
drive and the Medway, which was high and fast flowing.
Inside the house, there were no mouldering carpets, and
none of the representatives of the recovery teams that I had
seen elsewhere in the village; the Raikes had banished the
evidence of disruption – and yet there had been two inches
(five centimetres) of water in the house on Christmas Day.
Mr Raikes pulled back the curtain and showed me where
the white paint had sprung from the wall. 'The boards are
damp, as well,' he added, though he did not seem particularly concerned. The Raikes had taken the old-fashioned
approach: they had let the water flow through, and carried
on as normal.

Admittedly, it was very cold. Mrs Raikes, who was doing
a sudoku on a table in the corner of the room, was wearing
an overcoat, and Mr Raikes, who was an elderly man,
straight backed and white haired, was wearing a tweed
jacket. I wasn't sure if the heating had gone off or if they
always wore coats indoors; perhaps it was evidence of their
ingrained hardiness and frugality. After all, the lights were
working again.

The power had gone down for the first time in the storm
on the night of 23 December, and the river had been 'out

of its bank' on Christmas Eve. They didn't pay much attention to the Environment Agency's warnings. 'We make up
our own minds what we need to do,' said Mr Raikes. Their
warnings had proved unfounded in the past, and Mr Raikes
trusted his own observations. 'I think I can see rather better
than they what is going to happen, because I can look out
of the window – and I have a rain gauge.'

He didn't have an accurate reading at the height of the
storm, because his gauge had blown over, but he was surprised that the water came up so quickly and rose so high.
Yalding had 159 millimetres, or six and a quarter inches of
rain in January, which was approximately three months'
worth of rain in one month, or a little over two and a half
times January's average rainfall. It was less than the 174 millimetres of rain that fell in October 2000, the month of
the 'Great Millennium Flood', as Mr Raikes called it. Yet the
rain that falls in Yalding does not have a direct bearing on
the level in the Medway; the river was eleven inches (seventy-eight centimetres) higher than in October 2000, and, this
time, it had come inside.

On Christmas Eve, they decided to leave the house. 'We
couldn't go far,' Mr Raikes said. 'We were cut off from the
village and the station. The coastguard would have taken us,
but we thought we would rather be near the house, so we
could get to work as soon as possible. It's one thing to get
them to evacuate you – it's another thing to get them to
bring you back.' They stayed with their neighbours, whose
house had flooded as well, but they had 'a lovely party'
upstairs, and they were back home within days. It was too

cold to have a bath, Jennifer Raikes said – but even that stopped being annoying after a while. Mr Raikes was even less concerned: 'I didn't think it was too bad,' he said, adding that the flood's 'peculiar characteristics' had proved to their advantage, for the water had left as quickly as it arrived.

~

The flood of 1968 had delayed their arrival in the house. On the day they were planning to move in, Mr Raikes's grandmother had rung them up and told them not to come 'because the whole thing is under water.'

They were planning to live with his grandmother, for she was getting old and needed looking after, but she did not want to leave the house, to which she had a quasi-mystical attachment that Mr Raikes described with measured respect. She had grown up in Hertfordshire, and, on a pre-war visit to Cambridge, she had seen a postcard of an oast house beside a river. She bought six copies of the postcard because she 'thought it looked rather nice.' Later, her son had brought a house in Yalding, where Edward Raikes grew up, and, sometime in 1954, she had gone to stay with him. One afternoon, she went for a walk beside the Medway and saw the oast house from the postcard. It was a ruin, but she knew straight away that she had to buy it. She paid £1,000 for it, and set about converting it into the house she had always imagined. I was intrigued by the sense of destiny that had brought his grandmother to the house. He had known I would be – here's a story you might like, he had said, offering it up in a spirit of generosity to the anecdote-collector who had emerged from the darkness as the river began to subside.

Mr Raikes showed me the postcard that had inspired his grandmother's dream, and a photograph of the oast house during the conversion. Only the tall white conical chimneys denoted what it used to be. A narrow path ran between the sitting-room window and the river, joining the 'pleasure garden' at the back to the 'rough garden' at the front, and he showed me the point on the wall where a gantry had offloaded hops on to barges.

In 1968, they waited until the flood subsided and then moved in, a week late. Since the water hadn't come into the house then, or in 2000, they 'rather thought it was at the right height.' But being proved wrong had not diminished their affection for it, nor made them fearful for its future.

They were used to flooding; the house in Yalding where Edward had grown up was above the floodplain, but Jennifer grew up locally and she said they used to have a 'serious flood' every three or four years. Recently, she thought it was happening less often; it was quite an event if they got cut off from the village. The proximity to water had had no adverse effects on their three children. 'I used to say that I would rather live here than on the edge of a big main road – and none of them ever fell in,' Jennifer said. None of their friends had either. And there were pleasure boats and long boats from Holland and Germany passing by, and the view, and the sound of flowing water – all the delights of the pastoral dream of riverside life. 'It's a lovely place,' Jennifer said, 'a beautiful place.'

Edward agreed: 'We are very lucky to live here.'

~

I had only met one other person who was so unconcerned by the prospect of being flooded, or its effects when it happened. Geoff Parkin, who lived beside the River Wansbeck, in the Northumberland town of Morpeth, was even better qualified than Mr Raikes to assess the risks to his home. He was a senior lecturer in hydrology and water resources at Newcastle University, so when he opposed the Environment Agency's plan to build a flood wall on the bank behind his house – eight years before Morpeth was engulfed by the worst flood to hit the town for nearly fifty years – he did so from an unusually well-informed perspective. It was a question of balancing amenity and risk, he told me when I met him at his office in Newcastle. He knew that some people wanted defences at all costs – and he understood why they might – but other people bought their houses because they were close to the river, and they were prepared to accept the risk they might flood. 'So, when the Environment Agency came along and said, "We have to protect you," people refused. On balance, they said, "No, you are not going to build a wall across the top end of town."'

It was only a temporary reprieve – when I went to Morpeth in March 2013, five months after it had flooded for the second time in four years, they were cutting down trees on the banks in High Stanners, the low-lying area in the western end of town, to make way for the defences that Geoff Parkin and others had initially resisted.

It was a bitterly cold day. It had been cold when I left London, and I had seen it getting colder as we travelled north, as the standing water in the fields outside York gave way to a dusting of snow on the corduroy grooves in the fields near Durham. Even Alan Bell, the chairman of the local flood group, who met me at the station, conceded that it was 'cool out'. In typical Geordie style, he was wearing jeans, an open-necked shirt and a leather jacket, though he admitted that he didn't get out much. He preferred driving to walking, and, before we had left the station, he had begun talking about his Saab Aero, which 'beat the shit out of a GTi.' I had guessed he was a smoker when I spoke to him on the phone, and his wheeze was more pronounced in person. He drove me round town, pointing out the houses that had flooded in 2008, and showing me how the water had moulded itself to the contours of the land, so it reached the ceiling in some houses, but left other streets untouched. When we got to High Stanners, Bell stood, shivering, in the shelter of the trees, while I walked along the edge of the peat-brown river.

In most places, the water was a few feet below the level of the banks, though the way it coiled round the trunks of the riverside trees implied that it was higher than usual. In some places, the dark brown water slowed and circled, like peaty sludge, stirred by hidden currents, but in other places, it careered forwards, streaked with flecks of white foam. There were platforms under the trees that might have been for swimming or diving – if not for people, then for dogs, who were out in force.

I had left Morpeth when I was seven years old; I didn't remember much about the town, beyond home and school, but I remembered the way the village was built around its river, houses clustering on the low-lying banks, or arranging themselves on the hill for the best views of its snaking curves. It was easy to see why people valued the river – and yet those who wanted it to remain a living presence in the town, open and unconstrained, were losing out to those who feared its destructive force. High Stanners had become a lake in 2008 and 2012, as the swollen river rose from its channels and spread out across the banks towards the houses in the trees, where the land began to slope uphill – and, once it was under water, there was no way out, except by a muddy, unfenced path that climbed steeply through the woods. The work would alter the character of High Stanners and the other areas adjoining the Wansbeck River, because it would be 'canalized', or enclosed behind flood walls, as it was several hundred metres downstream.

~

The Wansbeck was quiet in the first half of the twentieth century, but, in 1963, it burst its banks in the centre of Morpeth. A butcher was rescued with a boathook after he fell into water eight feet (two and a half metres) deep, telephones at the police station failed when the electricity supply went down and abandoned vehicles blocked the road. The RAF helped with the clean-up. Hot-air machines were brought in to dry the houses. Afterwards, walls were built to contain the river in the centre of town. Yet, when Morpeth flooded again, in October 1967, two burns spilled out behind the walls, flooding houses and the lemonade factory in the riverside street called Goose Hill – site of the school of the same name, where I had learnt to read and write. Defences failed in the centre of town, and the library flooded. The staff saved books by carrying them upstairs. More work was done: the river channel was widened, walls and embankments were built, and the burns were modified to ensure they could still discharge into the Wansbeck when the river was high.

The work 'greatly diminished the natural amenity of the riverside to the town,' writes David Archer, a colleague of Geoff Parkin's at Newcastle University, in an evocative account of Northumbria's rivers called *Land of Singing Waters*, yet it also reduced the Wansbeck's propensity to flood. Alan Bell had grown up in a part of Morpeth that hadn't flooded in 1963, but he now lived behind Goose Hill, behind the new defences. His three children, who had gone to Goose Hill primary school after I had left, all remembered being shown a picture of a boat in the street outside the gates. The fear of the river did not entirely go away, even when the defences were built: people used to gather at the end of the Bells' road to check its height. Yet no one really thought it would overtop again, until

Saturday, 6 September 2008, when Morpeth was struck by a storm of rare intensity.

~

It started raining on Friday afternoon, and it was still raining on Saturday morning. 'In all my life, I have never witnessed rain like I did that day,' said Simon Davies, an old schoolfriend of mine who had got in touch through Facebook, forty years after we last met. I was pleased to hear from him. I sent him a copy of a photograph taken at my sixth or seventh birthday party, and Simon replied, identifying himself as the 'devilishly handsome dude in the tank top, next to your mam'. He had moved out of Morpeth in 2006, two years before the flood of September 2008, which was just as well, for the area where he had lived was inundated.

On the morning of Saturday, 6 September, Alan Bell walked to the end of the road several times to look at the river. It was high – the Mitford gauging station outside town would record its highest ever level – but the first flood came from the same source as in 1967. At ten o'clock, a culvert on the Church Burn behind Alan Bell's house blew a cover, and, within an hour, there was four inches (ten centimetres) of water in Goose Hill. Mr Bell went out to get a paper and found it hard to get through it. 'If it's static, it's like a pond,' he said. 'But six inches of running water is enough to knock you over.'

Driving through it was difficult as well, even with a

two-litre engine. His daughter, who was coming back from Newcastle, got to the entrance to Goose Hill at midday, and turned back. She went to her grandmother's house and Alan picked her up. 'You keep it in first gear and keep the revs high, and if it conks out, you use the starter motor,' he told me, but he admitted he didn't enjoy driving in those conditions. 'I thought, I'm not going to do that again.' The houses opposite were beginning to flood, and he went down the street with a tape measure, working out how high it would need to get before it came inside.

It was still raining. More than three times the long-term average rainfall for the whole month would fall on the town in less than forty-eight hours. Simon Davies went back into town to help his father, who lived at the bottom of King's Avenue, the street where we had lived, and together they filled fertilizer sacks with soil to act as sandbags. It was raining so hard that they couldn't see each other, though they were facing one another: 'he holding the sack and me shovelling,' he told me by email.

At four o'clock, Alan Bell decided to take the two younger children to his mother's, leaving via the footpath at the end of the lane, which was now the only exit. His wife took their eldest daughter to her boyfriend's house. At four thirty p.m., the Wansbeck overtopped the supposedly impregnable defences at Goose Hill, and by the time Alan's wife got back, the house had flooded. Mr Bell put bags of sand on the airbricks and fitted boards across the front door, but it didn't make any difference. 'You can't stop it,' he said. 'It comes through the floorboards. You're running around, trying to lift things – you put tellies on seats, things like that. But there are so many things you don't think about.'

Since the house stood at the extreme point of the flood, and on a slight rise, they had two inches of water in the ground floor, but, in High Stanners, the water was much deeper. Paul Gillie, who owns a B & B beside the bridge, which becomes a dam when the Wansbeck is high and can't get through its arches, was fighting a tide six feet (1.8 metres) deep. He had started bailing out the sewage-tainted water that was spilling from the gutters and washing through the ground floor in the morning, hoping that the Wansbeck would subside before it burst its banks, as the Environment Agency had said it would. But then there was a sudden surge and it came through the door. 'It's like tar – as black as the ace of spades,' he said. 'And the smell is disgusting.' To begin with, he was undeterred. 'The family had all gone, and it was a bit of an adventure – the adrenaline had started flowing.'

At four thirty p.m., he gave up trying to save the B & B and went to a friend's house. He helped her bail water and move furniture upstairs. He looked out and saw an RAF Sea King hovering over houses on the other side of Morpeth; he said it felt 'like a third world town'. Meanwhile, Simon Davies, who was going home, met 'a refugee column' of cars and people on the road. He was one of the last people to leave. As he came up the main street by Telford Bridge, there were torrents of water swirling around the foot of St George's church. He watched a car come up the street from the library; the water reached the bottom of its doors.

In Goose Hill, Alan Bell's neighbours were wandering around with plastic bags full of possessions, not knowing where to go. The electrics tripped soon after. Mr Bell had run out of cigarettes and tried to go and get some. He went out the back way, but he couldn't get across the footbridge into town, so he went home again. At eight o'clock, he looked out of the kitchen and saw a lifeboat going down the alley. 'That's when you know it's deep,' he said. Yet, once the water started draining, it went down very quickly; by midnight, it was possible to walk along the street at the back of the house without wellies.

~

As usual, the effects of the flood took much longer to subside. People were nervous, Alan Bell said, and it was plain that he was, as well. Whenever it rained and the river began to rise, he would start to worry – not only about his own house, but about other people's too. Since he worked from home, he was able to go to the many meetings called in the aftermath of the flood of 2008, and he became chair of the local flood group, which monitored the authorities' response when the river began to rise, and campaigned for improved defences.

Paul Gillie had known the B & B was at risk of flooding when he bought it, but he'd been reassured that there was a plan to build storage upstream. Yet the work hadn't started by 2008. It was finally approved in February 2012, but, before it began, the Wansbeck burst its banks and his painstakingly restored B & B flooded again.

'It's just anger – that's all I've felt since then,' he told me, as we sat in the hall that was being stripped out for the second time in four years. It was open to regulars, though his family had not moved back in yet. 'Anger and disappointment. Feeling a bit useless as well – the effect it has on your family life is quite profound. We all went back in. The first time we were flooded out, I just saw it as an inconvenience, because it was my business and we just happened to live here. Since then, it has become our home.' The cost of the repairs would be less than in 2008, but the strain had been worse; he wasn't sure how he had managed. 'Last time, I had a lot more help, but I'm working eighteen-hour days, and I'm exhausted.'

I asked him what he thought of the Environment Agency, and he sighed. 'I've got nothing good to say about them,' he said, though he did not like hearing himself complain. 'That's probably a little bit unfair,' he added. 'They've got to build flood defences everywhere – they've got to prioritize. But why they wouldn't say Morpeth was a priority, I don't understand. When it floods here, it's not just three or four houses that are affected.'

Geoff Parkin took a much more dispassionate view. He had never regretted the decision to refuse the defences. In fact, he had never even asked himself whether they would have helped in either of the floods. He assumed the wall would have been 'overtopped' in 2008, for it was planned to national specifications, which were inadequate for the scale of the storm that struck Morpeth that day, but he had never run the simulations to see where the water might have gone. 'I knew this point, but talking it through makes it a bit more obvious,' he said. 'It's a good point, actually. That would be quite interesting, because we could model that, which I hadn't thought of doing – we'll do that now. It is academic, now, because things have moved on, but in terms of decision making . . . that's a thought.'

I was fascinated to discover that he had never considered the idea. Across the country, people were furious with the Environment Agency for failing to build defences to protect them, and yet Geoff Parkin had not only done his best to stop the wall being built, he had never even considered whether it might have helped. Yet the flood had made an impression on him in other ways. He particularly remembered the sound the river made as it poured past his door. The contours of the land meant that, once it had burst out of its bank, upstream, it couldn't get back in, and it backed up until it was higher in the road than it was in the river. 'You open the door and it's like a waterfall, it's like the Niagara Falls going past.'

He had been moving possessions upstairs and watching the river rise in the back garden when his wife shouted that it was coming in the front door. Yet he was not concerned by any of the other elements of the flood that upset so many people: he wasn't upset by having water in the house, and he dismissed the process of 'recovery' with a shrug. The only part of it that he disliked was the effect it had on relations with his neighbours, particularly in the 'terrible scramble' that ensued the next day, when everyone who had been flooded had to find somewhere else to live. 'Everyone was walking up the high street with a £500 deposit, in cash, in their hands, and if you found a house in Morpeth, you said, "Yeah, we'll have it, done." I knew we were competing with other people up the street for the same house. That was horrendous.'

Conversely, he valued the community spirit that the clean-up inspired. For three years, he organized a Christmas party at the rugby club just up the road, because their neighbourhood had emptied as people refitted their homes. 'It was like a diaspora – people had scattered far and wide, so I organized this party and everybody came back. Virtually the whole street came in the first year, which was really good. I organized one the following year, which was reasonably good, and, in the third year, you could see that people were going back into their normal silos of existence, which was a shame.'

The community spirit was beginning to revive again, as the street united in opposition to the Environment Agency's plan to build what Geoff Parkin called 'this damn wall' across the back of their gardens. They wouldn't have to leave their houses, but they wouldn't be able to get into their gardens for nine months – and, for gardeners, that is not a trivial consideration, he said. He noted that he and his wife had been out of their house for seven months after the flood, which was more or less as long as it would have taken the Environment Agency to build the defences, and he seemed to think that being barred from the garden would have been as great an inconvenience as the flood.

Yet the flood had had at least one lasting effect on him, for it had changed the nature of his work. He used to specialize in ground water and water resources, but now he was running a 'citizen science' project that gathered eyewitness reports of downpours and flash floods, like the Toon Monsoon that had struck Newcastle in June 2012. He tried to 'get out and about' during 'flood events', gathering evidence that would allow him to reconstruct what happened and design 'alleviation schemes'. He had written a report on the Morpeth flood of 2008. *Information Gathering for Dynamic Flood Reconstruction* set out to identify 'flood generation mechanisms' – such as 'out-of-bank fluvial flooding', or flooding which was caused by the river, 'localised pluvial flooding', which was caused by the rain, backflow through urban drainage networks and overtopping of flood defences – and to use them to improve 'evacuation and emergency access . . . and flood protection measures.'

He was keen to make the point that flood defences might not help, no matter how well they are designed – in fact, they might make things worse, by creating a false sense of security. If a river bursts its banks in an undefended town, and rises slowly through the streets, there is time to react, but if a weight of water builds up behind a flood wall that gives way, or is suddenly overtopped, the town it was supposed to be protecting might be engulfed. There was such a 'tipping-point effect' in Low Stanners in 2008: once the flood defences were overtopped, the water rose so fast that puddles in the road became a flood that filled houses to the ceiling.

It wasn't easy conveying the nature of the risk, for the statistics were 'non-stationary'. The floods that struck Morpeth in 1963, 2008 and 2012 were classified as one-in-a-hundred-year events, which also meant they had a one-in-a-hundred chance of occurring in any given year, but, in fact, they were harder to read than that. You can't assess the probability of a flood occurring in any given time span, because the climate is changing all the time, and the odds are changing with it. Hence, the decision to increase the protection from one in a hundred years to one in fifty in Morpeth was political, driven by the perception that the risks are increasing. 'What probably matters to people is a lifetime's length, whether they think it's going to happen once in their lifetime, compared to once every five years,' Geoff Parkin said. 'Whether it's going to be one in a hundred years or one in a hundred and fifty years doesn't matter. Is it likely to happen lots of times within your lifetime or not? That's the sort of consciousness of risk that people take on board.'

There were other patterns to consider, too. His group at Newcastle University was studying evidence that floods come in cycles or clusters, which may be related to the way that heat is absorbed and released from oceans: temperature oscillations in the North Atlantic mean there is 'a kind of memory' in the ocean that drives global circulation patterns. 'So, you get more extreme weather for a period,' he said. 'People recognize that you get these periods like the mid-seventies, which was a drought period, and now we definitely seem to be in a wet period.' He laughed, perhaps recognizing the scale of the understatement – though, its measured nature carried more weight. 'So, there is probably evidence that things appear to be worse at the moment, but it might well be that, in five years' time, we get a sequence where people are saying, "Well, last year there was a drought, this year there's a drought. What's happening? Is it global warming?"'

This was not a new insight, he added; people had known it since Biblical times – you get seven years of plenty, followed by seven years of drought. Edward Raikes had made a similar observation in the newsletter I had seen in the window of the library in Yalding: in the twenty years he had been measuring rainfall, he had noticed a seven-year or eight-year cycle, with highs in 1994, 2001 and 2008, though he added that it would be 'imprudent' to make predictions on the basis of so small a sample. Geoff Parkin concurred: there were so many 'complex feedbacks' in the system that no one understood how they worked. He did not want to say that the recent floods had been caused by global warming, but he did offer one general prediction: 'There will be more extremes: there will be more floods, more droughts, and they will be more severe than they used to be.'

~

I thought about the way Geoff Parkin balanced the risk of being flooded against his love of his riverside home as I travelled back to London from Yalding. Before I had started meeting people who had been flooded, it wouldn't have surprised me to discover it was possible to treat the subject so calmly. But in the context of everything I had heard in the course of the year, it seemed extraordinary. As the train waited in the gathering darkness in a flooded wood, I wondered how many of the other people who had been flooded over Christmas felt the same way.

It was a long journey, for the train kept slowing or stopping. There were pools of standing water in the fields and the fairways of Kent, and I knew that nearby towns had flooded, including Tonbridge, eight miles south-west of Yalding on the River Medway. I had emailed Mary Dhonau that morning and she had advised me to stay away, as they were still clearing up. She had been in Boston helping with the recovery, and she was doing back-to-back radio and TV interviews – twenty-three on Friday, followed by more over the weekend. At that moment, she was waiting to do another. 'I'll have Christmas when this all calms down!' she said. Yet there was no sign of when that might be.

More storms had been forecast to hit the east coast. While I was in Boston in December, I had picked up a leaflet warning of an even greater tide that was due to arrive in the new year. But the storms of the winter were nothing if not thorough: instead of forming in the North Atlantic and descending the narrow channel of the North Sea, they came from the other direction, striking the south and west coast and travelling north towards Scotland. Natural and man-made features of the landscape disappeared, sometimes overnight, when no one was looking, and sometimes live-streamed to a mass audience. Storm watching became a national pastime; marvelling at the people crouched behind harbour walls as waves towered above them was a secondary sport. Several people drowned, washed away from beaches and breakwaters. Chiswell, which lies on the inland shore of the Isle of Portland, had only flooded once since the great storm in 1824, when thirty people drowned, but on the night of 6 January 2014, it had flooded again.

The next day, I left London and drove down to the south coast. I had left my boots on the train on the way back from Yalding, and I stopped at a supermarket on the edge of Bournemouth to buy another pair. I was half expecting to be told they had sold out, or to find queues of people stocking up on tinned foods and other essentials, for the floods spreading across the south of England were also spreading a kind of minor panic: 'Dorset was underwater as the county continued to be battered by wind and rain,' said the lead story in the local paper.

The day before, I had seen footage of people gathering on the steps of a church opposite the River Stour, as the water rose towards a retirement park on the other side of the road, but they had gone by the time I got there, and the park was closed. I didn't go past the chain that hung across the entrance, but I could see boxes stacked in the windows of the empty chalets. The river had gone down, leaving the pavements ribbed with silt, but it was still barely passing beneath the arches of the bridge. I followed a path through the wood beyond the park, splashing through pools of muddy water in the lime-green light beneath the trees, until I reached the edge of the fast-flowing river. It had seeped through the fence and filled the steps between the chalets. Garden gnomes and upturned chairs floated in the knee-deep water.

It was low tide when I got to Chesil Beach; the sea lay at the bottom of the steep shingle bank – though, two nights before, it had risen high enough to swamp the tombolo, the narrow shingle strip that connects the Isle of Portland to the mainland. It was fussing neurotically with the pebbles, picking them up as if to mould them together and throwing them back down with a discontented clattering. They were slick and polished, glossed in matching shades of blue, orange and grey. Rafts of weed drifted offshore, half hidden beneath the still surface of the water, and there were washed-out roots, like giant sticks of rhubarb strewn across the beach. A trail of wood, plastic bottles, shredded nets and plastic insoles ran towards a ruined pill box, as if they had burst from its collapsing interior instead of converging on it, on currents that had travelled across the Atlantic.

Further down the beach, I met a man from the mainland whose daughter lived in Fortuneswell, the main town on the Isle of Portland, with her mother. On the night of the storm, 6 January 2014, she had looked out of her window before she went to sleep and had seen water coursing through the streets below. At half past eight, the landlady of the Cove Inn had closed the shutters and gone upstairs to escape the six-metre waves. When I reached the pub, which stood high above the beach, in the village of Chiswell, I leant on the sturdy concrete sea wall and watched the surveyors measuring the new sea-sculpted profile of the shingle. The path inside the sea wall was littered with the stones the waves had flung against the windows.

Two days later, the sense of being under attack was fading. I had a drink and read the reports of the storm in the local paper. Then I climbed the coastal path past Chiswell Earthworks, which wind across the lower half of the cliff like frozen waves. Halfway up the cliff stood a school, which must have had the least impeded view in Britain; west of Portland, there is no land for more than 3,000 miles. The terraced houses had narrow gardens that ran like diving boards towards the cliff edge, and, further up, there was a basketball court set into a plateau below the quarried cliff top. I wandered round the white markings, imagining local kids shooting hoops or meeting to smoke and flirt, while, out to sea, ships passed unseen and storms gathered and dispersed, or turned to break upon the shingle below.

That night, I stayed in Dorset, near the source of the River Parrett, which runs past Thorney, and, the next morning, I drove north, into the flooded fields and lanes of the Somerset Levels, on the trip that took me to Thorney for the first time.

Part Two: Noah's Woods

A noble figure he was, that great and wise Canute . . .
trying to expiate by justice and mercy the dark deeds of
his bloodstained youth; trying (and not in vain) to blend
the two races over which he ruled; rebuilding the churches
and monasteries which his father had destroyed . . .
rebuking, as every child has heard, his housecarles' flattery
by setting his chair on the brink of the rising tide.
Charles Kingsley, *Hereward the Wake*

But I'd have you know that these waters of mine
Were once a branch of the River Rhine,
When hundreds of miles to the East I went
And England was joined to the Continent.
I remember the bat-winged lizard-birds,
The Age of Ice and the mammoth herds,
And the giant tigers that stalked them down
Through Regent's Park into Camden Town.
Rudyard Kipling, 'The River's Tale'

8: The Storm

I got to Burrow Mump two hours after the soldiers.

It was the end of January 2014. Two weeks had passed since I had drifted through Thorney in Glen Ward's canoe, and the army had been called in to address the crisis in the Somerset Levels. Major Al Robinson and Sergeant Leigh Robinson of 24 Commando Engineer Regiment were the first to arrive, and they did what many do when they want to orient themselves in the flat fields of the Somerset Levels: they climbed the low hill that stands above Burrowbridge, eight miles upstream from Thorney, at the limit of the tidal inflows on the Parrett and at the centre of its man-made system of rivers and channels. Burrow Mump is only forty-five metres tall, but it is to the southern Levels what Glastonbury Tor is to the north, though its associations are more warlike.

Royalist troops are supposed to have sheltered in the ruined chapel on the summit of Burrow Mump in the Civil War, and, in 1948, the hill and the chapel were given to the National Trust as a memorial to the Somerset soldiers killed in both World Wars. The gate that leads from the village of Burrowbridge, which is set either side of the ruler-straight banks of the Parrett, is decorated with a sword. It must have made the visiting soldiers feel welcome, if they didn't already. Their widely publicized visit was intended to reassure the locals that they hadn't been forgotten, though it wasn't clear how they were supposed to help. 'They came, they saw, there was nothing they could do,' the headline in the *Western Daily Press* would say, and when I reached the top of Burrow Mump's muddy slopes and saw the lake spread out beneath me, I understood why they felt like that.

The lake lapping at the fringes of the car park, and rising up the southern slopes of the hill, stretched as far the Polden Hills. Trees and hedgerows signalled the boundaries of the submerged fields, but every other feature of the landscape had disappeared. Burrow Mump was on the north-east corner of the smooth grey sheet of water. To the north, the land was dry, apart from a few pools that marked out hollows in the fields, but, to the south and east, the water stretched as far as I could see.

Before I climbed the hill, I had crossed the brimming Parrett and walked west along the A361, the main road that runs out of the village, towards Athelney. The surface was so littered with grass and dirt that it seemed to be reverting to a track, and there were bricks and rubble piled on the verge, as if in readiness for repairs. The red 'road closed' sign on the edge of the flood seemed redundant; no one would have thought of driving into the murky green water, which got deeper quickly. The wavering white line on the tarmac disappeared within metres, and only hedgerows marked the route of the road.

Athelney was 'the island' in the Levels that King Alfred had retreated to after the Danish invasion of 875; it was described as the last safe corner of his kingdom, 'surrounded on all sides by very great swampy and impassable marshes, so that no one can approach it by any means except in punts'. Exhausted and distracted by the campaign, he fell asleep and burnt the cakes that a peasant woman had asked him to bake, or so the story says. Three years later, he emerged from 'the fastness in the Fen', marshalled an army and defeated the Danes at the Battle of Edington. The floods had made Athelney as inaccessible as it was then, at least from Burrowbridge; the bevy of swans breasting the soupy green water in the nearest field stood a better chance of getting there than I did. The road north was closed as well, though the water hadn't spread across it, or reached the houses that stood on its right-hand side, between the flooded fields and the brimming river.

From the summit of the hill, the raised banks of the river were the only dry land in sight, a narrow bulwark between the slowly moving stream and the lake below. Two hundred metres south of the town, another parallel line of trodden earth converged on the Parrett. The Tone, which is the main river in the western half of the Levels, used to flow further north, past Athelney, but, in 1345, the monks of Glastonbury Abbey diverted it into a man-made channel that brought it across Stanmoor to meet the Parrett, south of Burrowbridge. It was the first significant step in the draining of the Levels, and subsequent efforts had also centred on the drowned fields beneath Burrow Mump. The River Cary used to flow across the fields to the east to meet the Parrett near the place that the Tone met it from the west, but, in the eighteenth century, it was diverted into a man-made channel that carries it further to the north, and, since the 1970s, another man-made river, called the Sowy, has taken water from the Parrett to the sea by the same course.

I couldn't see the man-made channel of the Sowy or the spot where it crossed the former route of the Cary, for it all lay beneath the water, but I had found a nice hand-drawn map that marked the route of the existing rivers in white, and the ghostly old ones in blue, and I sat down on the grass, with my back to the chapel, and tried to transpose the lines on to the grey sheet of water below.

It was half past two. I had stayed in Glastonbury overnight, and climbed the tor – Burrow Mump's taller and more venerated twin – in the peaty, predawn light. The supermarket in the high street was open when I walked past, though the shops selling tarot cards and aura cleansing weren't. I turned into a street lined with 1950s houses on the eastern edge of town. I passed an ashram on the side of Chalice Hill and followed a footpath to the road at the bottom of the tor, where a travellers' bus was parked. Its windows were obscured by bags and boxes, and the soles of a pair of boots faced outwards above the passenger's seat. The conical peak of the tor was silhouetted by the red glow of the rising sun. The steps cut into the path winding round its terraced slopes had been reinforced with concrete. A flock of starlings passed overhead, a dark shadow with trailing edges, constantly making and remaking itself. It was cold, even when the sun came up, and I sheltered from the wind in the ruined tower.

Queen's Sedgemoor, to the north, and Kennard Moor, to the south, were dotted with pools of water, and the town stretched along a low promontory to the west. Beyond it lay the village of Meare, where the first settlements were established, in 400 BC, in huts built on earth-and-timber mounds in the middle of a lake. They were 'a remarkable adaptation' to 'an adverse environment', the geographer Michael Williams writes in *The Draining of The Somerset Levels*. Rather than attempting to drain the land, the inhabitants led 'a semi-aquatic existence', until the water levels in the lake rose and they retreated to higher ground and laid down a series of trackways across the marsh.

When Glastonbury Abbey was established in the fifth century AD, it looked out across 200,000 acres of waterlogged fen. It was 'under water for nine months of every year, its still surface broken by clumps of alder trees, its waters alive with cormorants, pelicans, bitterns, otter and herons,' Michael Williams writes. Yet the pre-drained Levels were not as barren as they seemed to outsiders, any more than the Fens had been, or the carrs of Hull. The locals cut turf and collected rushes, caught fish and fowl, and pastured their animals in the summer. Fearing the loss of the shared amenity on which they depended, the locals resisted the draining of the Levels, yet the abbey's efforts to expand the areas of drained land and exploit the resources of the fens and pools were remarkably successful. When Richard Whiting, the last abbot of Glastonbury, was hanged, drawn and quartered on the tor in 1539, the abbey was said to be the richest in England.

~

Leaning trees with short, fat trunks and thin, tufty branches grew out of the drainage ditches in the sheep-dotted pastures and peaty fields of King's Sedgemoor, which lay between Glastonbury and the coast. They looked like truncated versions of the plane trees that line the roads of rural France. There were black plastic rolls of silage in the fields and the yards were stacked with pallets. The King's Sedgemoor Drain, which carries the diverted waters of the Sowy and the Cary, was full and fast flowing.

At Dunball Clyce, I dodged the fast-moving traffic on the A38 to reach the point where the King's Sedgemoor Drain rejoined the Parrett. The narrow clay belt where I was standing was the only natural defence between the sea and the low-lying moors. It had been strengthened with waste called fly ash when the M5 was built along it, but it was still subsiding towards the softer, lower moors, which lie as much as fifteen feet (four and a half metres) below the average spring tide. Sluices like the one at Dunball Clyce – which can stop the tide flowing up the King's Sedgemoor Drain – seal every river except the Parrett, though locking out the sea locks in the rivers. If the salt water doesn't get you, the fresh water does. Sometimes, they both do.

On 20 January 1607, 'the sea at a flowing water, meeting with land flouds, strove so violently together that heaving down all thinges yt were builded to withstand and hinder the force of them, the banks were eaten through and a rupture made into Somersetshire,' according to a document called 'A True Report of certaine wonderfull over-flowings of Waters, now lately in Summersetshire, Norfolke, and other places of England'. Two hundred square miles of farmland were inundated, and the water spread as far as Glastonbury Tor, fourteen miles inland. Two thousand people were said to have drowned. 'In a short tyme did whole villages stand like Islands (compassed round with Waters) and in a short tyme were those Islands undiscoverable, and no where to be found.'

Only the tops of trees and houses could be seen, as if the towns had been built at the bottom of the sea, and 'people had plaide the husbandmen under the Waters.' Ricks were borne away, one bearing a 'company of Hogs and Pigs', and rabbits, scoured from their burrows by the water, climbed on the back of sheep, 'as they swom up and down and at last were drowned with them.'

Another great storm struck the coast on 26 November 1703. The parish of West Huntspill, where I reached the estuary, 'receiv'd great Damage by the late inundation of the Salt Water,' wrote Daniel Defoe in *The Storm*, his account of the night, which collected testimony from around the country. Many people took shelter in the church in the middle of the village, drawn for practical as well as spiritual reasons – even now, it was the largest building for miles around, and it was pushed out furthest into the flat land that led towards the estuary. It was locked, and I couldn't get inside.

A brisk wind was stirring the trees, provoking expressions of surprise or consternation from the crows hidden in their branches, and tugging at the flag of St George that hung from the tower. The shape of a newly turned mound of earth on a grave was repeated on a larger scale by the sea wall beyond the churchyard. There have been defences along the Bristol Channel since the twelfth century, but, on the night of the storm in 1703, they were overwhelmed by water 'eight foot higher than ever was known in the Memory of Man', Defoe said. It broke the windows of the church, 'threw down several Houses,' and forced many people from their homes. An eighty-year-old woman drowned.

I left the church and walked to the point, half a mile west, where the River Huntspill joins the Parrett. The Huntspill was the final major engineering project undertaken in the Levels, though its purpose was not only to remove water, but to store it as well. It was dug in the Second World War, with gates at either end that turned it into a reservoir a mile long and ensured that the armaments factory at Puriton was guaranteed the supply it needed. No attempt had been made to disguise its artificial origins; it was as straight as the road that ran beside it, and it fitted neatly into the regular lines drawn by drainage ditches.

Like most of the rivers in the Levels, it has no natural fall or slope to carry it to the sea. It drops six inches (fifteen centimetres) in three miles. Upstream from the sluice, the water was so still that I could see trees and bushes reflected in the surface, but it gained speed as it funnelled towards the sluice, and, on the other side, it cascaded dizzyingly down a muddy ravine that wound through grassy banks towards the widening estuary of the Parrett.

The tide was out: the mudflats were sown with clumps of reddish marsh grass and studded with boulders carpeted with moss or seaweed. A TV, filled with straw, sat on a concrete wall. Softened shards of driftwood, sea-bleached cans and bottles and shattered pots showed how high the tide could reach – though, for the time being, the water was a narrow glossy thread in the centre of the wide, flat channel; there was no shortage of space for the Parrett to drain into. The sound of sea birds merged with the sound of traffic on the A38. The ground was very soft, but I followed a concrete causeway, which climbed higher as the estuary grew wider, curving into the mist beyond Burnham on Sea. My ears tingled in the cold.

On the Steart Peninsula, on the other side of the estuary, where the Environment Agency was establishing a nature reserve, green-tufted sand-dunes rose from a thin line of golden beaches. The locals sitting at the bar in the King Alfred Inn in Burrowbridge were complaining about it when I went in at lunchtime. The idea that the Environment Agency should allocate £31 million for a nature reserve on the coast, when it couldn't find £5 million to stop the

Levels flooding, was proof that it cared more about birds than people, one man said. I didn't see the contradiction: turning uninhabited parts of the coast into salt marsh recreated habitats lost to rising seas in the Bristol Channel and other places, but it also provided a buffer zone where the winter storms could waste their force. It was part of a plan called 'making space for water', and I thought its logic should have been apparent to the inhabitants of Burrowbridge, where the tide flows inland twice a day to meet the laggardly flow of the brimming river that was barely passing beneath the arches of the bridge beside the pub.

~

The crisis had brought other visitors to the town, besides me: there was a BBC van parked in a farmyard, upstream from the pub, and people were strolling along the banks with cameras round their necks. The emergency services were in evidence as well: there were fire engines parked on both sides of the river, and a helicopter passed overhead as I came out of the pub. The red phone box on the far bank was lined with shelves of books. Sacks of building rubble bound with black plastic sheets, and sandbags stamped with the Environment Agency's number, reinforced the banks beneath it. 'Stop the Flooding – Dredge the Rivers!' said the banner slung across the bridge. Downstream, two thick yellow arcs of water cascaded on to the dark brown surface of the Parrett: the pumps were lifting water from the flooded fields to the west and sending it into a river that was already full to overflowing.

~

Michael Horsington had farmed the land two miles downstream from Burrowbridge since 1975, and it had only flooded once. He wasn't local, he said, with a fine regard for county boundaries, as we sat round the table in the kitchen of Moorland Farm. He grew up near Cerne Abbas, in Dorset, thirty-five miles south of Burrowbridge, but his father sold the family land and gave him a chance to start elsewhere. He bought 150 acres, but, over the years, he had added to it. His daughter, Rebecca, who was sitting at the table with us, had been born six months after they arrived, and, three years later, the land flooded for the first time. 'It breached the sea wall in Burnham and overtopped,' Michael said. 'I went out to go milking and I thought it had been snowing – it was like a lake, out there. But it came and went in about a day; it didn't hang about.'

Their neighbour's house often flooded, but the Horsingtons usually escaped, thanks to the contours of the land, though the name of their road – Lake Wall – was a reminder that they were far from invulnerable. The farmhouse stood within one hundred metres of the Parrett, where the river made a sharp dogleg past the village of Moorland, or Northmoor Green, which stands on the other bank. The family had divided the house in two, with

Michael Horsington and his wife living on the far side, while Rebecca and her husband, Dan, lived in the side that faced the lane.

The TV was on in Dan and Rebecca's sitting room when I arrived, for they were expecting an announcement from the Environment Agency about its plans for the Levels. As we waited for the press conference to start, we stood in the kitchen next door, looking out across the fields that had been under water until two weeks ago. Beany-hatted Dan was drinking tea and making dinner. They were friendly, hospitable and argumentative, prone to talking over one another. 'What's happened to us is irritating, but it isn't devastating,' Rebecca said. She and her father had been standing on the bank of the Parrett near the house in January when it came over 'like a weir', and there were still patches of standing water in the field. Other people had been much more badly affected: their neighbour, James Winslade, who farmed on the other bank of the Parrett, had been flooded two years in a row, and most of his farm – 790 of 840 acres – lay beneath the lake that I had seen from the top of Burrow Mump.

Dan was a more recent arrival than his in-laws: he had moved there four years ago, when he and Rebecca got married, but he had read the hand-printed guide to the Levels that I had picked up in a local shop, and he was keen to talk about its topography and history. The whole area had been under water, all year round, until the abbots began to drain it, he said. It was a man-made system, and it had to be maintained. The tide carried silt upriver on the inflow, but didn't drain with sufficient force to take it out again, and it was getting to the point where it couldn't take a single day's rain.

'We're not saying that dredging would fix it altogether,' said Rebecca, who was part of the local Flood Action Group, which was leading the campaign for dredging. 'We will still flood from time to time – we know that. But it wouldn't come up so high and it wouldn't stay so long. It wouldn't come into people's homes.' The argument had been heard in Downing Street; earlier in the week, David Cameron had told the House of Commons that he had overruled the Environment Agency, and dredging would start as soon as the water had gone down.

Michael Horsington didn't think it would make much difference. 'You have an announcement like yesterday, and you think, Great! But you're still surrounded by water,' he said. Rebecca had offered to introduce me to him, and we had walked round the outside of the house and gone into the kitchen on the other side. 'A statement in Prime Minister's Questions doesn't change that,' he said. 'Everyone just wants to get back to normal – we're all upset, angry and frustrated.' He didn't seem it; he seemed remarkably calm and even-tempered, like many farmers I had met. He had noticed significant change in the Parrett over the years: it used to be so low that you could walk across it to get to the pub in Moorland, but it was much higher now, all year round. For the time being, the water had gone down, but it wouldn't take much more rain before it overtopped the bank again.

He also felt that the Environment Agency lacked local knowledge. Like most farmers on the Levels, he used to be part of the drainage board that managed the ditches or 'rhynes' that took water into the rivers, but the task had now been taken on by the Environment Agency, and he didn't think it was qualified to do it.

Even the name of its chairman, Lord Smith of Finsbury, seemed to condemn it, for it implied he was an urban dweller, with little sense of the realities of rural life. Yet it was only the senior staff that attracted resentment. Rebecca and Dan had jeered good-naturedly at the television when David Jordan, the Environment Agency's director of operations, came out of River House in Bridgwater and stood in the rain on the edge of a car park, talking about the new plan to dredge the rivers, but they didn't blame its other employees. They were very friendly and welcoming to the man who drew up beside us in an Environment Agency Land Rover, after we had left the house and walked up the lane to the flood wall. He wasn't local; he was one of the extra staff who had been drafted in to work in the Levels. 'I'm from Stafford, near Alton Towers,' he said, as if no one could pick a fight with someone connected to a funfair. Rebecca and Dan weren't even much use as protestors; when the Environment Secretary, Owen Paterson, had come to Northmoor Pumping Station, on the other bank of the river, two days before, they had gone out to 'harangue' him, but Rebecca had seen her father in the crowd, and she had been caught on film jumping up and down, waving at him instead.

As we walked along the edge of the field that the river had broken over in January, I asked them whether they thought global warming had contributed to the flooding in the Levels, but neither was prepared to consider the idea. 'No one round here blames global warming,' Rebecca said. 'They blame the Environment Agency.' She laughed as she said it, but Dan was even more dismissive.

'It's just incompetence,' he said. Sea-level rise or climate change had nothing to do with it. 'It's just the natural cycle. It's just weather, innit? The record doesn't show any difference. Storms happen – it doesn't mean the end of the world is nigh. There are more important things to worry about than a bit of carbon in the atmosphere.'

The Environment Secretary, Owen Paterson, was another 'climate sceptic', though that had done nothing to endear him to the locals. They even objected to the shoes he was wearing – smart black lace-ups – when he arrived at the pumping station. He tried to explain that he hadn't had a chance to put on his wellies before he was dragged from his car and engulfed by a crowd of people demanding answers, but it was too late to alter the impression he had created.

Northmoor Pumping Station was half a mile downstream from the farm, and the tide had turned by the time we got there; the river was moving faster, and the jets of water arcing from the mouths of the giant hoses slung across the bank and landing in the stream were sliding away rapidly in the dusk. It was an impressive operation. There were twelve pumps in all, plus two in the building, almost half the numbers brought in to supplement the battery of forty that drained the Levels all year round. It was the country's largest-ever pumping operation: 2.9 million tonnes of water was lifted into the engorged river every day from the lake that lay west of the Parrett.

Even the old pumping station, which stood upstream from the farm, had been pressed into use. Usually, the low redbrick building was a museum housing the old steam-driven pump that used to drain the fields, but a modern pump had now been set up in its interior. We met another Environment Agency employee on the riverbank beside it. He was there to stop the 'pikies' stealing the diesel, he said. He was from Stafford as well, though he didn't claim a connection to Alton Towers. 'We don't have much trouble with tidal rivers up there,' he said. He told me that dredging was only part of the solution; they needed a barrage on the Parrett, like the one on the Thames – though, even then, they would need to maintain the river. 'That's just a giant drain,' he said, gesturing at the Parrett.

It was a supportive assessment, but Dan still corrected him: 'It's not a drain,' he said. 'It's a high-level carrier – it's the same system they have in Holland – and if they looked after Holland the way we look after the Levels, there would be no Holland.'

God made the world, but the Dutch made Holland, the saying goes, and the people in the Levels wanted Dutch engineers to be brought in to drain the flooded fields.

It was dark. The man from Stafford was knocking off after a twelve-hour shift. Dan went to round up the horses, and Rebecca and I walked back towards the glowing square of the kitchen window, which lay beneath the level of the brimming river as it ran towards the sea.

9: A Drowned World

Rebecca Horsington had claimed that nothing would be done about the floods until places closer to London were affected, and she didn't have to wait long to find out if she was right. In Kent, the rivers were subsiding, but in Surrey and Berkshire, the Thames was rising fast. In Sunbury, where I stopped on my way back from the Levels, it had already burst its banks. It was like standing on the edge of a rush-hour motorway, inches away from the torrent of traffic. The river's blustering roar was intimidating, and yet I was conscious of a vertiginous urge to step into the flow. Shapes drifted past in the darkness. I knew that I was standing near one of the inhabited islands in the Thames, and I wondered if its houses had come adrift. It had happened before. On the evening of 31 January 1953, the 7.37 p.m. train from Hunstanton to Lynn collided with a floating bungalow as it travelled through the marshes, and, in the course of the night, many other houses on the east coast were lifted off their moorings.

Sometimes rivers shift houses around, as well. The Mississippi 'would enter the house and float the piano out of it, and the pictures off the walls and even remove the house itself if it were not securely fastened down,' William Faulkner wrote. Huck and his friend Jim, his former guardian's slave, come across a house floating down the Mississippi in *The Adventures of Huckleberry Finn*, when they escape on a raft. Jim goes inside and finds a dead man lying on the floor; he had been shot in the back.

The Thames is not as long as the Mississippi, and drains a fraction of the area, but, in the dark, it seemed as wild as any of the great rivers of the world. The barrier on its eastern reaches cannot always contain it. The plan for a barrier near the mouth of the river was conceived after the Great Tide of 1953, but it wasn't completed for another thirty years. My wife, who grew up in Fulham in the seventies, remembers drills at primary school to prepare them for the day the Thames burst its banks, as it would have done, more and more often, if the barrier hadn't been built. It was closed four times in the eighties, thirty-five times in the nineties and seventy-five times in the first decade of the new millennium. In the winter of 2014 alone, it would close no less than fifty times.

'People say we shouldn't live on a floodplain,' Rebecca Horsington had said, 'but they don't say that to people who live in London.' The Environment Agency had released a map that illustrated her point; it showed how far the Thames would have spread through its former floodplains, north and south of the river, if the barrier hadn't been in place. The translucent blue wash covers the City and Docklands and spreads north along the low-lying parts of East London bordering the River Lea. Battersea, Fulham and Hammersmith are flooded. So is Westminster, the Thorney Island in the Thames. Boat taxis would have crowded the flooded streets and stirred the reflections of the House of Commons and Westminster Abbey.

Yet there are places near London that the barrier can't protect. It can hold back high tides and coastal surges, and it can be closed at low tide during heavy rain, creating a reservoir in central London that can hold the water flowing downstream until the tide has turned. But it can't speed the flow of the swollen river downstream, which means it can't protect the suburbs of West London that lie beyond the Thames's tidal reach, nor the towns and villages of Berkshire and Surrey.

~

The next day, I took the train out to Cookham, the Berkshire village that the painter Stanley Spencer had reimagined as a Thameside Jerusalem, and tried to walk back along the banks of the swollen river towards London. I knew I wouldn't get very far, for long stretches of the riverside paths were closed. The scale of the disruption was apparent as we left central London and reached the outer suburbs. Many of the trains at Maidenhead Station had been cancelled, and the platforms were packed with people staring at departure boards, waiting expectantly for the display to change. It was like life behind the lines in wartime, when the irritation and frustration caused by the endless disruptions was offset by the exhilarating thought that the usual rules had been suspended.

The holiday feeling was particularly apparent on Cookham Common; only the causeway to the high street remained above the surface of the wide grey lake that the river had become, and the novelty of the flood induced people to talk to one another in a way they normally wouldn't. The locals were proud of their village. 'Nicer than working in Essex!' one shouted to an Environment Agency official. The complacency was striking – and so was the lack of anger. No one wanted to apportion blame for the flood, for the locals understood the Thames's propensity to burst its banks. Cookham is effectively an island, for it stands on a slight rise within the bend where the Thames turns abruptly south. In the past, the river may have run on the other side of the village, and the low-lying moors and meadows that surround it have always been prone to flooding. 'The winter rising of the river was anxiously watched,' writes Spencer's biographer Kenneth Pople. Yet the Thames wasn't just a threat; it was part of the magical landscape of a village that Spencer regarded as 'a kind of earthly paradise.'

He was born in 1891, in a house on Cookham High Street, the eighth child of a music teacher and organist, and he was taught in an improvised schoolroom at the bottom of the garden by two of his older sisters; yet, for him and his brother, Gilbert, who was also a painter, the village contained infinitudes: 'There were hidden bits of Cookham as remote as the Milky Way,' Gilbert said. Spencer called it 'a holy suburb of Heaven.' He said that 'the village churchyard held, somehow, the secret of the Garden of Eden, and

Heaven could not be further away than the other side of Widbrook Common.'

Miracles occurred everywhere. 'I like to take my thoughts for a walk and marry them to some place in Cookham,' Spencer said. He depicted many of the great Biblical scenes in the streets of Cookham: the Last Supper, Christ entering Jerusalem and Christ stopping Peter from attacking the servant of the high priest after his betrayal in the Garden of Gethsemane were all transposed to Cookham, and the sight of workers walking past his studio with ladders inspired his depiction of Christ carrying the Cross through Cookham High Street. He was so attached to the village that he was known as 'Cookham' while he was studying at the Slade; he came back every day, and, while he wasn't there, he secured his presence in its holy ground by burying a tin filled with sketches and drawings in 'a little place I know.'

Cookham Moor, which was under water, lay at the heart of Stanley Spencer's romantic entanglements, and his attempts to transfigure them in paint. I wouldn't have been able to work out where the river ran if it hadn't been pointed out to me by one of the locals, who took such pride in showing off their flooded village, but I had some idea of what lay beneath the lake, for I had seen it in Spencer's paintings. He had painted the common in many different guises, as manifestations of his spiritual, emotional and erotic desires. The top of the war memorial, which stood at the end of the causeway, where the road across the common slipped under water, became an altar to Priapus in *A Celebration of Love in Heaven*, and the common was the setting of a tribute to his first wife, Hilda: 'Spencer raised a statue of Hilda as the Goddess of Love upon the most sacred of all turf: Cookham Moor,' writes Duncan Robinson, in a book called *Stanley Spencer: Visions from a Berkshire Village*. It was to be the centrepiece of an unrealized dream to take 'the in-church feeling out of church' and make Cookham itself a place of worship: the main street would be its nave, the river a side aisle, the common its cathedral close.

Even the pub where I had lunch appeared in one of his re-imaginings of Cookham. Spencer completed six paintings in a series called *Christ Preaching at Cookham Regatta* but he did not finish the seventh and largest, which shows Christ sitting in the old horse ferry barge drawn up against the lawn of the Ferry Hotel, preaching to a group of children. 'The place is Cookham bridge,' he said in a letter to Hilda in 1944. 'I don't know yet whether he is a week-end guest sort of person or me-out-painting or not so much human as connected with the sedgy bank of the stream. But it will come.' The painting was intended for 'the river-aisle of the Church-house', but it now hangs in the Stanley Spencer Gallery in the high street, which was open despite the flood. It shows Christ sitting in a punt, leaning forward, almost bent double in his eagerness to communicate with the dimunitive children arrayed before him, while Mr Turk, the boatman, stands in the foreground, oars and mops resting on his shoulders, as if he was levering up the floor of a mysterious structure. A group of adults were standing on the bank in the background, their figures emerging from the empty canvas in a way that revealed the craft and magic of the illusion Spencer was creating.

The spot where they had been standing was empty; for the river was rising rapidly towards it. The manager of the pub said it would get higher still: the water had come up a foot overnight and there was more rain forecast. It was usually six feet (1.8 metres) below the terrace. Many of the riverside buildings had flooded, and he expected the pub to flood as well. Half the staff couldn't get in to work, though it didn't matter because there were no customers.

I walked to the middle of Cookham Bridge, but I couldn't go any further, for the road on the far side, which led into Bourne End, was flooded. A lorry pushed through the water, sending a bow wave spilling into the flooded foundations of a new block of flats beside the bridge. It was raining again. I leant on the railings of the bridge and watched a reporter doing a piece to camera on a boat beneath me, its bow slantwise towards the bank as its engines held it steady against the current.

Spencer had never painted the Biblical story of the flood, though he painted the Thames many times. *Turk's Boatyard Cookham* depicts boats drawn up on the footpath on the Cookham side of the bridge. In a letter to Mrs Andrews, who purchased the painting, he said he had painted it on 'mainly rainy days and "a rainy day" would have been a sub title for it'. Spencer had captured the Thames while it was still enough to hold the colours of the trees and the reflections of the pillars of the bridge, though the gondola-like boats had climbed the bank and were pressing inwards, as if lifted on a wave.

The graveyard of Holy Trinity Church, which lay behind the towpath where Turk's Boatyard had once been, had also flooded, and the water lay in pools between the graves. In *The Resurrection, Cookham*, Spencer depicted the dead bursting forth from the graves. Hilda is sleeping on a bed of ivy, and a pleasure steamer is taking the risen souls to heaven. The idea was 'not as far-fetched as it sounds,' he maintained, for the 'river was a sort of holy of holies' and the people who went past on the steamers had 'a kind of magicle [sic] feeling about them.' They were manifestations of another world that even Spencer's vision of Cookham could not contain. 'They did not stop at Cookham,' he said. 'They came from a world I did not know & disappeared into an unknown.'

~

The boy didn't hesitate when he reached the river pouring across the road and streaming through the gaps in the hedge on the other side. It was knee-deep and fast flowing; it had nearly knocked me over when I had waded through it. I wouldn't have tried to cross it on a bike, but the boy kept going. His back wheel skidded to one side, and he nearly fell off, but he shrugged his satchel back into place on his shoulders and stood up on his pedals to generate more momentum. His wheels dragged in the water, throwing up jets of spray. By the time he was halfway across, he was soaked to the waist. He didn't look behind him when he reached the other side: he picked up speed down the rain-slick road that led across Widbrook Common towards Cookham, as if he crossed knee-deep, ice-cold torrents every day on his way home from school.

I had been told that the road to Maidenhead was closed, and the causeway across the moor was the only way to leave the island Cookham had become, but I thought I would see for myself. I set off out of town towards Widbrook Common – yet another place Spencer regarded as holy, and commemorated in paint. 'Walking along the road he turned his head and looked into Heaven, in this case a part of Widbrook Common,' said his brother, Gilbert, and, in 1911, Spencer painted *John Donne Arriving in Heaven*, in which he imagined Donne walking across Widbrook Common, 'and here encountering heaven.'

It was raining heavily again, and the sky was dark. I was wearing a pair of waterproof trousers I had inherited from my father and they weren't waterproof anymore; I had never worn them in such heavy rain, and they were soon soaked through. They made a steady *swish-swish* as I strode along, the rhythm broken up when I had to jump across puddles. Even my waterproof coat, which was newer, had begun to leak, and, by the time I got to Widbrook Common, I was soaked.

The rain had transformed the Widbrook from a narrow stream into a lake. A large white house was mirrored in the shining sheets of water on the edge of the common. Cookham Station was hidden in the mist and rain that veiled the hills to the west. Spencer had lived near the station for the last twelve years of his life, in a house called

Cliveden View, which looked across Widbrook Common to 'the country seat of the Astor family', which stood in the woods on the far side of the Thames. As a child, Spencer had resented the Astors, because they had built a wall across the side of Widbrook Common, but he had gone to Cliveden often in his last years, for the grandson of the wall builder had become an important patron. Yet the distance from the working-class suburb of Cookham Rise to the stately home could not be measured in geographical or social terms; to Stanley Spencer, the water-silvered fields were measureless – though the sight of the boy going home on his bike made me think of the countless minor accommodations that the rest of us will be required to make as the weather subtly alters the places where we live.

~

The road into Maidenhead was long and straight, lined with large houses overhung by dripping trees that deepened the shadows around them. It had stopped raining, but the tarmac was black and glossy, and the air felt thick and damp, clogged with grit and dirt. The canal beside Boulter's Lock was very placid, but the Thames was fast flowing and streaked with yellow foam. It rose halfway up the trunks of the trees on the far bank, which found answering shades in the water – the evergreens merged with deep-lying tones of green-brown, and the bare grey branches of the deciduous trees picked up silvery filaments in the fast-moving surface. Two swans were keeping pace with me, effortlessly, undisturbed by the force of the current. The steps leading down to the water were fenced off; the towpath was submerged, and the water was only half a metre below the road. A man was fixing floodlights to the terrace of a Victorian house on the far bank, as if to monitor the water threatening to inundate the lawn – or in the hope that illumination might hold it back.

There was one car left in the basement of Chandler's Quay, but the others had been moved to higher ground. The residents knew it was time to move them, said one of the three people standing by the railings, watching the river. 'Too much building on the floodplain,' another one said. It didn't flood here anymore, not since they built the Jubilee River, which carries water past Maidenhead and dumps it in the Thames beyond Bray – but it flooded more down-stream. They were building a new school on a floodplain downriver – an enlarged version of one that was popular with locals. It will be built on stilts, like Chandler's Quay, but, even so, the man said it would flood, and they would have to move it. The three locals weren't sure how far the water had reached, but they knew that Widbrook Common had flooded. 'Well, that's a floodplain,' the man said: 'And they're planning on building on that as well.'

The schoolboy was not the only cyclist I had seen on the common. I had stopped to talk to a man who had set out to cycle from Oxford to London and was beginning to regret it. It was wet; he had decided to get on the train at Maidenhead, but he must have changed his mind, for he cycled past me on Maidenhead Bridge, heading away from the station. On the banks below, dog walkers whistled to unseen animals exploring the expanded edges of the sleek black river.

~

One of the residents of Chandler's Quay was sweeping out the basement car park when I went back to Maidenhead, two days later. She could tell when the water was going down because the ducks that lived on the island midstream came back. They weren't there yet. She had walked the Thames from source to mouth in the summer months, when the towpaths were clear, but you couldn't do it now.

A blustery wind was blowing. A hundred yards outside Maidenhead, a branch cracked and fell through the trees, landing on the towpath with a bump that made the sodden ground shudder. The river was fast flowing, spilling up the bank and pooling around the trunks of the trees that shaded the path. I passed a mock-Tudor mansion with a boathouse and a monkey-puzzle tree planted in the middle of the lawn that sloped down to the river, and another that looked like a plantation mansion, transplanted from Georgia, except the flag it was flying was a Union Jack.

There were traces of the rural origins of Eton Dorney, the rowing lake used during the 2012 Olympics, in the form of the sheep in the distance, beyond a fence, but the pursuit of fitness had displaced agricultural labour. There were people jogging and cycling, and others walking dogs. The flat grey sheet of water had become an arena of mortification, divided into lanes designed to test strength and endurance. Rowers skittered past in slim-hulled boats, while their coaches kept pace on bikes on the road in the middle, shouting instructions. The Eton College Boating Centre slowly came into view. There were schoolboys and girls unloading boats, some with their names engraved on the prow.

The cafes in Windsor had sandbagged their doors, and the path on the south bank of the Thames had flooded. Swans were congregating around a submerged pontoon. The meadow beyond Romney Lock was soft and squelchy underfoot; the standing water got deeper as it stretched towards the railway embankment that crossed the river. The top bar of a wooden fence marked its depth. I walked back to Windsor Station and caught the train to Datchet – the next village along.

Datchet had only flooded because a wall upstream had collapsed, the owner of the Manor Inn told me. The river was no higher than it had been several times since he had bought the pub in 1999, but the water had poured down the railway line from Old Farmer's Bridge at Eton End School and swept down the high street in a torrent, three or four feet (about a metre) deep. The distinction mattered, for it made a repetition seem less likely. The water had poured into the building through vents and seeped up through floorboards in the conference rooms. Yet it had also descended into the cellars. No one knew how far it had stretched. Workmen had taken up a trapdoor in the hall and were running pumps into the chambers below.

Some of the streets nearer the river were still flooded, and a long chain of sandbags known as the 'Datchet wall' had been stacked along South Lea Road, the damp hessian reminiscent of an improvised military installation. *Do not remove*, said the signs, as if they might be picked apart by sightseers or zealous bin-collectors. The Thames Path was closed. I turned away from the river, but I still found myself following a trail of water, in the form of the culverted stream that ran across the sodden grass of Datchet Common towards one of the reservoirs that supply London's south-west suburbs. The Queen Mother Reservoir was one of the many blue pools drawn on the map of the Thames Valley, among the thin blue lines of rivers and streams, though bright yellow danger signs and lifebelts hanging on the railings by the steps that led up the grassy slopes to the summit were the only signs of the mass of water that rose higher than the roofs of the houses on the other side of the road.

A rainbow – the symbol of God's promise that he would never send another flood – hung over the woods at Sunnymeads, but the air was heavy with the smell of sewage; even the faithful would not consider modern floods purifying. Yet a kind of calm had descended on the villages. Two days before, people had been rescued by boat from the riverside streets in Wraysbury, but as I stood by the railings that enclosed the green, ducks landed on the surface of the still grey sheet of water, ruffling the image of the cricket pavilion.

Outside Splash Studios, people had laid down planks so they could reach the corner by the bridge over the stream.

Even the old gravel pits that housed Wraysbury Dive Centre had been absorbed into the lake that had risen from the Thames. I passed dinghies and canoes tethered to lamp posts and saw people pulling on waders as they prepared to reach their homes.

Already the adaptations seemed routine, and, now I was surrounded by flooded houses, I was less concerned with seeing what they looked like. Perhaps I had learnt some manners since I had been in Thorney – or perhaps the idea of a flooded house seemed less extraordinary. In any case, I was less interested in the effects of being flooded, and more interested in trying to understand its causes, like many of the people I had met in the Somerset Levels.

~

It was hard keeping track of the places that had flooded. Cornwall was 'in recovery', as if the entire county had been afflicted by a bout of illness, and, in Somerset, only essential journeys were recommended. In Thorney, the water had gone down and come up again. Professor Temperley's family had begun cleaning up Thorney House, which had been flooded for thirty-two days, but, the very next day, it had flooded again. We would not be able to protect the Levels indefinitely, one expert said on the radio. At some point, it would be abandoned, though cities like Hull would be defended. The water reached record levels in the centre of Worcester, though only the 'usual suspects' had been affected locally, Mary Dhonau said. Even Kempsey had survived; the bund that Mr Oram had campaigned for was doing its work.

On 5 February 2014, I sat at my desk in London watching the sea punch holes in the causeway that Isambard Kingdom Brunel built to carry the railway line along the coast at Dawlish, in Devon. The last time I had been through Dawlish on the train, the sea had been a flat expanse that seemed to be tinted red by the sandstone leaching from the cliffs; now, it made the railway lines jump and buckle, and flung shingle at the windows of the houses on the far side of the tracks.

The next day, I caught the train to Shepperton, where J. G. Ballard had lived for nearly fifty years, and resumed my attempt to walk along the Thames. At Hampton Court, the river was high, but within its banks. Kempton Park Racecourse was dry, but there were pools of water on Sunbury Golf Course, and the Ash, the tributary of the Thames that runs through the common at the end of the road where Ballard used to live, had expanded into a widening pool, brushed by the branches of a willow. As I walked back down the road, past Ballard's old house, I passed a man in wellies and water-proof trousers.

In 1994, Ballard said the twentieth century had begun 'to transform the Thames Valley into a pleasing replica of Los Angeles, with all the ambiguous but heady charms of alienation and anonymity', banishing the 'spirit of Stanley Spencer's nearby Cookham', which had 'seemed to preside over the splash meadows and bosky walks' when he arrived. Yet I had never been anywhere that preserved the aesthetic of 1930s suburbia so perfectly. Most suburban streets have been absorbed into the mesh of other streets, or become entwined with the motorway access roads, airport terminals and research centres of Ballard's fictions, yet Shepperton still felt like an outpost on the edge of the city. When I stepped off the train on to the empty platform and emerged beside a parade of 1930s shops, I felt like I was retracing the path the first commuters had taken when they came home. Ballard's house, which was for sale, had the same period air, with its pebble-dashed facade and Crittall windows.

Yet Ballard had remade his surroundings in other ways, transforming Shepperton in his fiction as profoundly as Spencer had transformed Cookham in his paintings. In a novel called *The Unlimited Dream Company*, he imagines the Thameside suburb as a tropical forest, seeded by hand-fuls of semen distributed by a mysteriously transfigured protagonist, who arrives in Shepperton when he crashes a stolen plane in the Thames. The embanked masses of water that surround it on all sides prompted the idea that the Thames Valley was 'a marine world', in which 'the dappled light below the trees fell upon an ocean floor.' Shepperton was surrounded by water: 'gravel lakes and reservoirs, the settling beds, canals and conduits of the local water author-ity, the divided arms of the river fed by a maze of creeks and streams. The high embankments of the reservoirs formed a series of raised horizons.' Ballard, who had grown up in Shanghai, a city built around the Bund, the world-famous embankment that took its name from the flood defences beside the Tigris, had found himself in another place defined by bunds – the banks and walls that held back the masses of water stored among, and above, the villages and suburbs.

He returned to the idea of the Thames Valley as a 'marine world' in *The Kindness of Women*, a fictionalized memoir in which he imagines it inhabited by a 'new form of aquatic mammal' and describes his 'children playing on the grass and fishing for minnows along the reedy banks' of the Ash. 'I could almost believe that the bright summer frocks, fishing nets and children's voices were a dream conjured from this placid stream,' he wrote. Yet, in 1962, two years after he settled in Shepperton, he wrote a novel that offered a much less benign version of a world under water.

~

The global catastrophe in *A Drowned World* is not caused by human activity, but by 'a series of violent and prolonged solar storms' that deplete 'the earth's barrier against the full impact of solar radiation'. Tropical areas become uninhabitable, once-temperate areas became tropical, and 'entire populations' migrate north or south. The human population is reduced to no more than five million people, who survive in the subtropical zones on the polar ice-caps. 'The South' has been abandoned, and even London is too hot for most people; the city has become a tropical lagoon, where giant ferns sprout through the windows of the abandoned buildings and the air is thronged with giant bats and mosquitos. Reptiles are the dominant species. Ballard's flooded

London of the future recreates elements of its past. When the Thames first emerged as 'an observable entity', some thirty million years ago, it 'would have been a recognizable, tropical scene,' Peter Ackroyd writes. 'Termites and ants, beetles and spiders, flourished in the humid atmosphere; there were also turtles and crocodiles . . . as well as lizards that resembled modern iguanas.' There were 'palm-trees and laurels, vines and citrus trees, as well as oaks and beeches. There were water-lilies on the surface of the river, as well as long weeds that drifted through the warm water. There was also a new form of plant; grass began to grow.'

Yet Ballard's drowned world is far more hostile than the ancient Thames. Everyone has left, except the crew of a research station and Ballard's two protagonists, a man called Kerans and a woman called Beatrice Dahl, who self-consciously style themselves as a second Adam and Eve, living in a kind of inverted Eden in which there will be no birth or rebirth – only a dying swoon into the embrace of a planet that has become inimical to human life.

They do not want to leave London, because they are drawn by the deep, distant emanations of the increasingly powerful sun, and they welcome the re-emergence of the primeval world, with which we are all subconsciously familiar. 'How often recently most of us have had the feeling of déjà vu, of having seen all this before, in fact of remembering these swamps and lagoons all too well,' says the doctor of the research station.

Richard Jefferies' proto-science-fiction novel, *After London*, depicted the drowned city as a polluted swamp that no one could enter safely: 'the earth was poison, the water poison, the air poison, the very light of heaven, falling through such an atmosphere, poison,' he writes. Yet Kerans has no desire to escape London's flooded streets. An adventurer called Strangman, who arrives in London on a flying boat manned by a crew of pirates, drains the lagoons in his search for treasure. The submerged buildings emerge 'from the depths like an immense intact Atlantis,' but Kerans is unable to accept 'this total inversion' of his normal world. He blows up the barricades and re-floods the city, 'savouring the fresh tang that the water had brought again to the lagoon.'

Kerans does not fear the flood – he embraces it. Strangman sends him down to explore the halls of the planetarium and Kerans contrives to cut off his own air supply; he almost drowns, sinking contentedly into the 'deep cradle of silt' on the floor, which 'carried him gently like an immense placenta.'

'He *wanted* to become part of the drowned world,' Strangman says.

The novel's loving accounts of the drowned city, and Kerans' fascination for its lagoons and reptiles, have profound implications for our response to global warming; they imply that the reason we fail to address it is not because we do not recognize the severity of the crisis, or lack the energy to do anything about it, but because we do not want to: the drift to disaster is self-willed.

I had travelled through King's Cross on my way to Waterloo to catch the train to Shepperton, and I found myself standing in front of a poster advertising holidays in a luxury resort on a man-made island in the Arabian Gulf, called the Palm Atlantis. I had seen it many times in the course of the year, when I was reading about the history and mythology of flooding, and I always wondered what had been going through the owners' minds when they decided to name their artificial island after a continent that had sunk overnight. Had they forgotten what happened in the story, or were they consciously exploiting the allure of the name? To J. G. Ballard, who was fascinated by advertising's ability to articulate our subconscious desires, the attraction of a holiday in a drowned world would have needed no explanation.

~

Shepperton Green had flooded, and many of the roads were under water. The Thames had burst its banks by the jetty of the sailing club; the fast-flowing, wind-whipped water was as high as the benches on the riverside walks. It looked as wild and cold as a winter sea, thickened with a scurf of twigs and grass. Moored dinghies had tipped upwards, prows rising through the choppy grey waves. A houseboat called *Midnight Shadow* lay beyond the water's edge, parallel to the line of trees that marked the river's normal limit. The water had reached the back porch of the hotel on the riverbank. I stopped for a drink and a sandwich, and to get out of the cold. The barman had seen the river higher, but he said it never came inside. Ferry Lane was under water;

the line of foot posts marking the pavements was almost submerged. A man driving a four-by-four with outsized wheels and a raised body, like a jeep adapted for water, offered me a lift; he was running his own kind of ferry service to get people home. I said I was going the other way, but I waited until he picked up another passenger and watched him roll the vehicle forward into the lime-green water.

~

A tree had come down on Chertsey Road. It had fallen towards the house on the other side, and had caught in the branches of another tree, which held it like a crutch. If it slipped, it would crash into the garden. The owner of the house and her husband were standing in the road. They had called the police. As I walked on, I was conscious of the other trees dipping and swaying in the wind. The water lapping at their trunks was dark and muddy, but it was pale yellow in the shallows on the edge of the field, turning green as it got deeper. The further reaches of the lake were grey and opaque. The wind stirred up ripples on its surface and flung skin-tingling bursts of sleet in my face. My feet were frozen in my cheap rubber boots, and my ageing waterproofs were leaking again.

I wondered whether it was a coincidence that both *A Drowned World* and *After London* ended with their protagonists on foot. After Felix escapes near-death in London, in Jefferies' story, he becomes the leader of a band of tribes, but he does not stay for long, because he wants to find his lover, Aurora, and bring her back with him. He sets off into the woods as the sun sets: 'still onward', runs the last line, 'and as the dusk fell he was still moving rapidly westward.' The sentence anticipates the end of *The Drowned World* and its unforgettable closing line. After Kerans escapes his pursuers in London, he sets off through the swamps and lagoons of continental Europe, 'a second Adam searching for the forgotten paradises of the reborn sun.' Kerans is the only character drawn to the south; most had gone the other way, fleeing the ever-expanding zone around the tropics, where humans could no longer survive. Jefferies' vision of ecological collapse is not yet with us, but the northward exodus that Ballard imagined has begun. For the time being, most of the refugees arriving on Europe's shores are escaping war and civil unrest, but it will not be long before climate change drives many more to seek sanctuary in the north.

~

I reached Sunbury at the end of the day. The last stretch of road was closed, but a man in a petrol station, where I stopped to buy some chocolate, told me I could get through. Watersplash Farm hadn't flooded, but the stream by Fordbridge Road was level with the street and ringed the trunks of the trees on its banks. Ahead of me, cars were turning back, though two men in high-vis jackets were directing an ambulance through the water. It was knee-deep, and almost reached the top of my boots, but I could see that it was deeper in the flooded fields that stretched towards the river; it reached the top of the swings in a flooded playground and rose halfway up the goalposts in a playing field. The houses on the far side looked like houseboats.

A small red car had been left at the entrance to a long, winding drive, water lapping at the top of its wheels, and there were upturned benches and gas canisters beside a canoe and a life jacket in the garden. There was a rainbow over lower Sunbury, and the Thames was flowing fast between the shore and the island, where I had stopped on my way back from the Levels, two weeks before. A pair of waders hung above the gate at the entrance to Sunbury Court Island, and there was a UKIP flag flying above one of the houses. The river had gone down; it was lapping at the feet of the benches that marked its usual limits, but the main current was full and fast flowing. A canoeist came past, slaloming between the bins in the shallow water on the edge of the expanded river, followed by a line of joyriding ducks that made his progress seem effortful and clumsy.

10: The Sunken Hundred

The tide was going out so fast that the sea seemed to be receding even as I walked towards it, new expanses of gleaming sand appearing every few seconds. It even seemed to outpace my son, who was running towards it with the eagerness of a seven-year-old released from the car at the end of a long drive. It was easy to imagine it returning at the same speed, breaking over the defences at the entrance to the bay and crashing over the sixteen cities that are supposed to have stood on the sand.

Cantre'r Gwaelod, or the Sunken Hundred, the lost kingdom that lies beneath the sea in front of the Welsh town of Borth, was a Celtic New Orleans, precariously positioned below high tide, protected by defences that had to be constantly maintained. At its greatest extent, it stretched from Bardsey Island to Ramsey Island, which lie at the northern and southern ends of Cardigan Bay. According to the Welsh folklorist T. Gwynn Jones, it was 'a fertile territory', forty miles long and twenty miles wide, enclosed by Sarn Badrig, or St Patrick's Causeway, a bank of glacial deposits extending south-west from Shell Island, near Harlech, for twelve and a half miles. The causeway remains a hazard to shipping, says Robert Duck, in a book called *This Shrinking Land: Climate Change and Britain's Coasts*, and it is visible at the lowest spring tides. So are four main 'roads', also made of glacial deposits, that are said to have run across the kingdom. According to one version of the story, the Sunken Hundred was lost when a drunken keeper of the embankment forgot to close the sluices after a banquet. 'The sea broke through and only a few of the inhabitants escaped,' writes T. Gwynn Jones. There is no reason to believe the sixteen cities ever existed – and, if they did, they were not lost overnight. Yet land has been lost in the bay, and the storms of the winter had uncovered new evidence of how far it used to reach.

I saw the first of the tree stumps – Borth's own Noah's Woods – dotting the sands as I walked towards the receding sea. They were jagged triangles, like sharks' teeth, or miniature volcanoes, with sloping sides tapering to cratered summits. Some were turreted like sandcastles and moated by seawater. They were draped with moss or seaweed, or moored in beds of soft black peat. Some had roots twined around their base, like ribbons of dough. My son was soon soaking wet, and I took off my shoes and paddled in the shallows, where the stumps were gathered most thickly. The wood was turning white as it dried in the sun.

It was May 2014 – two months after the winter floods had come to an end – and it was a clear, fresh day, with a cool wind, and a pale blue sky draped with thin wisps of cloud. The noise of the sea was as steady as a waterfall.

Further up the beach, the struts holding up the groynes were a regular grid of dots shading into the speckled dots of the trees. There were lads sitting on the sea wall, smoking, in front of the pastel-coloured terraces and modern semis that lined the front. Beyond, lay the dyke-ribbed, river-threaded marsh that might, one day, fall within reach of the sea that had churned up the sands in the winter storms and exposed the stumps on the beach.

I had never been to Borth before, though my mother's family lived there during the war, and went back afterwards on family holidays. My mother remembered cine footage of her and her brothers eating ice cream on the beach – though she didn't remember the event itself. The town is supposed to have inspired 'Every Day is Like Sunday', Morrissey's post-Smiths ode to the drabness of British seaside life, though it seemed to me a fascinating place, enriched by the evidence of its past that kept emerging on the beach.

The storms had also revealed a wattle walkway that began near the lifeboat station, and the ancient footprint of a child, who was believed to be four years old. While we waited for the tide to turn, we had walked along the front to see if we could find them, and had come to a raft of peat beds that looked like models of the Grand Canyon: perfectly eroded formations, with streaked sides and flat overhanging tops. Sheets of drying water lay between the ribs of peat. I had been watching the tide running through the miniature canyons, like rivers, for several minutes before I looked up, momentarily disorientated by the shift in the scale, and saw that the sea had receded by hundreds of

metres, and the stumps beneath the high-water mark had
begun to appear.

The forests had flourished between 3500 BC and 2500 BC,
in the period when Stonehenge was being built. The trees
at Ynyslas, the village that lay less than two miles north in
the bay, were the first to go, while those at Borth survived
until 1500 BC. Some reports suggest there were trees growing at the southern end of the bay until 1000 BC.

Yet the legend of the Sunken Hundred is not the only
story that compresses the gradual loss of land, over thousands of years, into the events of a single, cataclysmic night,
prompted by human failings of one kind or another – an
act of drunken carelessness, or treachery, conducted in the
name of ambition or love. Henry W. Longfellow included
a poem in his anthology *Poems of Places* (1876–9) that gave
a similar account of the loss of Kaer-Is, a drowned land off
the coast of Brittany:

> Now curséd forever mote she be,
> That all for wine and harlotry,
> The sluice unbarred that held the sea!

The culprit is the king's daughter, who steals the key
'which bolts the sluice and bars the tide' from around her
father's neck as he sleeps off a drunken party, and gives it to
her lover.

The kingdom of Tyno Helig, which lies beneath the Great
Orme, the sheep-cropped headland beyond Llandudno, was
also lost to the sea when the floodgates were opened,

though the villain was not one of the daughters of the king, but the ambitious young man who wanted to marry her. He could only do so if he had a nobleman's golden torque or collar, so, when he was sent to escort a ransomed Scottish nobleman to his home, he murdered him and stole his collar. His treachery seemed to pay off at first, but the ghost of the dead man returned on their wedding day and said the family would be cursed to the fourth generation. The prophecy came true during the banquet to celebrate the birth of their great-grandchild: a maid went to fetch wine from the cellar and found that the sluices had given way, and the sea was pouring in. Already, the cellar was filled with fish.

The maid and her boyfriend, who was the court minstrel, ran for their lives, the story says. They heard screams behind them, but they didn't stop, and, when they looked back, they saw the waves racing towards them. They escaped to dry ground, and, at dawn, they saw that the palace had disappeared beneath the waters of the bay.

There are no comparable stories on the east coast. The archaeologist Vincent Gaffney tentatively attributes the absence of folk memories of Doggerland to cultural discontinuity, caused by successive waves of settlement and colonization. Native Britons were displaced by Romans, who were displaced by Anglo-Saxons, and each wave of invaders brought their own memories and overwrote those of their predecessors. On the west coast, where settlement was more continuous, memories of lost lands endured. The fact that it was lost more recently than Doggerland may have helped as well. Tacitus' account of the Roman invasion of Anglesey in AD 60 testifies that the sea in the Menai Straits, where Tyno Helig was supposed to stand, used to be much lower. He said the infantry crossed in flat-bottomed boats, while the cavalry followed 'by fording, or, in deeper water, by swimming at the side of their horses'. What's more, Lavan Sands, or the 'Place of Weeping', as the inter-tidal area is called, was occupied in a way Doggerland never had been. In 1864, a man from Llandudno set out to look for the ruins of Tyno Helig, and found a seaweed-covered wall, and, in 1908, a geologist who had accompanied him on the original expedition came across even more substan-tial ruins. 'The underwater archaeological evidence for former occupation . . . is compelling,' writes Robert Duck. Yet I was more interested in the accounts of the way the land was lost, for I had heard similar stories of floods caused by the opening of a floodgate in several places I had been to in the last two years.

~

John Wynne-Jones saw the wave sweeping towards him as he stood on the raised bank of the River Elwy, in the North Wales town of St Asaph at ten past four in the morning, on 27 November 2012. Mr Wynne-Jones was a flood warden, responsible for implementing the evacuation plan for St Asaph, where he had lived for twenty-seven years.

Two days of heavy rain had triggered flood warnings on the Elwy, and Wynne-Jones had gone round the estate the day before, warning his neighbours that they might have to leave. Midnight was the cut-off point: if the river hadn't flooded by then, they would be safe. John Wynne-Jones got the all-clear at half past eight, and passed it on to his neighbours. Yet he wasn't convinced.

At midnight, he walked up to the river, which runs within half a dozen metres of the back gardens of the houses on the estate, and he could see that the water was still rising. Every twenty minutes, he checked the gauge beneath the massive concrete pillars of the flyover that carried the North Wales Expressway above the river and through the outskirts of town. At three thirty a.m., it was higher than it had ever been, but, even so, he was not prepared for what came next. It wasn't just the force of the wave emerging from the darkness that shocked him – it was the direction. The Elwy, swollen by the water pouring off the sodden Denbigh Moors and obstructed by debris beneath the Spring Gardens footbridge, had backed up and reversed its course. In effect, John Wynne-Jones said, it had begun to flow upstream.

The 'wall of water', as Wynne-Jones called it, swept him down the path to the estate, and dumped him in the corner of the foaming pool that was spreading out towards his neighbours' houses. It could have been worse: had he been a few metres closer to the footbridge, the wave would have carried him down the side of the bank, which was both footpath and defence, and trapped him in the dip at the bottom, against the fence that enclosed the back gardens of the nearest houses. He was convinced that he wouldn't have been able to get out, and, when I met him, eighteen months later, on a warm, windless summer afternoon, he was still preoccupied by the narrowness of his escape.

St Asaph is dominated by the cathedral on the steep high street, which had earned it city status, and by the River Elwy, which winds through the fields and houses below. The name means 'enclosure on the Elwy', and a former mayor, who spoke with the soft Scouse accent that I recognized from my childhood on the Wirral, told me that most people were drawn to the town because of its riverside setting.

The pub where I met John Wynne-Jones, which stood on the main road into town, a hundred metres from the river, was one of many buildings that had flooded. The previous owners had sold up, but Wynne-Jones knew the people who had taken it on, and he often used it for meetings. He was a former town councillor, who had spent his working life in the NHS, but, these days, his time and energy were devoted to the flood and its consequences for the town. As soon as he walked into the refurbished bar, he started talking, nervously and compulsively, about the night he nearly drowned.

At first, I found it difficult to follow his descriptions of the landscape, which he seemed to inhabit constantly, and he took my notebook and sketched the configuration of river, road and bridges before we got in his car and drove half a mile downstream to see it for ourselves. We parked on the Roe Parc estate and walked up the path that had become a water slide on the night of the flood. It was the kind of path you see all over the country: a narrow strip, enclosed by overgrown borders and wooden fences, running from bollard to bollard, shaded by trees that made it feel dark and damp.

The river was very low – it came to the knees of the man fishing below the footbridge – and its murmur was overlaid by the chatter of gulls, who had made the short journey inland. The pillars of the flyover were fifty metres to the right; the concrete had begun to moulder and fade, turning the green-brown shade of the trees that overhung the river. It was cool and shady beneath the bridge, and, on the bank, the light was dappled by the shifting branches overhead. It seemed a peaceful place, to me, but it was evidently unsettling to John Wynne-Jones; he paced up and down the bank between the gauge and the footbridge, measuring the short distance between the top of the path, where the wave hit him, and the perilous stretch beside the fence, where he would have been, seconds later.

Yet it wasn't just the nature of the flood that preoccupied him – it was its source. There was only one way to explain the sudden surge that nearly drowned him: someone had opened a gate in the Llyn Aled Isaf reservoir, which lay upstream, and released the tide of water that came crashing through St Asaph with such force that it turned heavy bins into floating battering rams and tore out steel railings. John Wynne-Jones did not want to criticize individuals – he was too polite and generous for that – but he believed that Natural Resources Wales was to blame, and he was not alone in holding bureaucrats responsible for a flood that overwhelmed his home.

~

Several months after the storm surge of December 2013 had passed down the east coast, I drove along the Wash with an official from the Environment Agency, who showed me the places where the water nearly broke through, threatening the fragile-looking holiday encampments that had sprung up on the shores in the estuary, in the same haphazard and defiantly idiosyncratic way they had in coastal Essex. It had been a close thing, he said. In some places, the water had broken through and got trapped in a gap between the outer line of defences and the newer ones, which had been built on higher ground inland, though people's faith in their own security was so great that even those who lived in the shelter of the sea walls would not contribute to their upkeep. The Environment Agency couldn't maintain them all; some would be allowed to lapse – though, in the short-term, at least, the stubborn spirit of the seaside settlement would save them: someone's brother would turn up with a digger and they would build their own defences.

Yet the defiant self-sufficiency of the improvised coastal communities had its flipside in their suspicion of authority. In a previous job, when he was working on a river in Cambridgeshire, the Environment Agency official who had given me a tour of the Wash found himself arguing on live

TV with a man whose house had flooded. The man insisted that the official had caused the flood by opening a floodgate and releasing the wave of water that engulfed his home. The official said he hadn't, and couldn't have, even if he had wanted to, for there wasn't a floodgate on the river. 'I know every metre of it,' he said, on air, 'and, if you don't believe me, I'll show you. We'll get in my car and drive along the river, and you can show me the gate I opened.' It didn't make any difference; nothing could displace the notion of the spectral official cranking open a gate to release the flow of water that engulfed their homes.

I heard the accusation so often that I began to wonder whether people meant it literally or not. Shakespeare, the maker of so many phrases in our modern English language, was the first to use 'opening the floodgates' metaphorically. In *Othello*, Desdemona's father, Brabantio, says his 'particular grief' at the news of her marriage,

> Is of so flood-gate and o'erbearing nature
> That it engluts and swallows other sorrows.

The idea was particularly apt in sea-threatened Venice, but it is now used to describe uncontrollable surges of many different kinds – outpourings, upheavals, and influxes, such as the imminent arrival of 'floods of refugees'. I sometimes wondered whether people were not accusing the officials of releasing waves of water, but waves of care and sadness. Different eras succumb to different fears. In 1936, W. H. Auden wrote a poem called 'As We

Like It' that evoked the anxieties of the years before the Second World War:

> For the wicked card is dealt and
> The sinister tall-hatted botanist stoops at the spring
> With his insignificant phial, and looses
> The plague on the ignorant town.

Yet the figure that haunts the contemporary imagination is not the malevolent scientist of the 'low, dishonest' decade of the 1930s, as Auden famously called it, nor the drunken embankment-keeper or the scheming suitor of folklore – it is the unaccountable bureaucrat, recklessly indifferent to other people's safety.

~

Some people feared that gates or defences might give way of their own accord. Graham Chapman-Brice and his wife, Sarah, had already lost one farm to the Lake District reservoir of Thirlmere and they feared they might lose another. Sarah's family had owned a farm in Wythburndale, the valley that was flooded in the nineteenth century to create the reservoir, and they now lived beside St John's Beck, which was straightened and embanked to carry the overflow to Keswick.

The water had never reached their farmhouse, for it stood on a patch of high ground at the side of the valley, but their fields had flooded several times since they moved to St John's in the Vale in the early eighties – 1985, 1995 and 2005, with 'a few narrow squeaks in between'. Yet the flood of 2009, when Keswick was also overwhelmed, was unprecedented, Graham Chapman-Brice said, when I went to St John's in the Vale on a rainy autumn day. He and Sarah were generous hosts. I had been told that she was a good baker, and the home-made bread and cake lived up to its billing. We sat in the kitchen, which was a light, airy room, with windows that looked up the valley towards the Helvellyn, and across the low-lying fields to St John's Beck.

Sarah had 'stupidly agreed' to do a stand at the knitting and stitching show in Harrogate on Thursday 19 November 2009. She had taken the car out the night before, in the hope that, if she did, it wouldn't flood, regardless of what the forecast said. Yet in the morning, the beck was already so deep that she had to get her son to take her across in the tractor. Normally, the clouds blow through, Graham said, but this time, the weather system stopped: 'The rain arrived – and stayed: it rained and rained.' It wasn't raining very hard in Penrith when Sarah got there, and in Scotch Corner it was dry and sunny, but in St John's in the Vale, they had a foot of rain. They estimated that 10,000 million litres overflowed from Thirlmere down St John's in the Vale in one day. 'The water comes so deep and so fast it is frightening,' Graham and Sarah wrote in a collection of stories about the flood of 2009. 'The entire valley fills and you would think it another lake.'

There had been storms before – Sarah remembered August 1967, when a cloudburst sank Borrowdale – and they weren't sure whether it was getting worse. 'We had a friend who lived here for a long time and he said, "We have never had a normal year,"' Graham said. 'I would say that it's becoming more intense, but it's hard to know – perhaps we are becoming more aware of it.' Yet heavy rain only mattered if the reservoir was full and had no room to absorb it. 'If the lake is low, we don't flood, even if we have torrential rainfall, but if the lake is full, everyone is at risk.' The local postman would check the level when he drove across the bridge in the morning, and pass on the news as he did his rounds – he'd say, 'It's two bricks down,' or whatever it might be.

Outsiders recognize its destructive potential as well. In a poem called 'Civic', the Liverpudlian Paul Farley describes a walk through the predawn woods to the edge of Thirlmere, where he plans

> . . . to break
> the great stillness and surface of this lake-
> cum-reservoir by peeing quietly into the supply.

He was impelled by 'a keen sense of civic duty', for he is a Liverpudlian, and the reservoir supplies Manchester. No one would be harmed by it, he says, explicitly dismissing the fear of the 'tall-hatted botanist' of Auden's poem:

> . . . no citizens
> will draw a cold draught
> of LSD, or run a hot bath
> of nerve agent in two days' time.

Yet, as he walks back to 'the quiet road in the green shade' he reaches a point where he looks out across a wall that holds back the water,

> at chest height
> and gasped at the thought of the pressure,
>> the pounds-per-brick

resting against it. If the wall was to collapse, or there was a landslip on Helvellyn, the tidal wave would engulf the valley, generating more of 'those rumours that seem to follow reservoirs around':

> a drowned village, church bells on rough nights,
> the souls who stood their ground
> calling from the depths.

The flooding of Wythburndale to create Thirlmere was controlled, but sometimes dams burst unexpectedly. Two hundred and sixty people were killed in 1864 when the Dale Dyke Dam in the Peak District burst, and there were fears that the 'Great Sheffield Flood' would be repeated in 2007, when the rain that flooded Tewkesbury and Hull tested the walls of the Ulley Reservoir. Each reservoir has flood inundation maps, showing what would happen in the event of a collapse, yet the people most likely to be affected are not encouraged to talk about it, Graham said. 'It's naughty and scaremongering and you get told to stand in the corner.' In France, people who live within fifteen miles of a reservoir have sirens fitted to their houses, but the only warning the people who live beneath Thirlmere would get would be a message on Facebook.

~

The only authority that people seemed to have any faith in was the royal family. I had walked through Windsor as I made my way along the flooded banks of the Thames, in February 2014, and as I passed beneath the castle on the hill above the expanded river, I remembered the unlikely alliance between Prince Charles, Windsor's resident architectural nostalgist, and a modernist architect called Darren Ward, who had worked together to restore the Cumbrian town of Cockermouth after it had flooded in 2009, in the storm that also overwhelmed St John's in the Vale.

Darren Ward lived in an impeccably renovated house with a Le Corbusier print on the wall, in a narrow alley between the high street and the River Cocker. There had been warnings of heavy rainfall before the flood, he said. He had gone out to check the river level early, when the first warnings came through, and saw cause for concern. There had been warnings before, but, this time, the river was 'looking angry – incredibly angry. And the Environment Agency people were looking very worried.'

Even so, the speed of the flood was a shock. Suddenly, the town filled with rapids. 'It was so fast and dramatic, it was like a Hollywood disaster movie,' the owner of the toy-shop in the high street had told me. Water poured through the entrance to Cockton's Yard, where Darren Ward lived, as if the alley had become a hosepipe. On the night I was there, the lights in Cockton's Yard had failed; it was so dark that I had to check the numbers on the door with the torch on my phone, and, when I turned back towards the high street, I could see light spilling through the gap between the shops, just as the water had done on the day of the flood. A wave, eighteen inches (forty-six centimetres) deep, chased Darren back into his house. Floodgates didn't help; the water came through the front door, which opened straight into the whitewashed kitchen on the ground floor. He treated it as an inconvenience, at first. 'I was like, "Oh my God! There's half an inch of water in the house."'

The water kept rising for the next ten hours. He was struck by the deafening roar of the river flowing down the high street. It was six feet (1.8 metres) deep and travelling so fast that the rescue teams couldn't get their boats through it. They were going over the rooftops, identifying the houses in which people were trapped, but there were so many people in need of rescue that they couldn't get them out straight away.

At one o'clock in the morning, Darren got a message saying that a helicopter was on its way, but, before it arrived, Mountain Rescue got a canoe through the narrow mouth of the alley. Even then, he decided to stay, as he couldn't take the cat. He said he dived into the flooded kitchen to rescue a cheque he'd received from a client, and I assumed he meant it literally, for, when he got back upstairs, he realized he had used all the towels to stop the water coming in, and couldn't have a shower. He sat on the first floor and watched the water climb the spiral stairs that he had renovated himself. 'It makes you humble,' he said. 'It makes you realize that the world can just remove you without any concern whatsoever – if it wants to kill you, it can. I work for myself – I feel like I have total control of my life, and yet I felt totally powerless.'

He strung up a belay and sent a cup of tea to a neighbour without spilling it, though he knew that such minor triumphs would make little difference if the houses collapsed. 'It would only have taken a couple of courses of bricks to go, and whole streets would have been swept away.' Cars were found stranded in some of the yards; the current had picked them up, flipped them on their side and forced them through the gaps at the end of the alleys. He finally left his house the next day, when the water had started going down, and all he took with him was a piece of parmesan – emblem of his sophisticated tastes, and of the curious decisions that people say they make when they find their lives overturned by a flood. The water was still knee-deep and fast flowing; it had shattered windows and flooded shops. Coloured yarn had streamed out of one, snagging on obstacles in the current.

He came back a day later and climbed into the house through an upstairs window. 'It was emotional,' he said. 'I work from here – so, potentially, I had lost everything. I remember standing in here and thinking, What do I do? Where do I start? You've got to make a start somewhere, because it's the drying-out period that delays everything. So

I stripped the plaster. It was good to do that – it was taking control.'

The council asked him to survey buildings, which meant breaking in, for people weren't allowed back into their homes for several days. But he didn't expect to have such a prominent role in the regeneration of the town. Traumatic though it was, he knew the flood was an opportunity to make improvements. Cockermouth depended on its shops, and if they were lost, it would die. He also knew they didn't have to put them back exactly as they had been before; they could make them better. 'Nature had bitten me, and I wanted to bite it right back.'

He went to a meeting and said, 'If we are going to restore it all, we should think about how we do it.' He expected to get shouted at. Instead, he got applause. He became the chair of the regeneration society and started producing sketches of how the high street might look. David Cameron, the Old Etonian Prime Minister, alumnus of the school Henry VIII established in the meadow opposite Windsor Castle, got in touch, because they were the 'big society' in action, and Prince Charles came as well, for he loved Cockermouth's Georgian high street. The conservation officer showed him Darren's sketches, and he liked them so much, he 'pulled strings' and they got the money to improve the shopfronts.

Darren did most of the work for free, but he got a lot of publicity out of it, and won awards. It was ironic that a modernist should be recognized for renovating Georgian shopfronts, he said, but it didn't matter; he was born in Hull and trained in Liverpool, but he had lived in Cockermouth for fourteen years, and it was his town. 'I don't want to walk down a street I am going to be pissed off with. I want a quality town – Georgian, Victorian, modernist, whatever it is. I want thoughtful, considered design.' Prince Charles wanted to be involved, but he couldn't be, publicly, so he appointed a friend, who 'banged heads together' and speeded up the process. 'Until then, I would have said it's ridiculous, this networking – but, by God, it works. If there was a logjam building up, we would have a word with Prince Charles's private secretary and, the next morning, it would be gone.'

He wasn't alone in praising members of the royal family. Unlike politicians, who were invariably greeted with contempt and hostility, the royals were always welcome in flooded towns or villages. People found their presence reassuring and valued the practical help they could provide. Yet even Prince Charles couldn't stop Cockermouth flooding again in 2015. He might have retained the ability to pull strings and call in favours, but he didn't control the budget for flood defences or decide where they should go. That power had shifted downstream from the royal territories on the western reaches of the Thames – from Windsor, Hampton Court and Richmond Park, where King Henry VIII was said to have stood on a mound to await the signal from the Tower that Anne Boleyn had been executed – to one of the places where King Canute is supposed to have conducted his experiment in holding back the tide.

~

Thorney Island used to be one of the bars of sand and gravel that stretched across the Thames, and, until relatively recently, it was still depicted as an island. There is a drawing, dated to 1537, which shows it on the north bank of the Thames, as it is today, but separated from the rest of London by the embanked River Tyburn, which runs around it on three sides. Half a dozen bridges join it to the rest of the city.

The island emerged between about 6,500 and 5,000 years ago, writes Robert Shepherd, in *Westminster: A Biography,* when 'the Thames was wider and shallower than today's embanked river, with gravel and sand bars dotted across its clay-covered flood plain.' The site was 'marsh within marsh and forest within forest,' said Arthur Stanley, a Dean of Westminster in the nineteenth century, but it 'presented several points of attraction' – including 'close supplies of timber for building and fuel; reeds and rushes for thatch and fodder, and meat from wildlife in the nearby marshes'; 3,500 years ago, the land was farmed and partly cleared; 2,500 years ago, an alder wood platform and post were installed on a site in Richmond Terrace – the oldest structure found so far. 'Celtic items discovered in the Thames near Westminster, including a bronze parade helmet by Waterloo bridge and a shield at Battersea suggest offerings were being made to the gods . . . about 2,000 years ago, by which time a rise in the river levels had submerged the sites of the Underground station, Westminster Hall and the Houses of Parliament.'

In Roman times, the river was twice the width it is today,

and shallower. Peter Ackroyd describes how it 'wove in coils, its broad curves moving through a marshy riverine landscape . . . The river was replenished by many tributary streams and rivers that have long since disappeared or vanished underground. At low tide it moved slowly through banks of clean gravel and sand. Downriver from Westminster, dotted among the waters, there were numerous islands that were submerged at high tide.'

The traders who lived in a hall on Treasury Green, near Downing Street, in the eighth century may have founded the first church on Thorney, and since it was to the west of the town then known as Lundenwic, it was called 'West-Minster'.

Canute, the Danish conqueror of England who became king in 1017, chose it for his capital because it was removed from the busy settlement to the east. His palace supposedly stood in Parliament Square, though no one knows where he set his throne on the foreshore as the tide came in, during his famous attempt to establish the limits of kingly power. Some sources claim he was trying to show that man was powerless in the face of nature, though the inscription on the statue of Canute's chair that used to stand on the seafront at New Brighton, on the Wirral, endorsed the popular idea of the hubristic king who believed he could hold back the tides: 'Sea come not hither nor wet the sole of my foot,' the inscription said.

The statue was vandalized in the 1950s and it had been removed. I went to look for it one day, but I couldn't find anyone who remembered it, and I might have doubted it existed, if New Brighton wasn't such a perfect place for Canute's experiment. The Wirral claims to be the only place in Britain with documented proof of Viking occupation, and Robert Duck says it has 'long been a microcosm of this shrinking land', for the waters beyond the peninsula, between the mouths of the Mersey and the Dee, conceal another drowned forest called Dove Point and the three islets of Hilbre Island, which used to be part of the mainland. During the reign of Elizabeth I, 4,000 foot and 200 horse troops camped on Hilbre on their way to Ireland, where the Earl of Essex was fighting a campaign. Even in the seventeenth century, it was a single island, a mile long, with a deep inlet on its south-west side, but it has now been reduced to three weathered, wind-sculpted reefs, joined by tendrils of sandstone that are exposed at low tide. As usual, the process has not been entirely one-sided; land has been gained further down the Dee Estuary, as its waters have silted up, and its ports have moved progressively closer to the Irish Sea. Today, only the highest of tides reaches Parkgate, the former port that had replaced Neston as the port for Chester, and, on the night of the Great Tide of 2013, people in the pubs and cafes on the front were startled to see rats swarming out of the marshes, as they fled the sea's advance.

New Brighton flooded as well; I had watched footage of the waves breaking through the old marine lake and surging through the tower blocks and shopping centre. Yet Westminster was also prone to flooding. In 1236, the water rose so high that people punted through Westminster Hall in boats, or 'rode through it on horseback to their chambers.' The construction of the Embankment fortified and extended Westminster, yet it couldn't protect it entirely. In 1928, as melting snows in the Cotswolds swelled the Thames, a wall collapsed near Lambeth Bridge, and water poured into the lower galleries of the Tate. Fourteen people drowned.

Given the way the island had disappeared, absorbed into the fabric of the city, it seems appropriate that the street that bears its name lies beyond its borders. Thorney Street runs behind the Embankment from Millbank Tower, and emerges on Horseferry Road, opposite Ergon House, the home of the Environment Agency. It is an unusually quiet street; there are no shops or cafes until you reach the far corner, and no street furniture, either – there is no need for parking bays or signs, for there are no parked cars. The emptiness is explained by the massive stone building that occupies the northern side of the street. The signs saying 'Threat level heightened' inside the numbered doorways are one clue to its purpose. The spiked strips or stingers on the ramps leading down into the basement car parks, the darkened windows and the surveillance cameras are others. They make the nature of Thames House, and the identity of its tenant, seem very plain – though, even if you don't know it was the home of MI5, you might guess it by the shadow it casts across Thorney Street.

I had paused outside the Environment Agency, but I hadn't tried to go in. There was no point; I had tried approaching it several times, and, each time, I had been dismissed. Even personal introductions failed. A friend of mine lived next door to a senior official who had apparently spent the winter of the floods 'pacing the incident room like Dr Strangelove'. The official was responsive at first, but said he had to consult colleagues before he could meet me. The conversation went no further; he couldn't talk to me at all, not even socially or off the record. I got the same reaction from other people I was introduced to: at first, they responded to my interest in their working lives, but none of them would meet me, and they soon stopped answering my emails.

I wasn't surprised that the Environment Agency had become so defensive. When the floods were at their height in Somerset, the Communities' Secretary Eric Pickles had said on national television that he was sorry the government had listened to the advice of the 'so-called experts' who had told them not to dredge the rivers. It seemed a cowardly betrayal, couched in knowingly provocative language, and it made me feel sorry for the few employees of the Environment Agency I had been allowed to meet, who seemed conscientious and hard-working. I had no reason to doubt their honesty or the quality of their advice, and yet, when I saw the location of their offices, opposite the MI5 building, at the heart of the unaccountable power of the state, I wondered why I had been so prepared to make excuses for them. Perhaps I was getting old and complacent, or perhaps it was a consequence of living in London for so long: I had become so accustomed to the view from the centre that I had forgotten the purpose of my trips, which was to try to capture life in the marginal places that were prone to flood. I should have been more prepared to take the stories I'd heard on trust. I had underestimated people's legitimate complaints and fears. Perhaps the Environment Agency was as remote and arrogant as they said. Perhaps it had been negligent and incompetent in failing to prevent the floods – or, worse, contributed to causing them. Even the idea that it had acted maliciously did not seem far-fetched as I stood outside its offices. Yet I only came across one recorded instance of someone opening a floodgate and inundating a village, and the culprit was not an Environment Agency official, but a resident of the Somerset Levels – and the place he flooded was Thorney.

11: Isle of Thorns

The Anchorage had been a post office as well as a pontoon in the flood. 'All day, there were people coming in and out, knocking on the door and getting the dogs going – it was never-ending,' said its owner, Rita Dobson. 'We got to know quite a lot of people. It was a nice distraction, in a way – I had other people to talk to, and shoulders to cry on when I was having a low day. On the other hand, you have people come along in their waders and on family outings to see the flooding, taking photographs through the windows. One man came along with a box of chocolates to give to the people of Thorney. And I said, "Well, you know what you can do with those chocolates."'

One day, a group of bikers rolled into town and drew up on the water's edge. Rita went out and asked them what they were doing. 'They said they do this trip every year. And I said, "Don't you watch the news? Half of Somerset is under bloody water. Piss off, before I do some damage."' The response from everybody in the country – from local school kids putting food bags together to people making donations – was sweet and kind, she said, though not necessarily very helpful. After the water had gone, eight imams from South Yorkshire turned up with a cheque for the church relief fund. One of her neighbours asked if she would mind having a chat with them, and eight of them came to the door with a film crew. She laughed. 'So we took them round the house, where we had all the drying equipment, showed them the road where the water had come in. They were lovely. They didn't need to do that.'

Seven months had passed since I had first gone to Thorney, and the road from Langport to Muchelney, which I had tried walking down in the floods in January, was clear. It was a hot day, but the road across the moor ran through a cool green tunnel that retained an intimation of the water that had subsided. Tall reeds marked the lines of the rhynes and drains in the surrounding fields. Muchelney was closer than I expected; I reached it in five minutes. Thorney was less than two miles further on. I passed the path behind the village that I had walked along in the dark, and crossed the bridge into Thorney, where the water had begun.

Its absence had shrunk the village: in the car, in the bright summer sunshine, the distance from the Wards' house to the Anchorage seemed much less than it had when I had done the same short journey in Glen's canoe. I parked beside the cottages by the path to Thorney Mill, where I had parked on the evening of the flood, and walked back to the point in the road where the canoes had been beached. Evidence of the clean-up was everywhere: there were portable toilets, cement mixers and skips in the gardens of the houses, and sandbags stacked outside the thatched house that used to be the pub. Its walls were propped up with posts, and there was talk that it might have to be demolished.

Yet, if the buildings had suffered, then the gardens hadn't. The trees and shrubs had emerged unharmed from their drenching in the polluted water. Roses and climbing plants obscured the windows and front doors of the houses, and there were runner beans, broad beans and tomatoes in one garden. Even the sign on the front of the Anchorage, which had seemed so improbably prominent on the evening of the flood, had faded into the resurgent foliage.

I met Rita Dobson on the path beside the river, where the Parrett Internal Drainage Board was building a bank to divide Thorney from Westmoor, from where the winter flood had come, and we walked back to the Anchorage and sat at a wooden table in the garden. There were flowers in a wheelbarrow and garden furniture on a raised patio. Two steps led up to the bank that overlooked the river, which was far below the top, shallow and slow moving. It had nearly reached the top in the winter, Rita said, for it was so silted up, it wasn't flowing as it should have, but the water that got inside her house had come from elsewhere.

In 2012, the road had flooded, and they couldn't get to Muchelney, but the water stopped short of their house. This year, it had come inside on 6 January, a day after it flooded the Wards, because of the way it flowed. 'The water table was so high, it pushed up the pond liner and spilled more water in the garden, thanks very much, as if we didn't have enough already,' she said. When it breached the flagstone floor, they gave up trying to stop it. 'Somebody said this to me – and I didn't believe it until it happened – but it's almost a relief when the water's in, because you can stop worrying. It's in, and then you can deal with it. You thought, "Oh, well – that's that."'

There was still a skip in the yard, but most of the work was done. The house had new stone floors and a sleek fitted kitchen. The 'last fiddly bits and bobs' were the worst part, Rita said, but she did not want to complain; there were people in Moorland who weren't finished, seven months on, and people who had flooded the year before and hadn't even moved back in before they had been flooded again. 'I feel really bad for those who had it worse than me,' Rita said. 'All I could think was that it happened here and it's only so deep and it's bad enough. You know, I've got a brand-new downstairs, which I wouldn't have had. But I'd rather not have gone through that and got my house back as it was.'

She came from Croydon, like Glen Ward, her neighbour in Thorney, though she grew up on the Holloway Road, near where I live, in North London. She moved to Thorney because she wanted to escape the rat race. The flood hadn't made her love the house or the area any less, but she wished the people responsible for maintaining the rivers had been doing what they were supposed to do. 'If it's a natural phenomenon, if it's Mother Nature doing what she does, then fine,' she said. 'But if it's because they couldn't be bothered to spend the money to maintain the waterways, then I don't think it's acceptable. They have neglected their duties and that's why people are so cross. Some people will tell you that we didn't have much more water than normal that month. But we had a wet summer, so the land was already wet, and it will only hold so much. Of course, the weather was part of the problem. I don't think it was all the problem.'

~

The Parrett, which had been a dark, foam-flecked channel when I walked along it in the dusk, seven months before, had subsided to a narrow trickle, at the bottom of a deep, wide ditch. The bank that divided it from the houses seemed unnecessarily high, though I had seen for myself that it wasn't. Its transformation didn't surprise me, for I had seen the same thing many times before. Yet there was one element of the short walk behind the village that I could not reconcile with my memories of the previous time I had been there: halfway along the path, I reached a fence and had to clamber over it.

'You don't remember it because it wasn't there,' Glen Ward said, when I arrived at his house. The farmer had taken it down during the flood, but as soon as the water had gone down, he had put it up again, for he was tired of people lumbering across his land. The Thorney bypass, as people called it, was closed, and other barriers were going up again.

Glen felt 'a slight sadness' that everything was back to

normal. One of his neighbours had told him that a lot of good things would come out of the flood, and he thought that was true, though you had to be careful who you said it to. 'There are a lot of different characters, and the people who seem to be coping with it sometimes aren't. Emotions seesaw. It wasn't like 2012, when it was over in a week – blink and you miss it.' It had lasted a long time: the Wards' house was flooded for two months, though the water had come and gone three times, which made it worse. It didn't finally go down until early March.

At first, he enjoyed using the canoe, and it had given them some self-sufficiency, but the flood had been all-consuming in other ways. He didn't work for two months because he had to tend the pumps. They camped out in their bedroom, which was in the loft, though they had to put on wellies to come downstairs. Later, they brought in a caravan and lived in the yard.

Most of their neighbours had left. The Australian woman who lived next door went home to visit family, and, when she came back, the house was still flooded. Their other neighbour, Professor Temperley, still hadn't moved back in. At first, they had been ignored, but once the scale of the disaster was apparent, the police took over, and they were wise enough to send in officers 'with people skills', Glen said. 'When all the agencies turned up – too late, though that wasn't their fault – they were quite good. All the people helping were good; they were very mindful that we had been sorting ourselves out for three weeks, so they came in light-footed.'

The insurance company appointed a builder to do the repairs, but he wanted to lock them out of the house, put a canteen in the yard and turn it into a building site. Having looked after the house throughout the flood, Glen wasn't going to have that, so he took a lump sum and did the work himself. He had stripped the walls and floor in the hall and had taken up the floor in the kitchen. The rest of the house was coming together. He made most of the furniture himself; he said it was easier to point out the things he hadn't made, in the kitchen where we were sitting, than the ones he had. It hadn't been entirely straightforward. He had stepped on a nail when he was taking down a stud partition, and had to go to hospital. He got the fire engine to take him to Muchelney, where he got the boat to Langport. It was the only time in two months that he made the trip.

His memories of the flood were already hazy. Looking back on it, he said, it seemed surreal. The thick blanket of water that had been drawn across the Levels had a lulling, disorientating effect. Yet Glen remembered laughing more than he had for a long time, and he remembered meeting people that he might not have met if it hadn't been for the flood. 'It was nice talking to people – and you had time to do it. Somerset's a really friendly county – I've never come across a friendlier place. You always have time to get to know people, but add water into the mix and there's even more time. So there was an upside to it.'

The American writer Rebecca Solnit described a similar

feeling in the aftermath of the Loma Prieta earthquake in San Francisco, in 1989: 'I was thrown into an intensely absorbing present,' she wrote, in a book called *A Paradise Built in Hell*. There was no word for the post-disaster realm 'in which the wonderful comes wrapped in the terrible, joy in sorrow, courage in fear,' though she attempted to define how it felt: 'that sense of immersion in the moment and solidarity with others caused by the rupture in everyday life, an emotion graver than happiness but deeply positive.' Unlike J. G. Ballard, who suggests we are energized and enlivened by the descent into chaos, Solnit says, 'we cannot welcome disaster', but 'we can value the responses, both practical and psychological', for, in the 'suspension of usual order and the failure of most systems, we are free to live and act another way.'

Floods are transformative, as well as earthquakes: they create as well as destroy. The hurricanes and storms that devastate the Caribbean at intermittent intervals also strip vegetation and renew the soil. They drive migrations to America and Europe, seeding new communities around the world. The devastating Mississippi floods of 1927 drove the spread of the blues, for they forced the musicians from the Delta to move north to cities like Chicago.

And some practical-minded people relished the prospect of a flood as a challenge to be met: I had heard about someone who had built his own defences around his house in Somerset and was eager to try them out; and a friend of a friend was building a lighthouse in Glastonbury, on the northern edge of the Levels. Yet Solnit's idea of a paradise that 'arises in hell' was tested by Hurricane Katrina, which struck New Orleans in 2005. 'Katrina wasn't a disaster,' she wrote. 'It was a catastrophe, far larger in scale than almost anything in American history . . . 80 percent of New Orleans was flooded, all vital services were wrecked or suspended, and ninety thousand square miles of the coastal south were declared a disaster area.' The storm was only the start. The 'somewhat natural disaster' of Hurricane Katrina was compounded by the 'strictly unnatural disaster of the failing levees', and then by the 'failure or refusal of successive layers of government to supply evacuation and relief, and the appalling calamity of the way that local and then state and federal authorities decided to regard victims as criminals and turned New Orleans into a prison city . . .'

The trauma of Katrina was not only the terrible storm and flood – 'the waters in which bodies floated and poisonous snakes swam, the heat that blistered skin and killed many, the apocalyptic days in which people gave birth and died on freeway overpasses surrounded by unclean waters' – it was also the sense of 'being abandoned by their fellow human beings and their government.' The disaster in New Orleans was 'so horrific that it begat little of the ebullience of many other disasters,' she wrote. Besides, New Orleans didn't need to assert community spirit in the way of other cities, for it had it anyway. So did Somerset, Glen Ward said. Even Rita Dobson, who had found less to enjoy in the flood, felt closer to the people who had flooded than the ones further up the road who hadn't.

Yet there was one person who confounded the stories of a community united in the face of a crisis in the most egregious way, by directing the flood waters away from his house and towards his neighbours. Lee Goddard lived in Hambridge, four miles west of Thorney, and only a few hundred metres from Slabgate Sluice, which controls the flow of water from the River Isle on to Westmoor. Slabgate Sluice is often opened during the summer to irrigate the moor for cattle grazing, and, as the weather worsened and the rivers rose in December, Goddard smashed the padlock with a crowbar, releasing 45,000 litres of water into Westmoor. He then filled the mechanism with screws, so it couldn't close again.

He didn't try to disguise what he had done; he boasted about it at a New Year's Eve party. The Parrett Internal Drainage Board heard the story and brought a case against him. Thorney would have flooded anyway. But his intervention meant that the water rose higher and stayed for longer. 'I believe my father is not in his house today because of the actions of this man in Hambridge,' Julian Temperley said, when Goddard's conviction was reported, and Rita Dobson said they might not have flooded at all, given that the difference was a matter of centimetres.

He was fined £1,000 and will go down in the records as the first person in Britain to be convicted of opening a sluice gate. Yet he is not the first person to have done it. In the Somerset Levels, villages often turned against each another in an attempt to save themselves. In one recorded instance in 1894, water reached the upper storeys of the houses in

Langport, and a group of villagers set out to cut a bank and divert the flood to Aller, only to be turned back by people from Aller who were guarding their embankment, which had been cut three years before. Not surprisingly, people have always acted in unneighbourly ways when floods threaten their houses. Yet even such interventions did not distract people from the real target of their rage.

~

It had started raining again at the beginning of February, and, on the night of 5 February – the day that the storms ruptured the railway lines at Dawlish – a police helicopter equipped with loudspeakers had flown over Moorland and told the residents to get out. The marines of 40 Commando were sent in to help evacuate the village: the colleagues of the soldiers who had surveyed the drowned fields from Burrow Mump were finally given a role.

The water had been rising on the moors since Christmas, but people were used to that and they didn't pay much attention, said a man cutting a new path in the turf in the front garden of his house by the church in Moorland. He didn't want to tell me his name, but he did want to tell me what had happened, for he felt they had been let down.

I had walked to Moorland along the banks of the Parrett, following its straight course through the fields that had flooded in the winter. It was a clear day, with a bright blue sky, though a strong wind was blowing. The Parrett was low within its banks, a dark brown stream overhung by clumps of yellow weeds. The river began to slow as it reached the glass-and-concrete frame of Midelney Pumping Station, which was emitting a low, contented hum. Other reed-planted channels converged on the Parrett from the west, in an arrangement as complex as a motorway interchange. During the flood, Glen Ward and his wife used to walk up to the pumping station and look back across the lake to the village. 'There is a magnificent side to this extreme weather,' he had said. 'You just don't want to be in the middle of it.' I understood what he meant; and yet, as Burrow Mump came into sight, beyond Langport, and I realized I was walking across the bottom of the lake I had surveyed from the summit of the hill, I was conscious of the double-ness I had felt in other places – an awareness that the water had only just gone down and might come up again, for flooding was not an aber-ration, but the restoration of a natural state. The houses beside the road from Burrowbridge to Moorland were being renovated, and, further on, diggers were stripping the bank, reducing it to sloping strips of mud: the dredg-ing of the rivers, which the locals had wanted, had begun.

There were vans waiting at the entrance to Moorland, for the road is only open at certain times of the day. There were piles of bricks and building materials stacked in the gardens of the boarded-up houses, and Portaloos, skips, shipping containers, vans and mobile homes were parked in the driveways. Builders – shaven-headed and tattooed – moved in and out of the gutted buildings.

A Portakabin had taken the place of the town hall; inside,

it was papered with letters from schoolchildren sending best wishes for a speedy recovery. There was much to do, for the roads that forked in the centre of the village and ran in diverging lines towards the Parrett had become rivers in the flood, the man who lived beside the church told me. The water had poured along them, in two directions, and along the road from the village hall.

It hadn't come from the Parrett – the closer you were to the river, the safer you were. No one knew exactly where it had come from. Some people said the Environment Agency had released water because it feared that the Boltmore Wall, which the monks of Glastonbury Abbey had built to hold water on Curry Moor, was going to collapse, but others said it came from Clatworthy Reservoir, which was also under strain.

The man who lived beside the church had left, and he had come back on 8 February to find a foot of water in the house, and a lot of 'very cross people'. An aerial photograph showed the spire of the church rising above the flooded houses, and a small patch of dry land by the river, where it rises slightly. Car roofs and the top of a float that had been taken out of the sheds where it was kept in readiness for Bridgwater Carnival broke the surface. Fifteen or sixteen properties were saved, but the rest flooded, and still the water kept rising. 'Beyond the village hall, it was above your armpits,' the man said: 'Here, it got just above the windowsill. There was eighteen inches in the church. The Environment Agency did a runner – no, that's not fair,' he added. 'But they abandoned the village.'

As if causing the flood by releasing the water and then disappearing was not enough, the Environment Agency then prolonged its effects, the man said, through its incompetence. Its employees didn't know how to operate the machinery that kept the Levels dry. In 2013, the local council wanted to take out a noise abatement order because people living near Northmoor Pumping Station complained about the noise. The Environment Agency said it wouldn't run it until it had to, so it ran it in the daytime, until the floods began, when it was turned on twenty-four hours a day. The noise and vibration were terrible, the man said, until an old chap who used to service the pumps offered to take a look at them. With a little love and attention, they ran 'as sweet as a nut'.

In some cases, the Environment Agency didn't even know the machinery existed. There was a floodgate on the junction of the Tone and the Parrett that had been kept at two metres 'forever and a day', and it wasn't until the height of the flood that someone remembered to open it. The man made it sound like they had tripped over themselves running upstairs, like a householder rushing to pull the plug in the bath after the kitchen ceiling has fallen in. It didn't work, of course; the gate had seized up through lack of maintenance, and it took a day to lower it. The effects were immediately apparent – the water level in the man's bungalow fell a foot within twenty-four hours.

I was listening carefully, and yet, my doubts were growing again: I was finding it hard to sustain the sense of the perfidious nature of the Environment Agency which had seemed so strong when I stood in Thorney Street and felt a rush of rage at its secrecy and ineptitude. The Environment Agency seemed guilty of more failings than any single body could reasonably attain, for it was assiduous in doing harm and yet idle in other ways, simultaneously sinister and calculating and comically inept. I had begun to think that the stories we have always told ourselves weren't relevant anymore: neither the Noah myth, which imagined the flood as a longed-for purging and rebirth, nor the legends of floods caused by incompetent or malevolent individuals could encompass the nature of a crisis generated by the day-to-day activities of billions of people. When it comes to climate change, we are all to blame. I believed that the flood was caused by the natural vagaries of the weather, aggravated by the pressure that humanity exerts on the planet, not government policies or bureaucratic mistakes. Yet even Glen Ward – who seemed unlikely to subscribe to conspiracy theories – said that Moorland had been cynically sacrificed to save a housing estate downstream, and I found it hard to discount the testimony of two elderly farmers who lived on the edge of the village, between the moor and the river.

~

Mary and Brian Hutchings had met at a young farmers' ball more than fifty years ago and had known straight away that they were meant to be together. They had lived at Battens Farm for forty years, and they had never seen anything like the winter flood of 2013–14 – nor had the old farmer down the road, they said, and he had been there even longer.

There was often water in the fields, they told me, but usually you could still get out on the land. Some seasons were wetter than others, but that applies whether you are on top of the hill or in the Levels. Usually, the water was low, so the moor would act as a reserve to soak up rainfall, but, in the winter, the ground had been sodden to begin with. English Nature and the RSPB believed – wrongly, Mary said – that birds liked water, and the Environment Agency had designated Northmoor as a lake, without telling anybody. 'They're playing God with other people's property and it won't be tolerated,' she said.

Yet the long-term failures were compounded by the decision to release the flood of water that engulfed their farm. They had never seen anything like it, Mr Hutchings said. 'It was a vast area – miles of water. But we never heard a whisper officially to explain how it happened.' They were in no doubt; there was only one way the water could have risen so quickly.

'It was in the fields before Christmas, but it came here out of the blue,' Mary said. 'It came from nowhere. Obviously, it was let in, to come up that quickly.'

'And it wasn't just water, either,' said her husband. He was a tall man, bony and angular, with work-hardened hands. He was dressed in green trousers and short-sleeved check shirt, for he had just come in from the fields.

There had been wind to contend with as well; it lifted the roofs off the sheds and pushed over some of the outhouses. Yet it was the water that came up so fast, and stayed so long, that did the damage, and it was not a natural disaster: 'It was caused by management neglect and a decision to flood us out.'

There was still no official explanation of the cause of the flood, though the Environment Agency had published details of a twenty-year plan intended to prevent it happening again. It planned to repair fifty 'assets' – embankments, pumping stations, sluices, floodgates and coastal flood defences – and to install new barriers and pumps. There was a hint of defensiveness apparent in the hyperbolic claim that it had been 'the largest flood event ever known' – and yet the figures were undeniably impressive. The Environment Agency estimated there were one hundred million cubic metres of floodwater spread across an area of sixty-five square kilometres, and it did not seem surprising that it was unable to contain them.

When the helicopters passed over Northmoor, telling people to get out, Mr and Mrs Hutchings wouldn't leave, for they had to stay and look after the animals. Two days later, when the water was knee-deep in the cattle sheds of Battens Farm, they started moving their cows, and, two days after that, they moved out as well – they had no choice, as the farmhouse had also flooded.

Their animals were their first concern. They weren't back in their house, but that mattered less, for they were comfortable enough in the mobile home that had been set up at the end of the muddy yard, facing the drive, so it was the first thing you saw when you turned into the farm from the road that ran along the southern edge of the village. There were plant pots lining the steps leading up to the front door, and a sign saying 'Battens Farm'.

Inside, it was equally neat and tidy. There was an L-shaped sofa inside the door, with a kitchen beyond, and bedrooms at the back. It was very hot, even with the doors open to admit the breeze that made the net curtains flick and sway. 'It's lovely,' Mrs Hutchings had said when I arrived. 'We couldn't have wished for anything better. But, at the end of the day, there's nothing like home.'

Not everyone was forced to leave. The water rose on Wednesday night, and on Thursday the Environment Agency built a wall to protect properties further down the lane, so those people were able to stay. Yet all ninety acres of the Hutchings' land ended up under water. They sent some of their animals to different farms, but they had to sell half of them, because the water was too deep for tractors, and they couldn't get round to them all. Yet the farm hadn't been entirely abandoned; the cats were still there, and Mr and Mrs Hutchings had come back in their waders, delivered in the police's amphibious vehicles, so they could feed them. It was very eerie, Brian said, because the garden walls had been knocked down and the fences had floated away: there was nothing except the unbroken expanse of water.

They found the LPG gas tank under the apple tree, upside down, and their domestic heating tanks had tipped over, spilling oil into the village. They lost their car. Even then, the rain hadn't abated: fourteen millimetres of rain fell on 24 February, and the Environment Agency said that 'access to the area remains extremely difficult'. 'If you are in immediate danger, please call 999,' said another bulletin on 27 February 2014. 'There remains a significant risk to local properties.'

Additional pumps were running, and they were needed. Battens Farm was flooded for twenty-six days, and once the water started going down, it took two days to disappear. Mr and Mrs Hutchings moved back to the farm on 16 March, and found nothing left, except the brick buildings, and even they had been damaged. Even the grass had disappeared: 'The grass on the moor has largely survived, because it's used to being wet,' Mr Hutchings said. 'But, back here, where we've never had floods, it killed it.'

Their neighbour was pleased to see them, for it had been very eerie being there on his own. His house had been built on higher ground, but it had flooded nonetheless. 'It was a shambles, down here,' said Mr Hutchings, who was plainly not given to exaggeration. 'It really was.' Yet they took consolation from the offers of help that came from all over the country. One day, forty-three members of the Young Farmers Association arrived, and there were local volunteers as well, including the man who came in and washed his hands at the sink while I was there. 'He's one of the gentlemen who moved the animals out and he's come back and he's helping us rebuild our farm,' Mary said, when he had gone. He was an angel, Mrs Hutchings said, and her husband agreed: 'Marvellous. He's in the council and he knows who to contact. We'd be struggling tremendously with that. The kindness we've had is wonderful.'

Despite their age, they were determined to restore their herds and remake the farm as it had been before, and things were improving slowly. It was hard to remember how bad it had been, because it was looking better, they said, though it still looked bad enough to me. There was a new shed that housed a young herd of cows, but the house was a shell, and the sheds and barns that had been flattened in the flood were marked by strips of tarmac.

The house still smelt damp. They were turning the kitchen and sitting room into a single room. Mr Hutchings seemed pleased with the idea of transforming the old farm-house into a bright, open home. They hoped to be back at the end of September, though there was still much to be done, inside and out. Even the garden had gone; behind the house, there was nothing but an area of hardstanding and a swing-seat in the middle of the muddy patch of earth that used to be the lawn. Beyond it lay the scrubby fields through which the water had come, a black wave rising through the darkness, flattening out the dips and hollows in the moor as it sped towards Battens Farm.

Acknowledgements

I am grateful to all the people who appear in the book, and several others that I interviewed who did not. They include: Adrian Durrant and Simon Tobin in Southwold; Ivor Kemp in Hickling and Malcolm Kerby in Happisburgh; Mark Jones and Steve Wragg in Hull; Joanne Ellison and John Owen Roberts in St Asaph; Mark Gilbert and Joe Martin in the Fens; Lynn Jones in Keswick; John Leach in Thorney; Richard Coutts of Baca Architects; and Sue Tapsell in the Flood Research Unit, Middlesex University.

I would also like to thank Kris Doyle, my patient and insightful editor, and everyone else at Picador who worked on the book with great care and expertise, especially Paul Baggaley, Chloe May and Gabriela Quattromini. I am grateful to my agent Caroline Dawnay for her guidance during the last twenty-odd years. Jason Cowley and Helen Lewis at the *New Statesman*, Marina Benjamin at Aeon and Simon Grant at *Tate Etc.* commissioned articles about floods and rivers. For other kinds of support, I am grateful to the following people: Charles Fernyhough, Alexa de Ferranti, Linda Garforth, Nicholas Garnham, Cassian Harrison, Geoff Hewitson, Leo Hollis, Josh Lacey, Carol MacArthur, Robert Macfarlane, Matt McAllester, Johann Perry, Catherine Platt, Judy Shedden, Rebecca Whittle and

Kim Wilkie. I would like to thank my parents, John and Liz Platt, for introducing me to many of the places that I visit in the book. Most of all, I would like to thank my children, Benjy, Eliza and Ava, and my wife, Sophie.

Notes and References

p.10   **the Red Lady of Paviland – who was in fact, a man**   There is a full account of the discovery of the skeleton, and the ways it has been interpreted, in *Bones and Ochre: The Curious Afterlife of the Red Lady of Paviland*, by Marianne Sommer.

p.11   **'a *poured* landscape'**   From *Wetland: Life in the Somerset Levels* (p.10), by Patrick Sutherland and Adam Nicolson, which is a rich and evocative guide.

p.12   **'the gift of the river'**   *The Histories*, Herodotus, translated by George Rawlinson, p.117

p.12   **'Normally the Nile would start to rise in late June'**   *Flood: Nature and Culture* (p.56), by John Withington, is a very useful introduction to the art, literature, history and mythology of flooding.

p.13   **'a devout Marxist to an equally impassioned anti-Marxist'**   Simon Schama, *Landscape and Memory*, p.261.

p.13   **'grandiose' and 'overdrawn'**   *The Evolution of Urban Society*, Robert McCormick Adams, p.67.

p.14   **'Heaven commanded Yu'**   *Early China: A Social and Cultural History*, Li Feng.

p.20   ***If I were called in***   The lines are from Philip Larkin's poem 'Water', in *The Whitsun Weddings*.

p.21   **'For anyone under the age of 30'**   https://www.lrb.co.uk/blog/2018/october/the-rising-sea

p.22   **nine of the ten warmest years on record in the UK have occurred since 2002**   https://www.theguardian.com/environment/2018/nov/26/uk-flooding-threat-people-moved-michael-gove-climate-change

p.22   **globally, the last twenty-two years have seen the twenty warmest years on record**   https://www.theguardian.com/environment/2018/nov/29/four-years-hottest-record-climate-change?utm_term=RWRpdG9yaWFsXod1YXJkaWFuVG9kYXlVUyoxODExMjk%3D&utm_source=esp&utm_medium=Email&utm_campaign=GuardianTodayUS&CMP=GTUS_email

p.33   **'At the eastern extremity the Lake narrows'** *After London: or, Wild England,* Richard Jefferies, p.37.

p.38   **'confusion of small brooks'** *Portrait of Elmbury,* John Moore, the first book of *The Brensham Trilogy,* p.13.

p.43   ***The gods' load was too great***   The translation is from the poem dated to *c.* 1700 BC, known as *Atrahasis,* by Stephanie Dalley. The lines from *Gilgamesh* are from the Penguin Classics edition of *Gilgamesh,* translated by Andrew George, and the account of the significance of the flood is from his introduction.

p.45   **an expert in Mesopotamian cuneiform at the British Museum**   *The Ark Before Noah: Decoding the Story of the Flood* is both a learned account of the evolution of the ark legend, and a great adventure. The story of the attempt to build a new ark is also told in the TV documentary *The Real Noah's Ark.*

p.45   **There are at least two versions in Greek mythology**   The story of Deucalion and Phyrra appears in *The Library of Greek Mythology* by Apollodorus (p.36 of the Oxford World's Classics).

p.45   **'sacrificed kava, pigs, and coconuts'**   *The Oxford Dictionary of World Mythology*, Arthur Cotterell, p.285.

p.50   **She wanted 'to visit all the fairest cities of the kingdom'**   There is an essay by Liam Rogers which retells the stories of the Severn. It references *Worcestershire's Hidden Past* by Bill Gwilliam. http://www.whitedragon.org.uk/articles/sabrina.htm

p.51   **The Severn has flooded many times**   The descriptions of the floods (and many others) are taken from a fact-sheet I picked up in Tewkesbury. The floods of 1620, 1795 and 1852 are referred to here: http://ct-files.glos.ac.uk/igd/showcase/web/floodproject/bewdley_p2.htm

p.62   **'Offa's Charter . . . speaks already of ditches in the Pevensey Levels'**   *The Making of the English Landscape*, W. G. Hoskins, p.78.

p.63   **the water builds up behind an *argae***   The Landreader defines an argae as 'an earth bank built to hold back or retain flood water' (http://www.thelandreader.com/glossary/argae).

p.68   **'still exert an influence upon the world above them'**   *Thames: Sacred River*, Peter Ackroyd, p.44.

p.76   **Blake who was heavily influenced by beliefs in the lost city of Atlantis**   The references to Blake and his time in Felpham are from Peter Ackroyd's biography *Blake*, p.52.

p.78   **They were hard people**   'Why fishing produced so much cruelty is not clear,' write E. Gillett and K.

MacMahon in *A History of Hull*, p.304. 'Later, attempts were made to deny that there was any cruelty at all, but the record is quite certain: there was a great deal.'

p.80   **the 'flatness of the land'**   *A History of Hull*, E. Gillett and K. MacMahon, p.42. *The Draining of the Hull Valley*, by June A. Sheppard describes the reclamation of the carrs (http://www.eylhs.org.uk/dl/121/the-draining-of-the-hull-valley).

p.91   **When the diarists' thoughts were published in a report**   Whittle et al. '*After the Rain* – learning the lessons from flood recovery in Hull, final project report for Flood, Vulnerability and Urban Resilience: a real-time study of local recovery following the floods of June 2007 in Hull', Lancaster University, Lancaster, UK. Rebecca Whittle organized the writing group.

p.92   **'three massive wooden planks'**   *The Ferriby Boats*, Edward Wright, p.7.

p.98   **'Nothing but a change of sea level'**   *Submerged Forests*, Clement Reid, p.5. Also quoted in *Europe's Lost World*, by Vincent Gaffney, Simon Fitch and David Smith, which tells the story of the rediscovery of Doggerland, and describes the history of our preoccupation with lost lands beneath the seas.

p.98   **'a wide alluvial flat'**   *Submerged Forests*, Reid, p.38.

p.99   **'the first real evidence that the North Sea had been part of a great plain inhabited by the last hunter-gatherers in Europe'**   *Europe's Lost World*, Gaffney, Fitch and Smith, p.20.

p.101   **early modern writers such as Thomas More and Francis Bacon**   *Utopia* and *New Atlantis* were published in 1516 and 1624 respectively.

p.101   **The number of stories about lost continents is**

'beyond count' *Lost Continents: The Atlantis Theme*, L. Sprague de Camp, p.284.

p.101 **'its roofs open to the sky'** *Twenty Thousand Leagues Under the Sea*, Jules Verne, pp.167–168.

p.102 **'the Garden of Eden; the Gardens of the Hesperides'** *Atlantis: The Antediluvian World*, Ignatius Donnelly, pp.1–2.

p.103 **Blavatsky believed that Atlantis was one of several lost continents on which humanity had evolved** *The Secret Doctrine: The Synthesis of Science, Religion and Philosophy*, Helena Petrovna Blavatsky.

p.103 **Its existence had originally been proposed** Philip Sclater proposed the existence of the lost continent of Lemuria in an 1864 essay called *The Mammals of Madagascar*.

p.104 **'His stature was gigantic'** *The Lost Lemuria*, William Scott-Elliot, p.23.

p.104 **the American writer Frederick S. Oliver** *A Dweller on Two Planets* is available online, at: http://www.sacred-texts.com/atl/dtp/index.htm

p.105 **'the continents of Atlantis and Mu [often synonymous with Lemuria] did exist and still do'** So says the Lemurian Fellowship on its FAQ page: https://www.lemurianfellowship.org/faq/#faq6

p.110 **'I suspect he felt increasingly disappointed'** *The Norfolk Cranes Story*, John Buxton and Chris Durdin, p.15.

p.111 **'The fun of the thing to me'** *Fisherman Naturalist*, Anthony Buxton, p.189.

p.122 **the most landward of the three cottages** Juliet Blaxland describes life on the cliff in Easton Bavents in a book called *The Easternmost House*, which is due to be published in 2019.

p.133   **'You do not need to remind a Fenman'**   *Waterland*, Graham Swift, p.10.

p.138   **'Never in any history of which we have record'**   The accounts of the Fen flood are from *Harvest Home: The Official Story of the Great Floods of 1947 and their Sequel*, Dudley Barker.

p.149   **'Jaywick has succeeded'**   *Villages of Britain: The Five Hundred Villages that Made the Countryside*, Clive Aslet, p.251. Fred Gray has written about seaside architecture, and the significance of the bungalow within it, in *Designing the Seaside: Architecture, Society and Nature*.

p.151   **'By the afternoon of Saturday 31st January'**   *North Sea Surge: Story of the East Coast Floods of 1953*, Michael Pollard, p.28.

p.152   **'wall of death'**   *The 1953 Essex Flood Disaster: The People's Story*, Patricia Rennoldson Smith, pp.37–39.

p.162   **'the largest and highest'**   *A Tour through the Whole Island of Gt. Britain*, Daniel Defoe, Letter 7, p.414.

p.182   **The Wansbeck was quiet in the first half of the twentieth century**   The accounts of the floods of 1963 and 1967 are from David Archer's book about Northumbria's rivers, *Land of Singing Waters*.

p.203   **'surrounded on all sides by very great swampy and impassable marshes'**   The description comes from *The Life of Alfred* by a Welsh monk called Asser. It is the only contemporaneous account of his life. It is quoted in Adam Nicolson and Patrick Sutherland's book about the Levels, *Wetland: Life in the Somerset Levels*, which calls Alfred's retreat 'the great symbolic moment in the history of the Levels.'

p.205   **'a remarkable adaptation'**   *The Draining of the Somerset Levels*, Michael Williams, p.17.

p.207 **'the sea at a flowing water'**   This document is quoted
in *The Draining of the Somerset Levels*, Williams, p.87.
The Natural Environment Research Council says the
flood of 1607 was the greatest loss of life from a natural
catastrophe in the UK in the last five hundred years
(https://nerc.ukri.org/planetearth/stories/1812/).

p.207 **'receiv'd great Damage'**   *The Storm*, Daniel Defoe,
p.120.

p.212 **the hand-printed guide to the Levels**   The pamphlet,
which I found very helpful in understanding the
geography of the Levels, is *The Somerset Moors* by
Michael Stirling.

p.221 **'The winter rising of the river was anxiously watched'**
Stanley Spencer: A Biography, Kenneth Pople, p.3.

p.221 **'There were hidden bits of Cookham as remote as the
Milky Way'**   Gilbert Spencer, quoted in *Stanley
Spencer: Visions from a Berkshire Village*, Duncan
Robinson, p.10.

p.222 **'Heaven could not be further away than the other side
of Widbrook Common'**   *Stanley Spencer: Visions from a
Berkshire Village*, Duncan Robinson, p.9.

p.223 **'Spencer raised a statue of Hilda'**   Ibid., p.113.

p.233 **the twentieth century had begun 'to transform the
Thames Valley into a pleasing replica of Los
Angeles'**   *A User's Guide to the Millennium*, J. G.
Ballard, p.183.

p.234 **'the dappled light below the trees'**   *The Unlimited
Dream Company*, J. G. Ballard, p.41.

p.235 **'new form of aquatic mammal'**   *The Kindness of
Women*, J. G. Ballard, p.123.

p.235 **'a series of violent and prolonged solar storms'**   *The
Drowned World*, J. G. Ballard, p.21.

p.237 **'the earth was poison'** *After London*, Richard Jefferies, p.113.

p.242 **'a fertile territory'** *Welsh Folklore and Folk-Custom*, T. Gwynn Jones, p.97.

p.253 ***The sinister tall-hatted botanist*** is from W. H. Auden's poem 'As We Like It'. The 'low, dishonest decade' is from 'September 1, 1939', by W. H. Auden.

p.254 **'The water comes so deep and so fast it is frightening'** *Weathering the Storm: Stories and photos from the Keswick Floods, November 2009*, Keswick Flood Action Group, p.58.

p.255 ***to break the great stillness*** 'Civic', Paul Farley, *Tramp in Flames*.

p.262 **'the Thames was wider and shallower than today's embanked river'** The quote, and the following ones in the paragraph, are from *Westminster: A Biography*, Robert Shepherd.

p.263 **'wove in coils, its broad curves moving through a marshy riverine landscape . . .'** *Thames: Sacred River*, Peter Ackroyd, p.68.

p.275 **'I was thrown into an intensely absorbing present'** *A Paradise Built in Hell*, Rebecca Solnit, p.5.

p.275 **The devastating Mississippi floods of 1927 drove the spread of the blues** They also changed attitudes to the great river. 'It ended forever the argument over whether levees alone could control the Mississippi River,' writes John Barry in *Rising Tide*. Since nothing could control the Mississippi, 'Man would have to find a way to accommodate it.'

Bibliography

Ackroyd, Peter, *Blake*, 1995

——*Thames: Sacred River*, 2008

Adams, Robert McCormick, *The Evolution of Urban Society*, 1965

Apollodorus, *The Library of Greek Mythology*, 1997

Archer, David, *Land of Singing Waters: Rivers and Great Floods of Northumbria*, 1992

Aslet, Clive, *Villages of Britain: The Five Hundred Villages that Made the Countryside*, 2010

Atwood, Margaret, *Oryx and Crake*, 2004

——*The Year of the Flood*, 2009

——*MaddAddam*, 2013

Bacon, Francis, *New Atlantis*, 1624, in *Three Modern Utopias* [OUP, 2008]

Ballard, J. G., *The Drowned World*, 1962

——*The Unlimited Dream Company*, 1979

——*The Kindness of Women*, 1991

——*A User's Guide to the Millennium*, 1996

Barker, Dudley, *Harvest Home: The Official Story of the Great Floods of 1947 and their Sequel*, HMSO 1948

Barry, John, *Rising Tide: The Great Mississippi Flood of 1927 and How it Changed America*, 1998

Baxter, Stephen, *Flood*, 2008

Blavatsky, Helena Petrovsna, *The Secret Doctrine: The Synthesis of Science, Religion and Philosophy*, 1893

Buckland, William, *Reliquiae Diluvianae*, 1823
Burke, James Lee, *The Tin Roof Blowdown*, 2007
Buxton, Anthony, *Fisherman Naturalist*, 1946
Buxton, John and Durdin, Chris, *The Norfolk Cranes Story*, 2011

Childers, Erskine, *The Riddle of the Sands*, 1903
Churchward, James, *The Lost Continent of Mu: The Motherland of Men*, 1926
Comfort, Nicholas, *The Lost City of Dunwich*, 1994
Cotterell, Arthur, ed., *The Oxford Dictionary of World Mythology*, 1997
Craik, Dinah, *John Halifax Gentleman*, 1856

Darby, H. C., *The Changing Fenland*, 1983
Defoe, Daniel, *A Tour through the Whole Island of Gt. Britain*, 1724–6 [Penguin Classics, 1986]
— *The Storm*, 1724 [Allen Lane, 2003]
Donnelly, Ignatius, *Atlantis: The Antediluvian World*, 1882 [1976]
Duck, Robert, *This Shrinking Land: Climate Change and Britain's Coasts*, 2011
Dugdale, William, *The History of Imbanking and Drayning of divers Fenns and Marshes*, 1662

Eddison, Jill, *Romney Marsh: Survival on a Frontier*, 2009
Eliot, George, *The Mill on the Floss*, 1860

Farley, Paul, *Tramp in Flames*, 2006
Faulkner, William, *Old Man* (in *Three Famous Short Novels*), 2011
Fiennes, Celia, *The Journeys of Celia Fiennes*, 1888
Finkel, Norman, *The Ark Before Noah: Decoding the Story of the Flood*, 2014

Fitzgerald, Penelope, *The Bookshop*, 1978
—*Offshore*, 1979

Gaffney, Vincent, Fitch, Simon and Smith, David, *Europe's Lost World: The Rediscovery of Doggerland*, 2009
Gee, Maggie, *The Flood*, 2004
George, Andrew, trans., *The Epic of Gilgamesh*, 2010
Gillett, E. and MacMahon, K., *A History of Hull*, 1980
Gray, Fred, *Designing the Seaside: Architecture, Society and Nature*, 2006
Grieve, Hilda, *The Great Tide: the story of the 1953 flood disaster in Essex*, 1959
Gwilliam, Bill, *Worcestershire's Hidden Past*, 1991

Hallman, Robert, *Canvey Island: A History*, 2006
Herodotus, *The Histories*, translated by George Rawlinson [Everyman, 1992]
Hoskins, W. G., *The Making of the English Landscape*, 1995

Jefferies, Richard, *After London, or: Wild England*, 1885
Jones, T. Gwynn, *Welsh Folklore and Folk-Custom*, 1930

Keswick Flood Action Group, *Weathering the Storm: Stories and photos from the Keswick Floods, November 2009*
Kingsley, Charles, *Hereward the Wake*, 1866

Larkin, Philip, *The Whitsun Weddings*, 1964
Layard, Sir Austen Henry, *Nineveh and its Remains*, 1849 [Routledge & Kegan Paul, 1970]
Li Feng, *Early China: A Social and Cultural History*, 2013

Mabey, Richard, *Turned Out Nice Again*, 2013

Macfarlane, Robert, *The Old Ways*, 2012

Malster, Robert, *The Norfolk and Suffolk Broads*, 2007

Matless, David, *In the Nature of Landscape: Cultural Geography on the Norfolk Broads*, 2014

Moore, John, *Brensham Village*, 1946

—*Portrait of Elmbury*, 1946

—*The Blue Field*, 1948

—*The Brensham Trilogy*, 1966 [Oxford University Press, 1985]

More, Thomas, *Utopia*, 1516 in *Three Modern Utopias* [Oxford University Press, 2008]

Morrall, Clare, *When the Floods Came*, 2016

Oliver, Frederick S., *A Dweller on Two Planets*, 1905

Pearce, Fred, *When the Rivers Run Dry*, 2006

Plato, *Timaeus & Critias* [Penguin Classics, 2008]

Pollard, Michael, *North Sea Surge: Story of the East Coast Floods of 1953*, 1978

Pople, Kenneth, *Stanley Spencer: A Biography*, 1991

Reid, Clement, *Submerged Forests*, 1913

Rennoldson Smith, Patricia, *The 1953 Essex Flood Disaster: The People's Story*, 2012

Roberts, J. A. G., *The Complete History of China*, 2003

Robinson, Duncan, *Stanley Spencer: Visions from a Berkshire Village*, 1979

Runcie, James, *Canvey Island*, 2006

Schama, Simon, *Landscape and Memory*, 1995

Scott-Elliot, William, *The Lost Lemuria*, 1904

Sebald, W. G., *The Rings of Saturn*, 1995

Shepherd, Robert, *Westminster: A Biography*, 2012

Sisman, Adam, *Wordsworth and Coleridge: The Friendship*, 2007

Solnit, Rebecca, *A Paradise Built in Hell*, 2009

—*Unfathomable City: A New Orleans Atlas*, 2013

Sommer, Marianne, *Bones and Ochre: The Curious Afterlife of the Red Lady of Paviland*, 2008

Spencer, Gilbert, *Memoirs of a Painter*, 1974

Sprague de Camp, L., *Lost Continents: The Atlantis Theme*, 1954

Storer, Bernard, *The Natural History of the Somerset Levels*, 1985

Sutherland, Patrick and Nicolson, Adam, *Wetland: Life in the Somerset Levels*, 1986

Swift, Graham, *Waterland*, 1983

Thompson, Ian, *The English Lakes: A History*, 2010

Verne, Jules, *Twenty Thousand Leagues Under the Sea* [Wordsworth Classics, 1992]

Wilkie, Kim, *Led by the Land*, 2012

Williams, Michael, *The Draining of the Somerset Levels*, 1970

Williamson, Tom, *The Norfolk Broads: a landscape history*, 1997

Withington, John, *Flood: Nature and Culture*, 2013

Wittfogel, Karl, *Oriental Despotism: A Study of Total Power*, 1957

Wordsworth, William, *A Guide to the Lakes*, 1810 [Frances Lincoln, 2004]

Woolley, Sir Leonard, *Ur of the Chaldees*, 1929

Worpole, Ken, *350 Miles*, 2005

—*The New English Landscape*, 2013

Wright, Edward, *The Ferriby Boats: Seacraft of the Bronze Age*, 1990

Zola, Émile, *The Flood*, 1880